HEGEL'S SOCIAL AND POLITICAL THOUGHT

The Hegel Society of America wishes to thank the following for their financial support in the preparation of this volume for publication:

Rev. John M. Driscoll, O. S. A.
Villanova University

George L. Kline
Bryn Mawr College

Joseph O'Malley
Marquette University

Kenneth Schmitz
University of Toronto

HEGEL'S
SOCIAL AND POLITICAL
THOUGHT

ℜ

THE PHILOSOPHY
OF OBJECTIVE SPIRIT

Edited by

DONALD PHILLIP VERENE
Pennsylvania State University

NEW JERSEY: HUMANITIES PRESS
SUSSEX: HARVESTER PRESS

First published in 1980 in the United States of America by Humanities Press Inc. and in England by Harvester Press Ltd.

These are the papers delivered at the 1976 meeting of The Hegel Society at Georgetown University

Library of Congress Cataloging in Publication Data

Hegel Society of America.
    Hegel's social and political thought.

    Includes bibliographies and index.
    1.   Hegel, Georg Wilhelm Friedrich, 1770-1831—
Political science—Congresses.   I.   Verene, Donald
Phillip, 1937-   II.   Title.
JC234.H36H43   1978   320.5'092'4   77-26183
ISBN 0-391-00543-X

Harvester Press Ltd.
ENGLAND ISBN 0 85527 307 0

Manufactured in the United States of America

CONTENTS

Editor's Preface   i

Notes on Contributors   iii

Hegel's Concept of Philosophy and the Mediations of Objective
Spirit   1
    Hans-Martin Sass
    Comment: on Sass's "Hegel's Concept of Philosophy
                 and the Mediations of Objective Spirit"   27
                 David R. Lachterman

Theory and Practice in Hegel: Union or Disunion?   35
    Stanley Rosen
    Comment: on Rosen's "Theory and Practice in Hegel:
                 Union or Disunion?"   47
                 Heinz Kolar

Hegel's Lectures on Natural Law (1802-1805/06) as an Early
Counterpart to the *Philosophy of Right* (1821)   . .   53
    H. Kimmerle

Economic and Social Integration in Hegel's Political Philosophy   59
    Raymond Plant

Relation Between Economics and Politics in Hegel   91
    W. Ver Eecke

Person, Property, and Civil Society in the *Philosophy of Right* . . .   103
    Peter G. Stillman

Of Human Bondage: Labour, Bondage, and Freedom in the
Phenomenology   119
    Howard Adelman

Hegel's Theory of Sovereignty, International Relations, and War   137
    Errol E. Harris

Hegel and the Nation-State System of International Relations   151
     Henry Paolucci
     Comment: on Harris's "Hegel's Theory of Sovereignty,
                International Relations, and War" and
                Paolucci's "Hegel and the Nation-State Sys-
                tem of International Relations"
                Joseph C. Flay   167
                Paul Thomas   172

Hegel's Concept of Marriage and Family: The Origin of
Subjective Freedom   177
     Rudolf J. Siebert

Hegel in St. Louis   215
     John E. Smith

Some Observations on Social and Political Philosophy among the
St. Louis Hegelians   227
     John O. Riedl
     Comment: on the Relationship of Habermas's Views to
                Hegel . . . .
Richard J. Bernstein   233
Kenley R. Dove   240
Response to the Commentary of Bernstein and Dove   247
     Jürgen Habermas

EDITOR'S PREFACE

The papers that appear here are from the fourth biennial conference of the Hegel Society of America, held at Villanova University, Villanova, Pennsylvania, November 11-13, 1976. They focus on both general and specific aspects of Hegel's social and political thought. In considering a particular area of Hegel's thought the conference followed the practice of the previous meetings of the Society. The first biennial meeting, held in 1970, concerned "Hegel and the Sciences," the second, in 1972, "Hegel and the History of Philosophy," and the third, in 1974, "Hegel's Logic and Aesthetics," considered as two particular topics. The Hegel Society had its origin in a conference on "Hegel and the Philosophy of Religion," organized by Darrel Christensen at Wofford College, South Carolina in 1968.

The papers that follow are arranged from the general to the specific. An attempt has been made to keep papers with similar concerns as near each other as possible. No more specific ordering is intended. Obviously the papers can and should be approached according to the order dictated by the reader's interest. This volume contains all the papers and commentaries presented at the meeting. In some instances somewhat shorter versions of papers were presented at the meeting. The reader may wonder why these specific topics and not others are covered in this wide and rich area of Hegel's philosophy. The answer is the simple one of the problem of the human limits of length of time for such a conference and the approaches and availability of participants.

These proceedings include two papers initially announced as part of the program, those of Heinz Kimmerle and Raymond Plant, but which, because of practical difficulties, could not be presented, and are, happily, included here. The final item of the volume presents an exchange concerning some aspects of Jürgen Habermas's views on Hegel. This exchange is presented, as it was at the meeting, as two comments with a response by Habermas.

Having served initially as Program Chairman for the conference and now as Editor of its proceedings, my debts to others are great. I am indebted to my fellow members in the Hegel Society who gave advice and suggestions, read and refereed papers, and engaged in correspondence in the construction of the meeting. I am also indebted to the then current officers and members of the Executive Council of the

Society, whose cooperation and support I have had and which I greatly appreciate: Kenley Dove, Errol Harris, George Kline, Merold Westphal, Joseph O'Malley, and John Smith. I am also indebted to the President of the Society during this period, Kenneth Schmitz, from whom I so often sought and received advice directly and helpfully given. Joseph O'Malley is especially to be thanked for acting as the representative of the Society in overseeing the practical arrangements of the publication of this volume. Finally, this volume owes a debt to my wife, Molly Black Verene, who assisted with her practical editorial skills for many hours in the preparation of the total manuscript for submission for publication.

Donald Phillip Verene

NOTES ON CONTRIBUTORS

HOWARD ADELMAN. Associate Professor of Philosophy, York University, Canada. Author of articles on political theory and explanation theory. Associate Editor of the journal, *Social Praxis*. Co-editor of *The University Game* (1968). Author of *The Holiversity* (1973) and *The Beds of Academe* (1970).

RICHARD J. BERNSTEIN. Professor of Philosophy, Haverford College. Editor of *John Dewey: On Experience, Nature, and Freedom* (1960) and *Perspectives on Peirce* (1965). Author of *John Dewey* (1965); *Praxis and Action: Contemporary Philosophies of Human Activity* (1971); *The Restructing of Social and Political Theory* (1976).

KENLEY R. DOVE. Associate Professor of Philosophy, State University of New York, College at Purchase. Author of articles and research on Hegel, contemporary European philosophy, and social thought. Translator of the Introduction to Hegel's *Phenomenology of Spirit* in Martin Heidegger, *Hegel's Concept of Experience* (1970).

WILFRIED VER EECKE. Associate Professor of Philosophy, Georgetown University. Author of articles and research in the philosophy of Hegel, contemporary Continental philosophy, and the philosophy of the social sciences with emphasis on psychoanalysis, linguistics, and economics. Author of *Negativity and Subjectivity* (1977).

JOSEPH C. FLAY. Associate Professor of Philosophy, The Pennsylvania State University. Author of articles on Hegel, Marcuse, Dewey, and the Greek poet, Nikos Kazantzakis.

JÜRGEN HABERMAS. Adjunct Professor of Philosophy, Frankfurt/ Main and Director, Max-Planck-Institut zur Erforschung der Lebensbedingungen der wissenschaftlich-technischen Welt, Starnberg, West Germany. Author of, among other works: *Theorie und Praxis* (1963), trans. *Theory and Practice* (1973); *Erkenntnis und Interesse* (1968), trans. *Knowledge and Human Interests* (1971); *Technik und Wissenschaft als 'Ideologie'* (1968); *Protestbewegung und Hochschulreform* (1969); *Zur Logik der Sozialwissenschaften* (1970);

iii

Legitimationsprobleme im Spätkapitalismus (1973), trans. *Legitimation Crisis* (1975); *Zur Rekonstruktion des historischen Materialismus* (1975).

ERROL E. HARRIS. John Evans Professor Emeritus of Philosophy, Northwestern University. Author of *The Survival of Political Man* (1950); *Nature, Mind and Modern Science* (1954); *Revelation Through Reason: Religion in the Light of Science and Philosophy* (1958); *Annihilation and Utopia: The Principles of International Politics* (1966); *Foundations of Metaphysics in Science* (1965); *Fundamentals of Philosophy* (1968); *Hypothesis and Perception: The Roots of Scientific Method* (1970); *Salvation from Despair: A Reappraisal of Spinoza's Philosophy* (1973); *Perceptual Assurance and the Reality of the World* (1974); *Atheism and Theism* (1977).

HEINZ KIMMERLE. Professor of Philosophy, Central Interfaculty, Erasmus University, Rotterdam. Author of numerous essays on Hegel, Marxism, theory of the human sciences, and philosophy of religion. Editor of F. D. E. Schleiermacher, *Hermeneutik* (2d ed. 1974) and G. W. F. Hegel, *Jenaer Systementwürfe I. Gesammelte Werke,* Vol. 6 (1975). Author of *Die Zukunftsbedeutung der Hoffnung. Auseinandersetzung mit E. Blochs 'Prinzip Hoffnung' aus philosophischer und theologischer Sicht* (2d ed. 1974); *Das Problem der Abgeschlossenheit des Denkens. Hegels 'System der Philosophie' in den Jahren 1800 bis 1804* (1970); *Die Bedeutung der Geisteswissenschaften für die Gesellschaft* (1971); *Die Gottesfrage im konkreten Theorie-Praxis-Zusammenhang* (1975).

HEINZ KOLAR. Research Fellow in Philosophy of the Department of Science and Research, Institute of Philosophy, University of Vienna. Author of articles and research on Hegel's *Phenomenology of Mind* and *Science of Logic,* nineteenth-century philosophy, metaphysics, philosophy of history, and philosophy of religion.

DAVID R. LACHTERMAN. Assistant Professor of Philosophy, Swarthmore College. Author of articles and research on ancient and medieval philosophy, Kant and German Idealism, and phenomenology and philosophy of mathematics. Editor and translator of *Selected Philosophical Essays of Max Scheler* (1973).

HENRY PAOLUCCI. Professor of Government and Politics in the Graduate School, St. John's University. Author, editor, and translator of books on the political thought of St. Augustine, Dante,

Machiavelli, Beccaria, and F. W. Maitland, and also on Kissinger and the Presidency of the United States. Founder and Editor of *State of the Nation* and co-ordinator of *Review of National Literatures*. Co-editor of *Hegel on Tragedy* (1962, rpt. 1975).

RAYMOND PLANT. Senior Lecturer in Philosophy, The University of Manchester, England. Author of *Hegel* (1973) and *Community and Ideology* (1974).

JOHN O. RIEDL. Professor Emeritus of Philosophy, Queensborough Community College of the City of New York. Author of articles and research on the St. Louis Hegelians. Translator of Josef Koch, *Giles of Rome, Errores Philosophorum* (1944). Author of *The University in Process* (1965) and *A Catalogue of Renaissance Philosophers (1350-1650)* (1973).

STANLEY ROSEN. Professor of Philosophy, The Pennsylvania State University. Author of *Plato's Symposium* (1968); *Nihilism: A Philosophical Essay* (1969); *G. W. F. Hegel: An Introduction to the Science of Wisdom* (1974).

HANS-MARTIN SASS. Apl. Professor of Philosophy and Head of the Research Center for History of Philosophy, Institute for Philosophy, Ruhr-Universität, Bochum, West Germany. Author of publications and research on modern philosophy with emphasis on Hegelianism, Feuerbach, Marx, and Heidegger, critical theory, and philosophy of environment and technology. Executive Secretary of the Allgemeine Gesellschaft für Philosophie in Deutschland. Editor of the new edition of Friedrich Ueberweg, *Grundriss der Geschichte der Philosophie im 19. Jahrhundert*.

RUDOLF J. SIEBERT. Professor of Religion and Society, Western Michigan University. Author of numerous articles on Hegel, particularly on Hegel's philosophy of religion and on the critical theory of society of the Frankfurt School, particularly its theories of religion. Director of the course on "The Future of Religion" in the Inter-University Centre of Post-Graduate Studies in Dubrovnik, Yugoslavia.

JOHN E. SMITH. Clark Professor of Philosophy, Yale University. Editor of *Contemporary American Philosophy*, 2d Series (1970) Author of *Reason and God* (1961); *The Spirit of American Philosophy* (1963); *Religion and Empiricism* (1967); *Experience and God* (1968); *Themes in American Philosophy* (1970); *The Analogy of Experience* (1973).

PETER G. STILLMAN. Assistant Professor of Political Science, Vassar College. Author of numerous articles on Hegel, utopian thought, ecology, and contemporary political issues.

PAUL THOMAS. Assistant Professor of Political Science, University of California, Berkeley. Co-editor of a special issue of *Political Studies* (March 1976) on Marx and Marx studies. Specific research interests: Marx and Hegel.

DONALD PHILLIP VERENE. Associate Professor of Philosophy, The Pennsylvania State University. Author of articles on Hegel, Cassirer, Vico, and topics in the philosophy of culture. Editor of the journal, *Philosophy and Rhetoric*. Editor of *Man and Culture* (1970) and Co-editor of *Giambattista Vico's Science of Humanity* (1976).

Hegel's Concept of Philosophy and the Mediations of Objective Spirit

by

HANS-MARTIN SASS

I

Hegel's speculative method claims to be superior to other methods of thought—dogmatic, rationalistic, and irrationalistic—and it claims to be superior in regard to both cognition and action.

1. Hegel's program of speculative philosophy is developed explicitly through a polemical confrontation with all previous and contemporary philosophical methods. The method of speculative philosophy is different from empiricism in that it does not merely collect and juxtapose facts in an unmediated way. Rationalism and dogmatism fall short of an adequate account of reality because their purely discursive mode of thinking, with its "wooden scholastic terms," approaches any given reality from the outside, and thus rationalism cannot essentially grasp it. Romantic irrationalism falls short of reality because it considers mere subjective randomness, the engagement of the heart, to be the entire world. These traditional philosophical methods are not only useless for the analysis of reality; they are also unproductive for any attempts at changing it. Thought and action both, therefore, require the application of the speculative method in philosophy and in particular fields of investigation. In philosophy of religion, for example, orthodoxy, rationalism, and pietism each represent unworldly and purposeless methods: "ihr gegen die Philosophie feindlich gerichtetes Gerede ist daher Schulgeschwätz das sich in leere, inhaltslose Kategorien einhängt, wärend wir mit der Philosophie nicht in der sogenannten Schule, sondern in der Welt der Wirklichkeit sind."[1] These methods, which are to be criticized and suspended, remain in the realm of non-committal idle talk; they are the result of subjective *Eitelkeiten* (vanities). The speculative method, however, is itself "die Vernunft, welche auf Einheit drängt."[2]

2. The speculative method: (1) as a *method of cognition* and criticism deals with ordinary language and with theoretical terms in an analytical and fluid manner; (2) as a *logic of research*, its procedure is necessary and

1

strict and it justifies itself at the end of the research process; (3) as a *dialectic of the real* it is the way that reality (i.e., the idea) moves itself, makes itself its own object, and reconciles and mediates itself with itself; and (4) as a *method of individual actions* in philosophical, theoretical, and above all, political contexts the speculative method takes the narrow path of achieving freedom between reaction and revolution.

In the *Logik* Hegel says that the speculative method consists "in dem Auffassen der entgegengesetzten Elemente in ihrer Einheit,"[3] and the *Philosophy of Religion* states: "spekulative Philosophie ist das Bewusstsein der Idee, so dass alles als Idee aufgefasst wird; die Idee aber ist das Wahre im Gedanken, nicht in der blossen Anschauung oder Vorstellung. Das Wahre im Gedanken ist mehr dieses, dass es konkret sei, in sich entzweit gesetzt und zwar so, dass die zwei Seiten des Entzweiten entgegengestetzte Denkbestimmungen sind, als deren Einheit die Idee gefasst werden muss. Spekulativ Denken heisst ein Wirkliches auflösen und dieses sich so entgegengesetzten, dass die Unterschiede nach Denkbestimmungen entgegengesetzt sind und der Gegenstand als Einheit beider gefasst wird."[4]

As *epistemology* the speculative method deals with its objects "nicht als äusserliche Reflexion, sondern nimmt das Bestimmte aus ihren Gegenständen selbst, da sie selbst dessen immanentes Prinzip und Seele ist."[5] Not without reason does speculative philosophy see mysticism as its methodically more inadequate predecessor.[6]

As a *logic of research,* speculation is "not purely subjective": "in der philosophischen Erkenntnis ist die Notwendigkeit eines Begriffs die Hauptsache und der Gang, als Resultat, geworden zu sein, sein Beweis und Deduktion."[7] This has application for theoretical philsophy as well as for practical philosophy, e.g., for the philosophy of law, history, and environment. This method of a logic of research recommends itself also as a didactic of philosophy for advanced students.[8] As *reality* which itself behaves dialectically, the world of being and the world of thinking consist of contradictions which mutually produce, resolve, and propel themselves; thus: "das spekulative Denken hat jeden seiner Gegenstände und die Entwicklung derselben in ihrer absoluten Notwendigkeit aufzuzeigen. Dies geschieht, in dem jeder besondere Begriff aus dem sich selbst hervorbringenden und verwirklichenden allgemeinen Begriff oder der logischen Idee abgeleitet wird."[9] Dialectic, however, includes the cognizing and the acting *subject* in the process of mediation itself. In this respect, the dialectical method is identical with the achievement of the liberty of the thinking and acting subject; consider, for example, the *Phänomenologie des Geistes* and the *Philosophie der Geschichte*. In this regard, the *Philosophy of History,* for example, contains within the speculative theory of the Protestant Reformation a theory of action for the individual, and the *Philosophy of Law* may be read as the application of such a speculative critical action by its author, Hegel.

3. Thus the Hegelian speculation represents itself as a theory and a practice of coherence and complexity. Hegel introduces the coherence of a highly flexible system of linguistic meanings and structures, a self-regulating system which is not, however, fixed and stabilized on a certain level once that level is reached. On the contrary, it is set on its own self-determined, self-overcoming course in such a way that nothing gets lost, but is preserved and reaffirmed in its essential factors. Consequently it is not a system in a sense of contemporary system-theory. Philosophy does not simply create some simulative model of something existing outside itself; rather, in its "simulating" or apprehending of the complex factors of reality, philosophy brings itself into a unity with the process and progress of reality. On the one hand, the philosophizing subject states the objectivity of factual conditions and reflects it in the word-play of the "self-movement of the idea." It post-performs this objectivity. On the other hand, this post-performing, this becoming aware, represents an act of joining in the process. This can be substantiated by all objects of Hegelian philosophy, by the history of philosophy, among others. The human being is not only tied into the self-mediating systems through the act of speculative cognition, but also through various different ways of acting, the political, the social, the artistic, and the religious.[10] Normally, the human being is woven into the carpet of world history, as into the process of self-mediation, by means of his passions, according to the model of warp and woof, through the "cunning of reason." Because this process has no other medium and no other goal than the emancipation of freedom, the human being is also the conscious agent, both in perceiving and describing, and also in a kind of conscious acting which demands that one conduct oneself really reasonably, corresponding to the speculative equation of "reasonable" and "real," i.e., a conduct appropriate to reality. One of the ways in which speculative theory can contribute to the process of mediations and

materializations in all fields of reality is to initiate self-fulfilling prophecies via the description of the necessary proceedings of self-fulfilling facts. This action-predisposing function of philosophical theory and its straightforward academic description of mediations in objective spirit is one of the essential variables (E.V.) in this self-mediating system. The term "system" is here used for something that is more than a philosophical system of cognitive contents in the narrow traditional sense.

Even Hegel's disciples, who put together the *Grosse Enzyklopädie*, only kept an eye on the one side, the traditional-academical side of philosophy. But the politician and Hegelian disciple, Konstantin Rössler, director of Bismarck's Bureaus of Information, hints at what is at stake here in the preface to his *System der Staatslehre*[11] where he maintains that monuments had been erected to Fichte and Schelling, but that a monument to Hegel was not appropriate, because in Hegel's case it was a matter of the German nation having to build up their state as a living temple of a purged reality.[12] Under the aegis of the practice of mediation and embodiment, a philosophical system in the traditional sense is itself material for mediation and embodiment, i.e., for everything, therefore, which is contained in the German word *Aufhebung*. The speculative method of dialectic is nothing else but the strategy and tactics of overcoming conflicts in theoretical thought as well as in society by the way of "sublation."

II

I wish to present three areas of mediation in the objective spirit. I will show: (1) how the speculative method not only mediates factual opposites in reality with each other; but (2) how this mediation is an achievement of the progressive emergence of freedom; and (3) how the appropriation of such mediations in the philosopher's thinking and acting and in his reader's thinking and acting takes on the function of mediation itself.

1. The speculative theory of history mediates the subjectivity of reason and even of passion with the objectivity of historical progress by describing subjective interest and passion as means by which the cunning of reason can execute the process of world history. Furthermore, it

mediates the individual's freedom—which is the goal and purpose, but not the subject and the promoter of history—with the self-movement of the idea in the objectivity of its necessity.

The view that history proceeds rationally establishes itself in the course of its application in the areas of the philosophy of history and of the philosophy of the history of philosophy. The opposition, the greatest one conceivable—that between the passionate and often even irrational practice of human beings and philosophically stated rationality—is, on the whole, not that of an antithesis that cannot be mediated. On the contrary, it is a question of a dialectical activity which happens within the law of universal progress. What looks at first glance like an irreconcilable opposition appears after speculative penetration as an occurrence which, for the initiated member, takes place on a higher level, namely, on the level of the puppeteer who holds the strings and directs the actions of the puppets fighting each other. Speculation, therefore, starts with historical facts: "we may affirm absolutely that *nothing great in the World* has been accomplished without *passion*." The other element, however, which helps weave the world-historical carpet is the idea; thus the two are *interwoven*: "the one the warp, the other the woof of the vast arras-web of Universal History."[13]

Hegel's philosophy also may be read as a theory of conflict, as it has been outlined, for example, in our time by Coser and Dahrendorf. In the Hegelian theory of conflict, subjective interests (rational and irrational ones) continually suspend the status quo and propel it into new situations, which mean new challenges, and which finally find their (preliminary) solution (sublation) in a more mediated degree of idea and matter, of rationality and nature.

> The History of the World is not the theatre of happiness. Periods of happiness are blank pages in it, for they are periods of harmony— periods when the antithesis is in abeyance. Reflection on self—the Freedom above described—is abstractly defined as the formal element of the activity of the absolute Idea. The realizing *activity* of which we have spoken is the middle term of the Syllogism, one of whose extremes is the Universal essense, the *Idea*, which reposes in the penetralia of Spirit; and the other, the complex of external things— objective matter. That activity is the medium by which the universal latent principle is translated into the domain of objectivity. . . .
>
> The building of a house is, in the first instance, a subjective aim and design. On the other hand we have, as means, the several substances

required for the work—Iron, Wood, Stones. The elements are made use
of in working up this material. . . . Thus the elements are made use of in
accordance with their nature, and yet to co-operate for a product, by
which their operation is limited. Thus the passions of men are
gratified; they develop themselves and their aims in accordance with
their natural tendencies, and build up the edifice of human society;
thus fortifying a position for Right and Order *against themselves*.

The connection of events indicated above, involves also the fact,
that in history an additional result is commonly produced by human
actions beyond that which they aim at and obtain—that which they
immediately recognize and desire. They gratify their own interests;
but something further is thereby accomplished, latent in the actions in
question, though not present to their consciousness, and not included
in their design.[14]

Because Hegel accepts two levels in the world-historical process and
appropriates the higher level to rationality, from which it can determine
the process, remaining itself untouched and uninjured, a very high place
is given to the technique of argumentation present in reason (*Vernunft*):
"*It* is not the general idea that is implicated in opposition and combat,
and that is exposed to danger. It remains in the background, untouched
and uninjured. . . . The Idea pays the penalty of determinate existence
and of corruptibility, not from itself, but from the passions of individuals."[15] This offers remarkable advantages compared to other theories of
history: (1) the possible opposition of world-historical necessity and of
subjective interest is dissolved; (2) in view of undeniable, unreason-
able, and inhuman factors in the historical process, reason by remaining
in the background can protect itself against reproach; (3) the present is
the legitimate result of a reasonable process, and is therefore to be
reasonably and affirmatively recognized. This establishes an enormous
engagement on the part of the individual. On the one hand it is an
engagement in terms of a process of progressive emancipation. On the
other hand it is an anti-revolutionary engagement, which consists in
first safeguarding accomplishments and then in passing these on. There
is a relatively high degree of reason already embodied in the present,
thus it is worthwhile to develop it further.[16]

2. The speculative theory of the state mediates the subjective conscience, "a sanctum, the offense of which would be a sacrilege" (*Philosophy of Law*, § 137), with the state and with right, as being, in a triple
sense, the objectified embodiments of freedom. *First*, civil society and
the system of needs see themselves, under the speculative acceptance of

the doctrines of the classical English national economy, as being on the stage of history, in which economic and social progress emancipates itself from history.

Joachim Ritter considered Hegel's application of the results of the classical English national economy as the relevant step beyond the previous speculative processional theory of history, and at the same time as a step beyond the static models of the national economic theories. Hegel, he maintains, "understands the foundation of society upon nature as being the form, in which it renders itself independent towards the history of its origin, from which it emancipates itself. The un-historical nature of society is its historical essence."[17] In this way, the possible conflict between the right of *existing* and the right of *progressing* is mediated. Consequently, the tension between history and law and the tension between the main part of Hegel's *Philosophy of Law* and the final paragraphs of the *Philosophy of Law* on the world-historical process is mediated. *Second*, only the formal side of freedom, the abstract right, becomes the content of the law of the state and of the rules of the pluralist society; the separation between the "system of needs" and the "true designations of freedom" only really liberates the latter.

Joachim Ritter clarifies how it is just the limitation of civic society to man's "natural will" which releases the "true designations of liberty": "In this release lies the positive historical significance of abstract liberty and of its emancipative constitutionalizing through *un-mediation (Entzweiung)*. Because the purpose of society lies exclusively in the 'welfare' of men, it does not establish any purposes which must annihilate the right of man's individuality and with that man's substantial liberty. Just through its abstract lack of history society releases the right of individuality to subjectivity."[18]

And *third*, the conflict is principally resolvable when and as far as the individual voluntarily forms itself according to the already fulfilled realizations of freedom in culture, politics, and society, and thus finally freely mediates itself with them.

Hermann Lübbe presents a truly Hegelian proposition of mediation for the antithetical formulation of § 137 of the *Philosophy of Law* when he describes how the individual conscience, as a rule, is not in an isolated way opposed to a given order, but in a "relatively unanimous coherence of communication": "thus the moral consciousness forms itself into the autonomous competence of conscience through the 'objective spirit' of the family, of the civic society and of the state, and finds its substance in its ethics."[19] All three aspects mentioned above are at the same time remarkable facts which clarify the measure of self-mediation of reason already realized in the present. What Hegel described thus as factually existing, and what he secured by means of a special technique of anticipatory argumentation in the story of the owl of Minerva, must exercise a strong influence on the public consciousness and on the self-understanding of any politically active person, simply and just because it exists in reality in rudimentary form. By means of the subsequent description of events and statement of what is reasonable in them the speculative theory of the state *mediates itself* as a social, political, and cultural force against the relatively settled factuality of the state. In this way it structures the predisposition of consciousness and horizon of expectation for a potential reformative action and it does so by way of *self-fulfilling prophecies*.

In the anniversary year of 1870, Hegel's biographer, Karl Rosenkranz, describes in detail to what degree the descriptions of the system of civic society *differ* from the reality of the factual conditions in the Prussian state:

> Hegel's science of politics could not satisfy any of the three parties in whose midst it appeared. It contradicted feudalism, which likes to call itself patriarchal constitution, through the demand for lawfulness; it contradicted abstract democracy, which flatters the sovereignty of the people, through the demand for monarchy; it contradicted aristocracy through the demand for a representation of the people. It contradicted the bureaucracy of a civil servant's government through the freedom of the press, of the trial by jury and of the independence of corporations; it contradicted the hierarchy of all denominations through the demand for the subordination of religion in its appearance as Church under the sovereignty of the State and through the demand for the emancipation of a science from the authority of the Church; it contradicted the industrial state, which attempts to catch the people for the slavery of the factory work via the bait of wealth and of material welfare, through the demand for morality as being the absolute purpose of the state; and finally it contradicts the enlightened despotism, which wants to do everything for but nothing through the people, through the demand for a constitution, not to mention the cosmopolitan socialism which it confronts with the historical and national character of the state. Hegel's contradiction was not, as it occasionally happens, the contradiction of a still uninhabited adolescent naivety, but the contradiction of a critically penetrated mellowed judgement, well aware of its

significance. Therefore, he thoroughly incensed all parties against
himself.[20]

Rosenkranz is right in remarking that Hegel exacerbated all parties
against himself. But at the same time Hegel set *standards* for the public
consciousness such as to enthuse the individual to behave according to
the "already" factually and necessarily existing. This means just the
intention to first *provoke* the annoyance of the different parties and then
to *mediate* the one-sided annoyance and its causes with each other. The
citizen is supposed to conduct himself in terms of a self-evident affirmation of a political structure, the historical necessity of which is speculatively proven. In that way, a self-fulfilling prophecy is started, and
hardened and immobilized structures are dissolved through criticism of
the same, or rather they are brought along the way to self-dissolution
and further development. That is exactly the speculative relationship
between philosophical theory-making and political practice. The
philosophical theory indirectly activates political practice, in an unrevo-
lutionary, nay in an anti-revolutionary way, because the way things
should be, the reality and the ideal, are not confronted with each other
harshly and strictly, but are mediated with each other. For reasons which
are connected with the strategy of this kind of political practice of
speculative theory the picture of the "owl of Minerva" cannot be turned
into the object of such a speculative interpretation *within* the *Philosophy
of Law* itself.

3. The speculative theory of environment mediates idea and matter,
human practice and nature. It does this first in the forming and shaping
of matter and products into house and home and also in the speculative
representation of these transformations. Hegel differentiates between
the forming of a thing as a more intense form of taking possession and
the mere grasping of it, the mere marking it as ours. In the picture of the
construction of a house he described the way of taking possession
adequate to the spirit: "to impose a form on a thing," it says in §56 of
the *Philosophy of Law*, "is the mode of taking possession most in conformity with the Idea to this extent, that it implies a union of subject
and object." Even the taking possession of one's own body happens
according to this paradigm: "It is only through the development of his
own body and mind, essentially through his self-consciousness's apprehension of itself as free, that he takes possession of himself and
becomes his own property and no one else's." That is why private

property is one of the ways of taking possession of things and with it an embodiment of liberty. That, however, is only one aspect, not the most important or the central one. The central element in the shaping and forming of things is the "correspondence of the concrete ideal with its external reality":

> The general law which in this connection we can assert consists in this, that man in his worldly environment must be domesticated and at home, that the individual must appear as having his abode, and therefore as being free, in nature and all external relations, so that both sides, (i) the subjective inner totality of character and the character's circumstances and activity and (ii) the objective totality of external existence, do not fall apart as disparate and indifferent to one another, but show that they harmonize and belong together. For external objectivity, in so far as it is the actuality of the Ideal, must give up its purely objective independence and inflexibility in order to evince itself as identical with that (subjectivity) of which it is the external existence.[21]

Private property, landscaping, technique, trade, and all accomplishments of civilization are mediations and embodiments of the processes of work, of the self-emergence of freedom. In this respect, the idyllic stage of a direct unity of mind and nature is followed by the heroic stage, which in turn is followed by the stage of universal mediations.

Hegel distinguishes three different ways of looking at such harmony: the first situation of the correspondence of the concrete ideal with its external reality is that of the so-called Golden Age, the idyllic life: "Under such conditions on the one hand nature satisfies without trouble to man every need that may stir within him"; but Hegel points out: "Man may not pass his life in such an idyllic poverty of spirit: he must work. What he has an urge for, he must struggle to obtain by his own activity."[22]

On the contrary, there is the situation, in Hegel's words, of "universal culture": "In this situation the long and complicated connection between needs and work, interests and their satisfaction, is completely developed in all its ramifications, and every individual, losing his independence, is tied down in an endless series of dependences on others." He critizes this situation, too: "The individual is not at home even in his immediate environment, because it does not appear as his own work. What he surrounds himself with here has not been brought about by himself; it has been taken from the supply of what was already available, produced by others, and indeed in a most mechanical and therefore formal way, and acquired by him only through a long chain of efforts and needs foreign to himself."[23] Between those situations in which man is eliminated, midway between the "Golden Age" and the "perfectly developed universal mediation of civil society" (midway in the process of history, not as the final result of history), there is the "Heroic" or "Ideal Age" which, for example, Homer describes. This third and ideal situation is an idyllic one, but not in the limited mode of the first one; "on the contrary, within this original mode of life deeper interests arise in relation to which the whole external world is there only as an accessory, as the ground and means for higher ends, yet as a ground and an environment over which that harmony and independence is diffused and comes into appearance only because each and everything produced and used by human hands is at the same time prepared and enjoyed by the very man who needs it."[24]

These universal mediations, however, do not suspend art, religion, and philosophy, do not abolish the theory and the individual, and do not dissolve them in a panlogical materialization of total organization and techniques. On the contrary, Hegel maintains, using Goethe's *Hermann und Dorothea* as an example, that even in the various mediations present in economy, technology, trade, and medias of information, the material and the motives of the heroic art of the epic poem are not yet obsolete. On the contrary, in such situations, situations in which there is a leaning towards universal and infinite mediation, the arts, for example, must illustrate the degree and the means of all forces of mediation and of materialization—i.e., man in his self-gained moral, political, and cultural self-determination. This is a different goal than that of industrialism, economy, and total administration.

Hegel poses the question whether heroic ways of representation and the horizons of problems from earlier times could and might be transferred to our times. He comes to the conclusion that this transferral would only mean great difficulties and danger. Not only was that permitted, however, it was even necessary. In *Hermann und Dorothea*, Goethe had presented such an outline for the ideal mediation in the present age, an outline meant to be critical of culture, civilization, and techniques, and meant to serve as a model. In the bad idyll of *Luise* by J. H. Voss, the self-sufficient country life is connected to the outside world via the consumption of imported coffee and tobacco, but the connection is merely external and pleasure-bound: "Coffee and sugar are products which could not have originated in such a circle, and they point at once to a totally different context, to a strange world with its manifold interconnections of trade and factories, in short to the world of modern industry. That circle of country-life is therefore not wholly self-enclosed." In the more examplary story of Hermann and Dorothea, who belong to and are at home in their families, their circle of friends, their country, and their environment is not such an egotistically consummating one; on the contrary, this mediation of culture and nature, of country, history, and human being is in close contact with the great interest of the age (the battles of the French Revolution, the defense of their own country, the aid to the refugees from France). Thus the scene of bourgeois liberality and of a humanely shaped environment is "transferred into the broader scope of a fuller and richer life" through conversation, readiness for defense, and active help.[25] They don't smoke and don't drink coffee, they enjoy the homegrown wine: "With care the gammer brought clear, excellent wine in a cut-glass flask on a shining pewter plate, along with greenish runners, the proper goblets for Rhine wine."[26]

Thus the Hegelian mediation is not liquidation of nature through civilization, and not violation of soil through the idea, but the taking shape, the embodiment of the idea in the reality, the acclimatization of liberty and humanity in the reality of this world. The function of art, of which it is said elsewhere in the *Enzyklopädie* that philosophy had deprived it of its function as it had deprived religion of its function, is just the following: to keep up the vision of something more than operationalistic-rationalistic mediation in times marked by the rational forming of products in civilization and technique, and to demonstrate to the world the self-fulfilling prophecy of ideal and humane mediations which has been alienated by industrialism, economics, and total administration. In this respect, even in the industrial age, where idea and matter are mediated not merely for purposes of illustration on the screen, but which exist in fact in the real mediations of industry and administration and which are determined to expand their mediations to totality, thus transgressing the individual and individuality, art, as criticism of such tendentiously totalitarian mediations, is not outdated. Art is not obsolete so long as these mediations transgress the region in which the self-responsible and free citizen exists as its center.[27]

The mediation between idea and matter appears under double perspective as an indispensible contribution to the self-mediation of reason: as a forming, shaping, and predisposition of matter and nature to be man's house and home, and as the result of man's striving for an embodiment and formation of his ideal freedom. Such a theory of environment has a double character of appeal. First, it offers the justification of the rationality of shaping the world into house and home for man. Second, it entails a description in which one cannot fail to find the civic subject understood not only as a means, but also as the goal of any formation of nature, not forgetting that in a dialectical way the human being itself has its "natural side."

III

In the sphere of practical mediations and materializations, the above-mentioned methods of mediation in the field of the objective spirit show remarkable achievements. These achievements consist first in a "compensation" of factual antitheses, then in a plausible contribution of this compensation to the "emancipation" of freedom, and finally in the "mediation" of the philosophizing individual in these processes of reconciliation and of embodiment. Yet there are elements in these mediations which are not logically cogent, which are, in fact, even contradictory in parts.

1. Hegel's theory of history is neither convincing in terms of the unavoidability and necessity of the self-mediation of reason by means of passion, nor in terms of the thesis of the cunning of reason, which constitutes an unacceptable disrespect for individual morality. Finally it is not convincing in the sudden necessity for the French Revolution, after "the new the latest standard round which the people rally," had been developed in the Protestant Reformation.

What is it about the particular quality of individual rationality and morality, if not it itself, then its opposite (passion and egotistical interests), that constitutes the support of historical progress? Is morality here not deprived of any justification in the historical process through the intention to make "necessity a virtue," namely, to declare the real (the actual existence of interests and passions) to be rational? This would mean an intolerable domination by the absolute and by objective ration-

ality in its mysterious procession-like advance and would involve im-
plausible mystery-mongering in the choice of its means, so that individual rationality, desiring to be or actually being rational and moral,
could only be frustrated.

Indeed, Hegel explicitly called the socially and politically involved
morality an unbearable, unacceptable, a "terrible" liberty:

> Robbespierre set up the principle of Virtue as supreme, and it may be
> said that with this man Virtue was an earnest matter. Virtue and Terror
> are the order of the day; for Subjective Virtue, whose sway is based on
> disposition only, brings with it the most fearful tyranny. It exercises its
> power without legal formalities, and the punishment it inflicts is
> equally simple—Death. This tyranny could not last; for all inclinations,
> all interests, reason itself revolted against this terrible consistent Lib-
> erty, which in its concentrated intensity exhibited so fanatical a
> shape.[28]

In that respect the French Revolution can actually appear only as a
world-historical calamity, as a calamity of the Catholic Principle, which
is justified in view of the incapability of Catholicism to liberate first
from the inside the consciousness and the conscience, and then to mate-
rialize in reality bit by bit and in a non-revolutionary way. But what are
we to think of the universality of the Protestant Principle, of which it is
said, in the first chapter of the *Philosophy of History* on "The Modern
Time":

> Time, since that epoch, has had no other work to do than the formal
> imbuing of the world with this principle, in bringing the Reconciliation
> implicit (in Christianity) into objective and explicit realization. Culture
> is essentially concerned with Form; the work of Culture is the produc-
> tion of the Form of Universality, which is none other than Thought.
> Consequently Law, Property, Social Morality, Government, Constitu-
> tions, etc., must be conformed to general principles, in order that they
> may accord with the idea of Free Will and be Rational. In virtue of that
> degree of intensity which Subjective Free Spirit has attained, elevat-
> ing it to the form of Universality, Objective Spirit attains manifesta-
> tions.[30]

Irrationality is the reality which follows the Protestant Reformation
and the French Revolution, of which Hegel himself said: "it is a false
principle that the fetters which bind Right and Freedom can be broken
without the emancipation of conscience—that there can be a Revolution
without a Reformation."[31]

2. In the theory of the modern state, an unmediated opposition

remains between the self-supporting and flexibly stabilizing system of civic society, its liberties, its positive disunions, its essential variables (police and institutions) on the one hand, and the procession-like advance of the historical process, on the other hand, which is conjured up at the end of the *Philosophy of Law*, and which does not allow for any such systems which flexibly stabilize themselves against external and internal influences.

But even the attempt to represent the Revolution as necessary for the Roman Catholic countries[32] is not very plausible, as the Reformation itself had sprung up in a Catholic country. The opposition of the self-stabilizing system of national economy in the main part of the *Philosophy of Law* cannot logically be mediated with the picture of the self-surpassing system and the unflagging process painted by the final paragraphs of the *Philosophy of Law*. In final analysis, even the opposition between law and conscience, between the rights of materialized freedom and the single, insignificant individual's right of conscience is maintained in § 137 of the *Philosophy of Law* in terms of an indissolubility of the opposition. There only remains the hope that in case of the failure of individual morality, of its disregard by the state, of its prohibition or its persecution and eradication, the promoter of the historical process as a whole (this promoter is not man but God) will indeed represent the "higher" interests of morality and of liberty against the individually oppressed and suppressed morality and will then turn it into reality in the future as well. Nevertheless this is purely a consolation.

Julius Binder's interpretation, which one-sidedly accords significance to the state and to the legal system, has a certain plausibility when he demands, "that even the properly speaking free will cannot lead an existence outside the law, and that a realm of liberty which is not at the same time real as law, is an absurdity."[33]

The same is true, however, of the panlogical interpretation of Hegel by Friedrich Jonas, who sees the goal of speculative mediation in a universal mediation in technical organizations, encroaching on the individual subject and resolving it in its subjectivity. According to Jonas mediation is "in as much as it finds its concept in certain interest, in a certain spirit . . . no longer pure organisation."[34]

And further there is the interpretation of Hegel by the Frankfurt School which, no less plausibly, wants to defend the "autonomy of the individual" against "the central regulation of life, the administration

planning each detail, the so-called strict rationality" against the "right
of the yet living subject." With Max Horkheimer, this support for the
sovereignty of individual morality and self-designation plucks up cour-
age for a late conjuring of the liberalism of the possessive individual
against totalitarian currents in the East and the West. "The epoch shows
tendencies to liquidate all that which is connected with the individual's
autonomy, even if it was a relative one. The citizen in Liberalism was
able to unfold his strength within certain limits, to a certain degree his
fate was the result of his own activities."[35] Herbert Marcuse starts with a
similar diagnosis of the "one-dimensional man" and demands the rebellion which should contain "a strong element of spontaneity, nay, of
anarchism."[36] He proclaims the rebellion of the subjective conscience of
the individual citizens, "there is no other judge above them except for
the established authorities, of the police and of their own consciences. If
they use violence, they do not start a new chain of violent acts, but they
break the established chain. As they will be beaten, they know the risk,
and if they are willing to take it upon themselves, no third person, least
of all the educator and the intellectual, has the right to preach absti-
nence to them."[37]

The thesis of liberty as a rebellion against unbearable conditions, as
the emancipation of liberty against the system of prevailing norms of
injustice cannot be formulated any more plausibly than can Binder's
thesis of liberty as a right. To support the students' rebellion, Marcuse,
too, could affirmatively quote the following sentence of Hegel to describe the French Revolution: "Never since the sun has stood in the
firmament and the planets revolved around him had it been perceived
that man's existence centres in his head, i.e. in Thought, inspired by
which he builds up of the world of reality."[38] As a whole, all the
above-mentioned positions in their one-sidedness do not do justice to
Hegel's thesis of liberty.[39]

And finally, it is unsatisfactory that the achievement of philosophy
and of critical theory within the state itself does not become a topic for
the theory of state and law within the *Philosophy of Law*. Indeed, if
philosophy is only a reflection of already developed phenomena, the owl
who wrote Hegel's *Philosophy of Law* had poor eyesight, for the formations actually carried out in state and society were not at all so rosy and so
rational as the owl subsequently saw them.[40]

3. It is not logically sound in the theory of environment to block the

process of total materialization in technique, the sciences, and organization and to criticize it via the concrete utopia of a philistine idyll *à la* Goethe's *Hermann und Dorothea*. In any case, the thesis of the necessity of the *Aufhebung*, of even sublating civic subjectivity in greater mediations would be plausible from the angle of the model of reason which mediates itself with itself.

The bourgeois idyll of Goethe's *Hermann und Dorothea* represents itself as a system which statically maintains itself in itself in a flexible way. The system continues steadfastly against the total and universal organizations of commerce, industry, and administration, it safeguards the interests of civic subjectivity and behaves selfishly in this respect. To present such a system of mediation of man and environment as exemplary means to criticize and to want to block off the formations emerging in the process of universal mediations and reconciliations between nature and spirit, between idea and reality according to the demand for the embodiment from a certain level, namely, from that level where the civic subjectivity—which could be called the center of such a philosophy—would then become itself substance and matter for the *Aufhebung* in such supra-individual mediations.[41] The rehabilitation of art is an interference and attempts to preserve something against the course of time which should necessarily suspend itself. Art only represents mediations and materializations of the ideal, with very limited technical means, in a very limited area, and furthermore only for illustration, in times which provide better mechanisms of mediation and embodiment.

To just that degree by which the achievement of mediation grows in industry, administration, and organization at large, such partial mediations of idea and substance as found in the arts, such mediations of the world here and the world beyond, as found in religion, and such mediations of rationality and reality, as found in academic philosophy, lose their right to existence. They need not be fought against, they are eliminated more and more with each new level; they themselves and their functions fall victim to the *Aufhebung* in universal mediation. Not only the end of art, but also the end of philosophy should be discussed as a business which is alien and hostile to materialization, as a theory which confronts practical mediation apart and unalloyed. Traditionally speaking, J. E. Erdmann's interpretation was consistent when he called the Hegelian system *in toto*, Panlogism.[42] However, does it not rather lie in the consistency of the Hegelian system, described here as a system of mediation between theory and practice, that philosophy is also in its exposed position to be "suspended" in the universality of mediations and embodiments? And one would have to ask, with Jonas, are not the presuppositions, functions, and goals of philosophy necessarily eliminated in the progress of more and more universal mediations and materializations, along with the sovereign objectivity of the thinking and acting citizen? Is it therefore cogent to claim that philosophy, even if in the shape of speculative philosophy, should be at the end of a process which is destined for mediation and embodiment, as the system of the *Enzyklopädie* suggests? Is not the sovereign, unmediated philosophy indeed still the representation of an idea not yet totally and completely enough embodied as reality, having a function only for as long as it is necessary to evaluate the already existing degree of mediations, to contribute to the mediation of the spirit and of itself, and through this becoming aware of the process itself to create, by way of self-fulfilling prophecies, predispositions for further mediations which, however, would surpass also the individual and his product—philosophy! In the *Enzyklopädie* the philosophy of history also appears as a part of the philosophy of the objective spirit, because the creation of the state is meant to look like the achievement of history. It goes without saying that the philosophy of history is not an essential part of the philosophy of the subjective spirit, although superficially it deals with nothing else but single individuals, with their passions, goals, and actions.[43]

But it is also totally wrong in keeping with speculative philosophy to place the *Philosophy of History* next to the system of the *Enzyklopädie* which was constructed by Hegel's first disciples still entirely in the traditional sense. If that were done it would become evident how the forces working towards actual embodiment in law, government, technique, environmental formation, changing and forming of natural resources are just as important and as necessary elements of the processional self-mediations of the spirit as the mediations of religion, art, and philosophy introduced in the traditional system. But in view of the program of the mediation between idea and soil, between spirit and nature, those mediations which are objects of history (in which philosophy can only occur as describing and affirming philosophy of history and nothing else), are more comprehensive and more far-reaching. And yet Hegel writes not only the *Aesthetics* and the *Philosophy of Religion*, he also philosophizes in the academic lecture hall.

These pent-up tensions, the disunion and half-heartedness in the process of the development towards more and more mediated structures, always appear there where the emancipation of the perceiving, moral, self-responsible civic subject is first concerned, and where then the stabilization of this civic individuality, as opposed to more and more wide-spread mediations in organization, state, and environment is concerned. In the drafting of a system, therefore, it is not a matter of a constantly and purely self-overcoming system; it is a matter of a system which produces itself through overcoming by means of the essential variables "mediating" and *aufheben* and which finally maintains itself flexibly (dialectically) in high complexity. "Philosophy in any case always comes on the scene too late to give it [the instructions]. As the thought of the world, it appears only when actuality is already there cut and dried after its process of formation has been completed;"[44] thus philosophy only postperforms that which had already been factually shaped; "the ideal apprehends this same real world in its substance and builds it up for itself into the shape of an intellectual realm."[45] Not a word is said about a possible influence of such speculative reconstruction of the real world on its present and future development. Such an influence can and may be expected because what is described can no longer be considered as the latest actuality. It has itself already turned old and hardened, so that in case of a rejuvenating of such an obsolete structure this rejuvenating could come from everywhere but from philosophy; "by philosophy's grey in grey it cannot be rejuvenated but only understood."[46] Thus the remoteness from practice and the absence of influence on the formations of the real world becomes the *conditio per quam* and the *conditio sine qua non* of philosophy. Philosophy's business is thinking, not acting.

IV

If we are now asking for the philosophical reasons for these oppositions which speculatively are not harmonized or which are only superficially harmonized, we have to ask for the self-understanding of a philosophy, the unmediated existence of which is under discussion as well. Here it strikes us immediately that Hegel does not use an explicit theory, but that he uses pictures and stories to demonstrate a self-understanding of philosophy which indeed acknowledges and describes mediations and materializations, but does not wish to make itself the object of mediations.

The picture or image of the "owl of Minerva" is explicitly developed to answer the question whether philosophy might or shall be capable of "giving instruction as to what the world ought to be." This picture postulates the distance of philosophy from practical life and actions, and its competence for the inconsequential describing, nay the subsequent describing of things which actually are no longer of topical interest. The picture of the "Deeds in the World-Spirit" in the history of philosophy show the intimacy of philosophy with the hidden decisive subject and the laws of movement of nature and of history; it shows the necessity of their recording and the eminent significance of such abstractions which seem boring and superfluous at first glance. The remoteness from practice constituted by philosophy is more than balanced by this special intimacy of the philosophical abstractions to the essence of things. Hegel sharply and passionately refutes the reproach that philosophical works were "verbal abstractions only": "No, no; they are the deeds of the world-spirit, gentlemen, and therefore of fate. The philosophers are in so doing nearer to God than those nurtured upon spiritual crumbs; they read or write the orders as they receive them in the original: they are obliged to continue writing on. Philosophers are the initiated ones—those who have taken part in the advance which had been made into the in-most sanctuary."[47] What seems insignificant and superfluous at first glance thus becomes the servant of intrinsic things. And the everyday things receive a secondary, derived significance from these intrinsic things. That which philosophy formulates is not, by the way, subjective randomness, but it is necessary. It is dictated by the subject proper of world and history.

Philosophy's function in this picture is not a leading but a serving one. That which philosophy has over others—"others have their particular interests—this dominion, these riches, this girl"—is "the advantage of having objects which are past and dealing with abstraction."[48] Finally, the picture of the "Sanctuary Apart," of the "isolated order of priests who must not mix with the world," whose task is "to protect the truth," shows an esoteric area which constitutes and maintains itself through its distance to the ordinary world and which exhibits an elite and detached disinterest for the destiny of man and for the mediations and materializations of truth. The difficulties of the world are not the objects of the philosopher's business: "How the actual present-day world is to find its way out of this state of disruption, and what form it is to take, are questions which must be left to itself to settle, and to deal with them is not the immediate practical business and concern of Philosophy."[49] That means, indeed, that philosophy takes a keen interest in the realizations and formations of the objective spirit; however, this interest is secondary because the formations of the spirit are only interesting in terms of how and in what way the truth embodies itself in them. And should the truth not be able to embody itself in reality for reasons of many an adversity, "the isolated order of the philosophers" has the truth present as its own property, as elsewhere realized or realizable, or, in any case, as the object of veneration and adoration in the inner circle of the "isolated sanctuary." The philosophical self-understanding sketched in these three pictures is *nowhere* theoretically developed; on the one hand, it even contradicts the factual role of a philosophy which is preoccupied, and exclusively so, with these mediations; on the other hand, it contradicts the factual achievement of mediation which Hegel's philosophy had actually brought about in its academic, cultural, and political environment. In fact, Hegel's philosophy has a special degree of significance for the guiding of practice. It has an effect on the politics of theoretical thought and of philosophy. Above all, it has an effect just through the way and manner of its shaping of the historical material for purposes of the self-orientation of the contemporaries, and it has an effect through the way and manner of its exaggeration of the tendencies in the Prussian state and therewith going beyond any reality, that these tendencies are not postulated as philosophical necessity and as actually also existing structures, but are merely matters of "subsequent" description.

If the pictures conveying knowledge of the self-understanding of philosophy are to be taken seriously, two ways offer themselves as to how to mediate them with the factually existing practice which Hegel's philosophy describes and under which it places itself. The first way would be, indeed, to accept a sanctuary apart from an esoteric, self-loyal philosophy, a sanctuary which would then externally produce theoretical or philosophical theories for exoteric purposes. From the vantage point of such an acceptance even the above-mentioned contradictions in the mediations of the objective spirit would be explicable as inconsistencies taken into the bargain under the aegis of practice. I will not take that way because it will lead to insoluble epistemological difficulties as far as methods are concerned. Besides, this maxim of interpretation has helped to develop dangerous, but evidently not ineffective, dogmatics of criticism and of revolution in the Hegelian hermeneutics of Bruno Bauer and Karl Marx.[50]

The second way would be to interpret this opposition in the roles of philosophy as being speculatively intended and as being designed for the purposes of improving philosophical influence on the mediations and embodiments in the world. In such a case the tension in the practical mediating work, caused by this opposition, would have to be worked away bit by bit later on without, however, letting the materialized side have the certainty that the sanctuary apart would not now or ever be totally integrated into the mediation and would be suspended. For methodical reasons alone I prefer this way.

V

A philosophy which presents itself as being sacred, esoteric, necessary, as being descriptive and not active, that kind of philosophy can, by using all the potential trust the world offers to it, carry out its interests in the world all the more intensively, the less it pretends to be interested in the description of the identity of reason and of reality. Furthermore, if it always mediates itself only in a mediated way with reality, and should these mediations fail, it can withdraw, uncontested and unaccused, into the academic fields of theory-making, into speculative logic and into speculative theory of practice, and it can care for the "protection of truth."

1. But what are the concrete political interests of philosophy in objective spirit? From the descriptions in the *Philosophy of History* and in the *Philosophy of Law* the following can be named as such goals: the citizen's liberty and security, formal law, social plurality, reformation and not revolution. These concepts, however, are not developed theoretically and systematically in their substance and then presented as essential variables of a system of civil liberty. Rather, stories are told, stories about the necessary process of emancipation of liberty and history, of history of philosophy and history of religion, stories (as re-narrations) about the reasonable and the real condition of the contemporary political, cultural, and social world. In the stories about the process of history, these values appear as invariants yet to be emancipated.[51] In the story

about the reality of reason, they appear as essential variables which may sway only within certain limits unless the whole system of civil liberties shall be destroyed. The factor which performs the essential emancipation and stabilization here is the principle of mediating criticism, the Protestant Principle.[52]

Joachim Ritter presented Hegel's political goals as an interpretation from the *Rechtsphilosophie*[53] without elaborating on the level of these essential variables in Hegel's philosophical system and Hegel's philosophical system in its mediated relation to political practice (i.e., to the system of embodiment). The story about the exemplary nature of heroic idyllics in the modern industrial and economic state has for its theme the essential nature of man (not to be mediated) as man's right to autonomy and to a goal-in-itself within a world which should be man's house and home, but not a superordinated higher complexity.

One could, in connection with Hegel's preference for the principle of Reform over that of Revolution, outline a theory of pragmatic criticism of politics and law, a theoretical polemic against the theory of revolution developed by Herbert Marcuse, directed also against Julius Binder's conservative theory of the state, and against Friedrich Jonas's theory of organization, which suspends the individual. This could be done as a strategy and tactics of political critique, connected to the Hegelian dialectically mediated relation of philosophical theory and political practice. Hegel's practice of philosophy is an excellent example of the concept of critique that could be developed.[54]

2. The nature of such a strategy for efficiency is clear. Philosophy sees itself on the one hand as an essential part, even in its own perfection, of an ongoing great process of mediation and of materialization, and philosophy presents itself, on the other hand, as uninfluenced and detached, as on the outside of these mediations. The system to be developed on this basis and to be flexibly stabilized would be neither autonomous and perfect in itself, nor would it advance uninhibited in an infinite progress of more and more total mediations. Hegel outlined such a dialectical theory of environment and of technique in the passages quoted earlier from the *Ästhetik*. In 1845, Hegel's disciple Ernst Kapp developed in *Philosophische und vergleichende allgemeine Erdkunde* a detailed philosophy of environment which is an important alternative to Binder and Jonas's totalitarian structures.[55] And it is more assuredly not an academic philosophical system in the traditional sense, for example, in

the sense that the first Hegelians produced the *Encyclopedia of Philosophical Sciences*. In view of these difficulties in Hegel's attempt, which can be concretized in the meanings that are played upon in the German word *aufheben*, it is a fascinating attempt also from a methodical perspective. It is an attempt, namely, constantly to protect the degree of already achieved liberty against regressions, in an anti-revolutionary and at the same time completely emancipatory manner, and to develop this further into a flexible, self-maintaining system of civil liberties. An essential part of this method is the removal of oppositions concerning the aegis of practice in philosophy and of philosophy as the sanctuary apart.

3. The composition of a system composed for the purposes of self-mediation is plausible enough from the point of view of a strategy for efficiency. But even for the strategy of the self-assurance of philosophy, which must not lose its head in the mediations which it effects, the self-understanding of the sanctuary apart is indispensable. Should the maxim of esoterics-exoterics-interpretation be preferred, I could reply that the secret of Hegel's philosophy might coincide with or determine the strategy of both efficiency and self-reassurance. The secret would then be connected with the special raw material of the *humanum*, which must bring itself into reality, but in such a way that it would neither lose itself in mere external naturalness, nor surrender itself in the self-indebted process of strict rationality. This engagement in the *humanum* and in its "sublation" (emancipation and conservation) demonstrates itself in all of Hegel's descriptions of the mediations in objective spirit. Philosophy, however, on the one hand describes those mediations from an "unmediated" viewpoint, and on the other hand occurs as an essential material within these mediations and embodiments. The above-mentioned problems in the dialectical structures of objective spirit and the self-understanding of philosophy had to be mediated with one another for the purpose of demonstrating that, according to this genuine model of the system of Hegelian philosophy, neither the world nor philosophy have come to an end.

NOTES

1. *Jubiläumsausgabe*, Vol. 15, pp. 73f.
2. Ibid., p. 48. Cf. J. N. Findlay's understanding of dialectics in Hegel as a "fairly definite, very valuable method of higher-level comment on previously entertained notions and positions" in the Supplementary Note of his book, *Hegel: A Re-Examination* (New York: Oxford University Press, 1976), p. 354.
3. *Jubiläumsausgabe*, Vol. 4, p. 177.
4. Ibid., Vol. 15, p. 39.
5. Ibid., Vol. 5, p. 335.
6. Ibid., Vol. 8, p. 197.
7. Ibid., Vol. 7, p. 40.
8. Ibid., Vol. 3, pp. 315f.
9. Ibid., Vol. 10, p. 15.
10. The self-mediation of the idea in religion, art, and philosophy is the one side; the self-mediation of the idea as the embodiment in culture, politics, and technique is the other side of this Janus-faced system. In that respect, the *Heidelberger Enzyklopädie* of 1817 (1827) represents only one of the two sides; it is obvious that there cannot be a mere book-representation of the second side.
11. Konstantin Rössler, *System der Staatslehre* (Leipzig 1857), p. xvii.
12. Cf. Hans-Martin Sass, "Hegel feiern!" In *Deutsche Feiern* (Frankfurt, 1977).
13. Hegel, *The Philosophy of History*, trans. J. Sibree, rev. ed., p. 23.
14. Ibid., pp. 26-27.
15. Ibid., p. 33.
16. For details see H. M. Sass, "Das Verhältnis der Geschichtsphilosophie zur politischen Praxis bei Hegel" in *Hegel-Jahrbuch* 1968/69, ed. W. R. Beyer (Meisenheim, 1970), pp. 59-72.
17. J. Ritter, *Metaphysik und Politik* (Frankfurt am Main, 1969), p. 227.
18. Ibid., p. 229.
19. H. Lübbe, "Zur Dialektik des Gewissens nach Hegel," in *Hegelstudien*, Beiheft 1 (Heidelberger Hegeltage, 1962; Bonn, 1964), p. 258.
20. Karl Rosenkranz, *Hegel als deutscher Nationalphilosoph* (Leipzig, 1870), p. 162.
21. Hegel, *Aesthetics*, trans. T. M. Knox, Vol. I (Oxford, 1975), pp. 252f.
22. Ibid., p. 259.
23. Ibid., p. 260.
24. Ibid., pp. 216f.
25. Goethe, *Hermann und Dorothea*, p. 262.
26. Ibid., pp. 262f.
27. Cf. H. M. Sass: "Hegels Theorie bürgerlicher Umwelt," in *Hegel-Jahrbuch*, 1972, pp. 258-67.
28. Cf. H. M. Sass, "Die philosophische Erdkunde des Hegelianers Ernst Kapp," *Hegel-Studien*, 8, 1973, pp. 163-81.

29. Hegel, *The Philosophy of History*, p. 450f.
30. Ibid., pp. 416f.
31. Ibid., p. 453.
32. Ibid., pp. 419f.
33. J. Binder, "Die Freiheit als Recht," in *Verhandlungen des ersten Hegelkongresses,* ed. Wigersma (Tübingen and Haarlem, 1931), p. 167.
34. Fr. Jonas, *Sozialphilosophie der modernen Arbeitswelt* (Stuttgart, 1960), p. 216.
35. M. Horkheimer, *Traditionelle und kritische Theorie* (Vier Aufsätze: Frankfurt am Main, 1970), p. 9 (introduction to the reprint).
36. H. Marcuse, *Versuch über die Befreiung* (Frankfurt am Main, 1969, p. 130.
37. H. Marcuse, in Wolff, Moore, and Marcuse, *Kritik der reinen Toleranz* (Frankfurt am Main, 1967), pp. 127f.
38. Hegel, *The Philosophy of History*, p. 447.
39. Cf. H. M. Sass, "Hegels Rechtsphilosophie als Strategie pragmatischer Politik- und Rechtskritik." *Archiv für Rechts- und Sozialphilosophie*, 53 (1967), 257-76.
40. Cf. n. 20 above, Rosenkranz's judgment thereof, and n. 52, below.
41. H. M. Sass, "Meaning in Geography versus meaning in History," *Proceedings of the Bicentennial Philosophical Symposium*, 1976.
42. J. E. Erdmann, *Grundriss der Geschichte der Philosophie*, Vol. 2 (Berlin, 1866), pp. 594 and 611.
43. Against that cf. Erdmann, p. 605.
44. Hegel, *Philosophy of Right*, pp. 12f.
45. Ibid., p. 13.
46. Ibid.
47. *The History of Philosophy*, trans, E. S. Haldane and F. H. Simson, Vol. 2 (New York: The Humanities Press), p. 453.
48. Ibid.
49. *Philosophy of Religion*, trans. E. B. Speirs and J. B. Sanderson, Vol. III (London: Routledge & Kegan Paul), p. 151.
50. Cf. H. M. Sass, *Anmerkungen zur Vermutung von disciplina arcani in der Philosophie* (Festschrift Rudolf W. Meyer zum 60.Geburtstag, Basel, 1976).
51. Cf. my soon to be published essay, "Idealistische und materialistische Antithetik. Bruno Bauer und Karl Marx"; and my essay, "Bruno Bauer's Critical Theory," in *The Philosophical Forum*, 1977, issue 3/4.
52. Cf. H. M. Sass, *"Das Verhältnis der Geschichtsphilosophie bei Hegel."*
53. J. Ritter, "Hegel und die Französische Revolution," *loc. cit.*
54. *Archiv für Rechts- und Sozialphilosophie*, 53 (1967), 257-76.
55. Cf. H. M. Sass, "Die philosophische Erdkunde des Hegelianers Ernst Kapp. Ein Beitrag zur Wissenschaftstheorie und Fortschrittsdiskussion in der Hegelschule," *Hegelstudien*, 8 (1973), 163-81.

COMMENT ON

Sass's "Hegel's Concept of Philosophy and the Mediations of Objective Spirit"

DAVID R. LACHTERMAN

Dr. Sass has given us an interesting paper, at times highly challenging, at times somewhat obscure. I hasten to add that these obscurities are not of his own making; they stem, rather, from an almost unavoidable use of those key entries in the Hegelian lexicon that call out for conceptual and argumentative clarification. Before saying anything more about Dr. Sass's paper, let me urge on all of us at this conference the sense that terms such as "mediation," "reconciliation," *Aufhebung, Geist,* etc., are only so many placeholders, or promissory notes to be paid back in detailed analysis and non-technical paraphrase. If they are allowed to substitute, on their own, for such analyses, then we run the venerable risk of explaining *obscurum per obscurius.*

Within the exiguous compass of reply, it is impossible to speak significantly about all the issues Dr. Sass's lecture raises. Accordingly, I have singled out for scrutiny one small but, I hope, important strand in his complex argument; the remarks that follow are meant to complement his paper and to encourage further consideration of the problem. Stated most simply the issue is: Hegel's systematic speculation about human things presents itself as the *complete theory* of the so-called mediations that have occurred or are occurring in a multitude of humanly relevant domains; if we now include philosophy itself among such domains, then philosophy as a *complete* theory will have to furnish an account of itself, that is, it will have to display and explain the mediations within philosophy considered as one human domain and institution among others. This formulation becomes sufficiently less abstract in Dr. Sass's own words (sec. II): "How, third, the appropriation of such mediations [sc. in other domains] in the philosopher's thinking and acting and in his readers' thinking and acting takes on functions of mediation itself." This statement points us in even more concrete directions, first, because the conjunction of "thinking and acting" seems to specify in advance *what* it is for which Dr. Sass is searching and, second, because it hints that the relationship between what takes place in the philosophical domain and what takes place in the other domains to which philosophy is addressed, is not a linear juxtaposition of equals; instead, the intelligibility and thoroughness of what is to be accomplished in those latter domains is linked to the success or failure of what philosophy tries to achieve in regard to itself. If, in turn, philosophy's self-achievement is understood to depend, at least in part, on its practical or active involvement with the world in which it figures as a cultural institution, then a new criterion of the truth of a speculative system seems to recommend itself with forceful plausibility: The truth of a putatively complete philosophical system becomes bound up, in a decisive way, with that system's capacity to subsume and validate itself, not only or even primarily as still another *cognitive* formation which it must cognitively assess, but more importantly as an instance of a historically fixed and culturally influential activity that must be legitimated *qua* activity or socio-political *praxis*. In other and, I hope, clearer terms: we now need to distinguish between philosophy as an account *of* the union (of disunion) of theory and practice—where the first "of" is the grammarians' objective genitive—and philosophy looked upon as *both* a theory, i.e., an articulate discourse *and* a form of practice, more particularly, as a discursive practice that aims (or should aim) at bringing about changes in its auditors, and, through them, in the world at large. If, at first blush, Hegel's system, or more narrowly, his systematic account of "objective *Geist*", seems to be a logos of the non-philosophical or pre-philosophical deeds, the *erga* of others, on reflection, if Dr. Sass is right, the question emerges: What is the real or intended *ergon* of Hegel's own *logos*? In sum, if I have understood this part of his paper, Dr. Sass has shown us that the nowadays all-too-familiar matter of the relation of theory and practice is pertinently and inexorably applicable to the very philosophical discussion of this relation.

Let me stand back for a moment, before entering into some of the details of Dr. Sass's subsequent account. Certainly, the underlying question here is, or ought to be, patent to us all, even in its most homespun form. After all, Hegel wrote books and gave academic lectures; students, and others, read these books and heard these lectures. A complicated cultural apparatus of education, scholarly tradition, public discussion, and so on, provides the backdrop before which Hegel's literary activity enacts itself. Thus, the question—What we should do with the fruits of that activity, i.e., with Hegel's books, forces itself on us with a measure of obviousness (I say "obviousness" by way of asserting that it doesn't take current Parisian sophistication or older Talmudic wisdom to see this *as a question*).[1]

Is a Hegelian book a metaphorical ladder to be discarded at the end of my climb? Or a "self-consuming artifact"? Is a Hegelian book like an auto mechanic's manual that, once mastered, need be consulted again only when the "knack" I have acquired momentarily fails me? Or when a hitherto unseen case confronts me? Feuerbach, speaking, to be sure, of the *Science of Logic,* makes the point with comic immediacy:

> Of course, at the end [of the *Science of Logic*] I return to the beginning, but let us hope, not *in time,* that is, not in a way that would make me begin with the *Logic* all over again; for otherwise I would be necessitated to go the same way a second and a third time and so on with the result that my whole life will have become a circular movement within the Hegelian *Logic.*[2]

To raise the issue of the *ergon* of Hegel's discourse is to pose, as Sass and others have seen, a political question, in the broad, that is, Greek sense of the affairs and aims of the *polis.* More specifically, what is at stake in this question is, to use the title of Hans-Friedrich Fulda's monograph, *Das Recht der Philosophie in Hegel's Philosophie des*

Rechts.[3] Now it might appear to some that Hegel's own system, at least in its encyclopedic version, blocks a question of this kind; philosophy, together with art and religion, belongs to the sphere of *"absolute Geist*," while the political things fall within the antecedent sphere of *"objective Geist.*" This line of demarcation would accordingly seem to preclude assessments of philosophy that draw upon the standards and concepts of the second sphere rather than on those of the first. Nonetheless, using that demarcation for this purpose is artificial, for reasons Hegel himself indicates, although never in a thoroughly explicit and systematic manner. I can give only a quick sample of those reasons on the present occasion.

(1) In a long and crucially important footnote to Paragraph 552 of the Berlin *Encyclopedia,* the last paragraph of the section, "Der objektive Geist," Hegel takes up the "relation between the State and Religion" and in this context discusses the "famous or notorious" passage in Plato's *Republic* in which "Philosophy and State power must coincide, if the unhappiness of the peoples is to have an end." Hegel rejects the Platonic solution, *viz.,* that philosophers must become kings and kings, philosophers; at the same time, he argues that the principle of self-knowing *Geist* contains the "absolute possibility and necessity that state-power, religion and the principles of philosophy coincide." In this coincidence "the reconciliation of actuality with *Geist,* of the State with religious conscience and with philosophical knowing comes to completion."[4]

(2) Similarly, in the *Philosophy of Right,* Hegel, once again treating the relation of State and religion, speaks of the two-sidedness of religion as well as of cognition and science in their relation to the State: "they *enter into* the State in part as *means* for educational formation *(Bildung)* and the shaping of civic disposition *(Gesinnung),* in part, insofar as they are essentially ends in themselves *(selbstzwecke),* owing to the fact that they have an *external existence*.[5] However, the conduct of the State towards religion and philosophy takes the same form in regard to both these sides; the principles of the State are "applied" to them considered both as *means* and as *ends per se*.[6]

(3) Finally, the theme of "Bildung and Gesinnung" mentioned in this last passage has a central place in Hegel's thinking about the "office" of philosophy in the *polis*. If the philosopher is not to be king, he is nonetheless the potential educator of those who will rule, i.e., the members of what Hegel calls the "universal class." In this role the philosopher faces competition from rival claimants to comprehensive truth, religion especially, but also all other cultural institutions that shape "public opinion." (This is perhaps why Hegel dwells on the State's treatment of religion and the church in the *Philosophy of Right;* here the principle of tolerance works to undercut the political claims of religion since the multiplicity of organized sects guarantees a confused babble of disparate voices. Hegel is appropriately silent on whether the State should equally encourage a plurality of disparate philosophies.) I cannot enter any further into the theme of *Bildung* and *Gesinnung* here; it must suffice for me to point out that Hegel, in general, rejects the complete "privatization" of philosophy. In a very

strongly worded sentence about *Bildung* and philosophy from the early *System der Sittlichkeit* he even suggests that "the true, absolute reality of science" itself *is* "the 'people' as it educates itself, enters into discussion with itself, is conscious of itself."[7] In contrast, philosophy, when seen as a merely individual affair is "still quite ideal," i.e., deprived of significant actuality.

The upshot of this overly hasty survey is that philosophy, in Hegel's own eyes, is neither fully political, nor fully trans-political. In any event, thanks to its concrete or external existence *as* one of the many institutions of the *polis,* its deeds will be most conspicuously visible *as* political deeds. Consequently, the question I take Dr. Sass to be raising, the question of Hegelian philosophy as a form of political *praxis,* is a legitimate one within Hegel's thought-structures themselves. It is worth mentioning, however, that Hegel characteristically, and possibly with greater circumspection than his later partisans and critics, raises this question from the side of the state's behavior towards philosophy, its willingness or unwillingness to grant philosophy free public play. Alternatively put, it is only in certain political conditions that the question of philosophy's bearing on the State can come to light first of all and primarily as a matter of philosophy's freely chosen relationship to the State. It is certainly an irony reminiscent of Hegel's *List der Vernunft* that this lesson has been brought home most forcefully in our own day by the fate of the philosophers known as the "Praxis-group."

Having tried to bring out the legitimacy and place of Dr. Sass's inquiry, I have left myself little time to explore more consequentially his specific claims or to ventilate in detail plausible counter-claims. If I now plunge recklessly ahead with these two tasks, it is only in the hope of learning from the responses my remarks may provoke.

Sass's principal thesis, as far as I have understood it, is that philosophy, being the theory of ongoing and open-ended mediations in history, society, and culture, must of necessity take on these same features of "processuality" and "open-endedness" when it comes to see itself, as it should, as *another* case of a structure in need of continual mediation, that is, as one requiring continuous negotiation between the conservation of already established achievements and the emancipation of desires yet to be fulfilled or even presently recognized as such. This consideration brings him to allude to the "end of philosophy" and to ask whether, "in the progress of more and more universal mediations and materializations, the presuppositions, functions, and goals of philosophy [are not] necessarily eliminated along with the sovereign objectivity of the thinking and acting citizen?" (sec. III, 3).

I must limit myself to three very brief remarks on this thesis.

(1) Sass's portrait of philosophy is deliberately at odds with Hegel's own conviction or insight that philosophy, in the form of *Wissenschaft* or *sophia,* is the unique and comprehensive explanation of the *Real* or *Actual* and is, at the same time, the complete fulfillment of free subjectivity. Hegelian philosophy is, in Kojève's phrase, a "discours un et unique."[8] Now, Hegel may or may not be right on this score; what is important

here is to see that once these distinctively Hegelian claims are undercut, the resultant sequence of incomplete and non-unique philosophical discourses can only be described by Hegel's term, *"schlechte Unendlichkeit,"* "bad and worthless infinity." With this, the attempt of philosophy to secure and maintain its institutional place in the State overrides or replaces the attempt of philosophers to become wise or to communicate wisdom. If the success of the first attempt is a necessary precondition for philosophy's public or externally free existence, it is not a sufficient condition for philosophy's self-fulfillment as wisdom or science. In other words, once Hegel's conception of philosophy as an all-embracing discourse is abandoned, no principle is left by which to distinguish between philosophy and ideology, no matter whether this is ideology in the service of state-power or in the service of "the institution of philosophy." I hope we can discuss this issue in some detail later.

(2) The model of *praxis* itself that seems to me to be implicit in Dr. Sass's language of "materialization," "production," "work-processes," etc., is, I should want to argue, a model of *poiesis,* of making rather than of action or conduct. To put this differently, pre-Hegelian *praxis* was, in Hegel's eyes, necessarily poetic or productive since pre-Hegelian subjects could find their objective identities only *in* products other than and alien to themselves, whether material products in the strict sense or social and ethical products such as laws, customs, governments, etc. However, if Hegel is right, the necessity of making the *poetic* production of *otherness* the route to the actualization of subjects disappears when, in the language of the *Phenomenology,* self-consciousness comes *to know* itself as really at work in the whole series of self-externalizations it has brought about hitherto. The elimination of the necessity *for poiesis* leaves open the question of the form activity or conduct will take once, by hypothesis, self-consciousness has achieved the actualization of its knowing and willing. Does Hegelian *praxis* now, for the first time, become *praxis* in something like the Aristotelian sense, namely, as activity having its rationally desired end in itself, not in a product it issues into the world? If something of this sort emerges from Hegel's thought, then we shall have to consider the radical differences between Hegelian praxis and *both* the technological paradigm in play, for example, in Kant's essay on "Theory and Praxis," *and* the later instrumental or revolutionary paradigm of *praxis* exhibited in the works of the *Junghegelianer.* [9]

(3) To go on to make the further claim that Hegelian *praxis* is the same as, or an aspect of, Hegelian theoretical philosophizing itself, might seem to go against the grain, not only of Dr. Sass's argument, but of what most reasonable students of the matter would hold. Nevertheless, examination of an essential feature of Hegel's own thinking about the nature and intelligibility of actions (or activity) leads, so I would argue, very close to that conclusion. To put the argument in the briefest possible terms: Throughout the *Phenomenology* (and elsewhere) Hegel is concerned to analyze the tension between the finitude and singularity that mark each agent and his empirical deeds, and the infinite and comprehensiveness such deeds are intended by their

agents to signify or to embody. The case of unhappy consciousness, in Section IV of the *Phenomenology*, exhibits this tension in clear fashion, since here an unbridgeable gap opens up between the intended significance of what the "servant of Lord" does and the import of his actual performance.[10] Since the response of Kantian *Moralität* to cases of this kind—namely, pay attention to the intention, not to the performance—has been systematically overthrown by Hegel's arguments, we need to search for instances in which such a gap does not and cannot open. Secondly, in his rarely noticed early comment on Hume's *History of England*, written, in all likelihood, during his stay in Frankfurt, Hegel sees it as a distinctive mark of the modern world that no agent can perform on his own and as his own an action complete within itself or carrying the significance of wholeness. In his words, "Because the whole of an action, in which only a fragment belongs to each actor, is split into so many pieces, the whole work is also a resultant of so many single actions. The work is not done as a deed *(Tat)*, but as a planned result *(als gedachtes Resultat)*. The consciousness of the deed as a whole is not present to any of the actors."[11] Accordingly, the object of our search must also be an instance or kind of deed, the whole of which one agent alone can perform, and can perform with the consciousness of its (potential) wholeness. Hegel's world-historical individuals fail to satisfy the criterion of consciousness; world-historical peoples *(Völker)* fail to meet the first criterion since, as Hegel writes in Paragraph 549 of the *Encyclopedia*, "each *Volk* as a single people, having a natural or native qualitative character, is destined to fill out only *one stage* [in world-history] and to complete only one transaction [*Geschäft*] in the deed as a whole." That seems to leave the Hegelian philosopher as the unique case of an agent in whose deeds *Totalität* can be self-consciously achieved; that is, the Hegelian *ergon* is the total articulation of all the deeds and all the speeches of others.

NOTES

1. This topic, of Hegel as author and of his real or intended relations to his audiences, has remained far in the background of current Hegelian studies. It has obvious links with Hegel's pedagogical and journalistic activities and reflections. For an interesting, if one-sided, study of the importantly analogous case of Kant, see Jean-Luc Nancy, "Logodaedalus (Kant écrivain)," *Poetique*, 6 (1975), 24-52.
2. L. Feuerbach, "Towards a Critique of Hegel's Philosophy," in *The Fiery Brook: Selected Writings of Ludwig Feuerbach*, trans. Zawar Hanfi (Garden City, N.Y., 1972), p. 62.

3. Frankfurt, 1968.

4. *Enzyklopädie*, Par. 552, Anm. (ed. Nicolin & Pöggeler, pp. 436-38). (All translations are mine.)

5. *Grundlinien der Philosophie des Rechts*, Par. 270, Anm., note 1 (ed. Hoffmeister, p. 222, n.).

6. On the theme of "application" introduced here, see H. F. Fulda, *Das Recht der Philosophie in Hegel's Philosophie des Rechts*, pp. 16-23.

7. *System der Sittlichkeit* (ed. Lasson), p. 90.

8. Alexandre Kojève, *Essai d'une histoire raisonnée de la philosophie païenne*, Tome I (Paris, 1968), p. 31 *et alibi*.

9. On these two versions of *praxis*, see the helpful studies of Günther Bien, "Das Theorie-Praxis-Problem und die politische Philosophie bei Platon und Aristoteles," *Philosophisches Jahrbuch*, 76 (1968/69), 264-314, esp. 264-69, and Rüdiger Bubner, *Theorie und Praxis— eine nachhegelsche Abstraktion* (Frankfurt, 1971).

10. *Phänomenologie des Geistes* (ed. Hoffmeister), pp. 170-71.

11. The comments on Hume's *History of England* come at the end of a series of reflections on ancient and modern politics and society. Although the exact date of composition is uncertain, Hoffmeister places them in Hegel's Frankfurt period (1797-1801). German text in J. Hoffmeister, *Dokumente zu Hegels Entwicklung* (Stuttgart, 1936), pp. 273-74.

Theory and Practice in Hegel: Union or Disunion?

by

STANLEY ROSEN

As my title suggests, the following remarks are intended to raise a question rather than to provide a definitive answer. The question is whether Hegel succeeds, on internal grounds, in establishing the union of theory and practice that is an essential ingredient in his system. These remarks are therefore intended as a supplement to the discussion in my book, *G. W. F. Hegel: An Introduction To The Science Of Wisdom* (Yale Press, 1974), on whether Hegel succeeded in overcoming the "alienation" between the state and the philosopher. I shall limit myself here almost entirely to the *Encyclopedia* of 1830 which, however it needs to be supplemented, must stand as the one comprehensive and authoritative statement of Hegel's system. I am not concerned here with the various stages in the development of Hegel's thought, but solely with its most mature presentation. It should go without emphasis that, in the format of a brief paper, nothing more can be done than to explore part of the relevant evidence. Nevertheless, I shall claim to establish the legitimacy of questioning the success of Hegel's union of theory and practice. In order to do this, I must bring together a large number of passages from the *Encyclopedia,* almost none of which is contained in the section on objective spirit. However, it should be clear that my topic bears centrally upon that section of the *Encyclopedia.* My paper may therefore be taken as a commentary on paragraph 513 of that section, which begins with the sentence: *"Sittlichkeit* is the completion of the objective spirit, the truth of the subjective and objective spirit itself."

It will be useful to begin by reminding you of some passages that establish the connection between thinking and freedom in the *Encyclopedia.* According to Hegel, the highest interiority of spirit is thinking (11, 44): that is, spirit is satisfied in thinking.[1] This of course contains implicitly Hegel's intended union of theory and practice. Thus, for example, the thinking of true nature is in fact the production of nature by the thinking ego as *bei sich sein,* or as in accordance with the freedom of the thinking individual (23, 57). Freedom is contained immediately in thinking, which is always self-thinking or *my* thinking, but mine in the sense that I am simple universality. Therefore, in thinking nature, I am thinking myself: the process of self-knowledge develops co-ordinately with knowledge of nature. As Hegel puts it in the section on Natural Philosophy (245, 199), in practice, man applies the purpose contained within himself to the task of giving nature its form. One sees already the line of argument according to which practice unites itself to theory; in other words, it is practice that takes the initiative. However, it will be wise to go more slowly in building up the picture from its details.

The co-ordinate development between self-knowledge and knowledge of nature may also be called the co-ordinate development of interiority *(Wesen)* and exteriority *(Existenz)*: the unity in this case is actuality *(Wirklichkeit*: 142, 140). Actuality, taken in its totality, or as *energeia* of the Absolute that exhibits itself in the structure of totality, is necessity (149, 144; cf. 156, 148). The *"truth* of *necessity* is thus *freedom,* and the *truth* of *substance* is the *concept"* (158, 148). In other words, "the *concept* is herewith the truth of *being* and *essence"* (159, 149). As one might paraphrase this, the (self-) grasping (by spirit) of the identity-within-difference of the pure spatio-temporal continuum and our reflective or discursive thinking of that continuum is the truth in question. Still more simply: the concept is the thinking of the co-ordination of substance and subject in the necessary structure of actuality *(à la* Spinoza). But it is also (potentially) freedom. This transition by thinking, within the concept, from necessity to freedom, "is the hardest transition" we have to make, namely, to think freedom *as* necessity, as the co-ordination of actual subject and actual object in spirit. "The thinking of necessity is . . . the dissolution of this difficulty; for it is the coming-together of thinking with itself in the other—liberation *(die Befreiung). . . .* As existing for itself, this liberation is called *I,* as developed to its totality, *free spirit,* as feeling, *love,* as enjoyment, *salvation"* (159, 150). The passage I have just cited is of incidental interest, in view of those interpreters who exaggerate the religious or cultic elements in Hegel. For us, the point is slightly different. "The concept is free *power* as substantial for itself, and is *totality"* (160, 151). The concept is free because it grasps, or, as finally developed, is the self-grasping of, the whole. Nothing grasps it; there is no further transition to some more comprehensive level, but only *development* (161, 151).

We may pass by Hegel's analysis of the subjective concept and the object: "The Idea is the true, *absolute unity, in and for itself, of the concept and of objectivity*" (213, 182). It is the thinking of the whole in the "judgements" (self-articulations) of the system. It resolves all finite dualisms of the understanding (214, 183). It is the atemporal, and so eternal, dialectic of differentiation and integration (214, 184), the essential process of the absolute and free concept (215, 184). Let us now draw a preliminary conclusion. In Hegel, freedom means thinking the whole. To do this, of course, requires that we be alive, and the life-process must be assimilated into the activity of thinking. Hegel thus first discusses life, then knowing, and finally, he integrates these moments in the absolute Idea. One way to formulate the question of this paper is as follows: what is the exact contribution of objective spirit to freedom in the comprehensive or highest sense?

I now turn to a more or less detailed survey of the union of theory and practice in the section of the *Encyclopedia* on logic. We begin in part 3, section C (The Idea), with the transition from life to knowing: in itself, life is the identity of object and subject (223, 187). In other words, life is intrinsically the union of theory and practice, and life, of course, is always of individuals. The process by which the identity *in itself* is made *for itself* is knowing (*Erkennen*), by which Hegel means a combination of knowing and willing (225, 188). As he puts this in a general statement: "Reason comes into the world with the absolute belief in its ability to pose identity and to raise its certitude to the level of truth, and with the instinct (*Trieb*) to render as nothing the opposition which, for reason, is in itself null and void" (224, 188).

More specifically, in the activity of *Erkennen* or (as we may call it) practico-productive theory, the opposition of one-sided subjectivity and one-sided objectivity is overcome. Initially, however, this *Aufheben* takes place only "in itself." The identities are each finite; the circle of systematic theoretico-practical production of the totality of finite identities is not yet described. Hence the *Aufheben* falls apart into the distinct excitations of instinct (since reason is not yet working in a fully self-conscious way): (1) the one-sidedness of the subjectivity of the Idea is overcome by taking up the existent world into it, as true objective content; (2) the one-sidedness of the objective world (which is mere *Schein*, a collection of contingencies rather than a necessary structure) is overcome by defining and shaping it through the *interior* of subjectivity, which therefore functions here as the true existing objective. Sub-process (1) is the instinct of *Wissen* toward truth, hence *Erkennen als solches,* the theoretical activity of the Idea. Sub-process (2) is the instinct of the *good* toward the completion of the good, or the practical activity of the Idea (225, 188f).

We may now draw a more general conclusion. Theory originates in the process by which the world is assimilated into the subject, whereas practice originates in the process by which the world is formed by the subject. In both cases, the subject is active; there is no pure passive-receptive *Wesensschau.* That is, what Hegel calls the "theoretical activity of the Idea" is already practical, since *Erkennen* includes the practico-productive activity of will. It would perhaps be no exaggeration to say that, in Hegel's system, the unity of theory and practice is intrinsic to each as separate from the other. Thus the unity of the theoretical and practical Idea is already implicit in the purposiveness of reason. The separation of theory from practice is then the same as the separation of the objective from the subjective Idea in the necessary process by which the Absolute manifests itself in and as a world of extension and thought (the two principle attributes of Spinoza's substance). The purposiveness of reason, or the voluntative element in *Erkennen,* is the basis for what I called above the initiative taken by practice in its unification with theory. The unification of the theoretical and practical Idea is accomplished as the *truth* of the good, "that the good accomplishes in and for itself," namely, by the practical activity of the Idea (235, 193). This practical activity is that of the subjective Idea, the *will* to define the objective world in accordance with its purposes (233, 193).

Hegel says this even more sharply: "the objective world thus is in and for itself the Idea, as it together eternally poses itself as *purpose* and produces its actuality through activity" (235, 193). In other words, as we noted above, the purposiveness of reason (and ultimately, of the Absolute) is present from the outset in objectivity. What we may then call the "reunification process" of subject and object, or practice and theory, must take place at each level of the externalisation- and development-process of the Absolute. At the level of logic, the unity of the subjective and objective is *"absolute, total truth,"* but not yet as the whole; it is "the Idea that thinks itself, and indeed here *as* thinking, as *logical* Idea" or absolute Idea (236, 194).

The separation of theory from practice, although an essential part of the unfolding-process of the Absolute, is nevertheless in a fundamental sense an illusion. The overcoming of this illusion is equivalent to the completion of history, or to the co-ordinate completion of eternity and world history, of which the pivot is the state (that is, the "final" state or constitutional monarchy of Hegel's own time). On the other hand, the union of theory and practice is essentially the same as the union of objective and subjective, and this takes place in the Absolute. If this is so, then how can the union of theory and practice take place in the domain of objectivity, i.e., in objective spirit or the state? This is the question to which the balance of our analysis will lead us; it is already visible in the structure of the analysis of the Idea.

There is another question, subordinate but related to our main line of inquiry, for which a reply may perhaps be sketched. Does Hegel make thinking into *poiēsis*? Is the practico-productive nature of Hegel's theory a transformation of the Aristotelian distinctions of theory, practice, and production into a single *energeia*? If we define "theory" in the Greek sense as "looking" and "production" or *poiēsis* as "imitating" (natural forms or psychic ends), then a simple answer of "yes" is impossible. For Hegel, thinking or theorising is fundamentally an assimilation-process; it is a "making" only in the sense that it contains will, and it would be difficult to call it an "imitating" in any sense. The distinction between original and image is not present in Hegel except within the transitional stage of the "reunification" of subject and object at all levels of Hegel's thought up to the final or comprehensive one. From Hegel's standpoint, to call production "imitation" is to guarantee alienation or dualism between original and image. One could also say that the assimilative function of theory is analogous to the process in Aristotle by which the intellect or soul becomes "somehow" the thing thought. Hegel replaces the word "somehow" with the totality of his system.

Similarly, one might wish to call willing a *poiēsis*, but again, this is not altogether accurate, since subjective spirit "produces" but does not "imitate." Human production is the manifestation, not the imitation, of divine creation, but not, of course, of the orthodox Christian creation *ex nihilo*. Even here a qualification is necessary. The Absolute, or man, creates until such time as the truth is fully revealed and history is completed or fulfilled (as distinct from "terminated"). Once Hegel has finished speaking, it makes no sense to talk further of creation. Henceforward, the task of man is to preserve what has been created. With all these qualifications (and no doubt others could be added), we may nevertheless agree that, in Hegel, the tripartite distinction of theory/ practice/production is not maintained. It is present neither at the beginning nor at the end in Hegel's ontological eschatology. But it is scarcely fair to say that Hegel "confuses" the Aristotelian distinctions. He transforms them by marrying them to the Christian doctrine of spirit. If one wishes to criticize this aspect of Hegel's teaching, then it is the legitimacy of the marriage to which objection should be made.

I now return to our investigation of the union of theory and practice. It will not be necessary for us to consider the section on Natural Philosophy in the *Encyclopedia*. We go directly to the section on Philosophy of Spirit. And again the theme of freedom gives us our bearings. The essence of spirit is formally freedom or "absolute negativity of the concept as identity with itself." This means that it is immediate universality, or freedom from anything external to it (382, 313). Spirit must then develop or give content to itself as formal freedom. This development will have three stages: (1) subjective spirit: freedom *bei sich,* or the self-referential (=self-conscious) dimension of content; (2) objective spirit: the world of reality, of freedom as "existing *(vorhandene)* necessity"; (3) absolute spirit: "existing in and for itself, and eternally self-producing *unity* of the objectivity of spirit and of its Ideality" (=subjective spirit: 385, 315). This corresponds to the process of unification of the objective and subjective in the absolute Idea (in absolute, total truth as logical Idea) (236, 194). Absolute spirit is "spirit in its absolute truth," and so, it is the unity of the Idea and nature, hence of the subjective and objective, and so of the practical and theoretical.

In man, this process occurs as the development of self-consciousness, which negates the one-sidedness of subjectivity and objectivity in the activity of satisfying instinct or desire (426-427, 350). The subjective spirit is treated in three parts: anthropology, phenomenology, and psychology. The most important remarks about the unification of theory and practice occur in the section on psychology. As phenomenology is presented in the *Encyclopedia,* it is fundamentally about the development from consciousness to self-consciousness. This development makes the appearance of consciousness "identical with its essence, thereby raising its self-certitude to truth" (416, 364). So phenomenology, we may say, corresponds approximately to the section in the logic on essence.

We would anticipate that Hegel's analysis of the development of spirit will be co-ordinate with his analysis of the Idea. Of course, the section on the Idea is the conclusion of the logic, whereas the section on spirit is at the same level as that on logic. Nevertheless, it is in the development of the Idea that the subjective and objective are united in the absolute. However, in the Philosophy of Spirit, the subjective and the objective seem to be united in both the objective *and* the absolute spirit. Let us look at the details. I remind you that the initiative for the unification of theory and practice in the case of the Idea comes from the practical activity of the subjective Idea. When this unification is completed, we have the Absolute Idea. So the objective Idea is assimilated into the subjective Idea by the activity of the latter. But subjective spirit is, as it were, *exteriorized* (rather than assimilated) into objective spirit, that is, into the state and world-history. Are we then to conclude that the initiative for the unification of theory and practice in the domain of spirit comes from the activity of the objective rather than (as in the case of the Idea) of the subjective element? And if so, is this activity "theoretical" rather than "practical?" What sense does it make to refer to the activity of objective spirit as (primarily) theoretical?

It is true that subjective spirit (rational will, the Idea in itself) wills to unfold its content into existence, the actuality of the Idea, or objective spirit (482, 387). This unfolding is structurally co-ordinate to that of the subjective concept into the object world of theoretical science. The object is already the product of subjective desire or will, which motivates the unification of subjective and objective at this level. In the case of spirit, however, the object is the state. Hegel's doctrine turns upon the assumption that there is not simply an analogy, but an identity, between the subjective dimension of the conceptualized object, and that of the state. I find this assumption unacceptable. There is no reason to believe that the subjective dimension of the state (i.e., the satisfied ethical citizen) initiates a unification of subjective and objective spirit in art, religion, and philosophy. Correspondingly, one might allow that a reasonable development of objective knowledge returns us to the knowing subject, and hence to the unity of subject and object. But if "the reasonable development of the state" (whatever that is) is the unity of theory and practice in objective *Sittlichkeit,* is there not here a terminus of development (as perhaps in Maoist China)? How explain absolute spirit as a further consequence of that "totality"? In my opinion, the universality of the subject in objective knowledge is not even analogous

to, let alone identical with, the universality of the subject in the objectivity of the state. Stated simply, complete knowledge is not analogous
to complete political satisfaction because citizens are individuals, some
of them philosophers, most of them not (to say nothing of other differences). Perfect knowledge may be divine, but God is not a citizen of
Prussia.

Let us turn to some specific passages in the *Encyclopedia*. Just as
consciousness has as its object the natural soul, so spirit has consciousness as its object. Spirit develops by uniting objective content with its
own Ideality, and is thus: (1) theoretical: it treats the rational as its own
immediate determination (i.e. the world of reality or necessity is known
or assimilated); (2) will or practical: the rational determination is made
subjective (i.e., not merely known, but "owned" or stamped with "my"
mark or purpose); (3) free: this is the *Aufhebung* of the one-sidedness of
the theoretical and practical. This *Aufhebung*, or the unity of theory and
practice, apparently occurs in the state, that is, in the free activity of
objective spirit (444, 358), or in *Sittlichkeit*, "the fulfillment of objective spirit, the truth of the subjective and of the objective spirit itself"
(513, 402). Objective spirit is one-sided because it has its freedom
partly in external reality and partly in the good as an abstract universal.
Subjective spirit is one-sided because it defines itself abstractly in its
inner singularity in opposition to the universal. These are *aufgehoben*
through *Sittlichkeit*, and thus subjective freedom becomes "the self-
conscious *freedom* unto *nature*" (ibid). So the theoretical and practical
remain as not yet unified within the domain of the subjective spirit
(444, 358); they are unified within the domain of the objective spirit. In
the case of spirit, then, the unity of subject and object is initiated by
objective activity or *Sittlichkeit*. As I have already claimed, if *Sittlichkeit*
is itself motivated by the subjective element of purposiveness, this
cannot be in the same sense as in the Idea. If it were, the result would be
a universal homogeneous world state *à la* Kojève. This apart, once the
subjective spirit is "fulfilled" in *Sittlichkeit*, how does it move beyond
objectivity and the state to the absolute? That this is a problem for
Hegel himself is suggested by the fact that there seem to be *two* unifications of theory and practice because there are two unifications of subjective and objective. Or else, if the final unification of subjective and
objective takes place in absolute spirit, then the union of theory and
practice is antecedent to it, again contrary to the dialectic of the Idea.

Furthermore, we saw previously that freedom is thinking the whole, in other words, the absolute Idea. But now freedom is the *Aufhebung* of the one-sidedness of the theoretical and the practical (via the objective and the subjective) spirit, within *Sittlichkeit,* the completion of objective spirit.

The intelligence of theoretical spirit appropriates or assimilates the determinations of the world as immediate. Through the last negation of immediacy, intelligence poses within itself that its content is "for it": this is the transition to will or practical spirit (468, 379). As will, spirit steps into actuality; as *Wissen,* it is in the ground or foundation of the universality of the concept (469, 380). That is, practical spirit is the enactment of purposiveness in the world as known theoretically. The completion of this enactment is freedom. Freedom as concept "is essentially nothing but thinking." So thinking must be united with willing; willing must raise itself to the status of "thinking willing." And this "raising" is the process by which practical becomes objective spirit. In my previous formulation, subjective "exteriorizes" into objective spirit and is thus truly free. And "the actually free will," in other words, that of objective spirit, "is the unity of the theoretical and practical spirit." Again, "the will has this unity or universal determination as its object and purpose only insofar as it thinks, knows its concept, is will as free intelligence" (481, 387). To paraphrase, freedom is the thinking of politico-historical activity. In this case, it cannot be the thinking of art, religion, and philosophy, or the activity of absolute spirit.

We can sharpen the point as follows. Spirit that knows itself to be free is at first generally "the rational will, or in itself the Idea, and so only the concept of the absolute spirit" (482, 387f). That is, objective spirit, or the thinking of politico-historical activity, is the absolute Idea "in itself" (483, 389). Does it follow from this that subjective spirit is the absolute Idea "for itself," and that the two are *aufgehoben* in absolute spirit? Apparently not; in the opening paragraph on absolute spirit (553, 440), Hegel says that it is the identity of *Realität* and the concept of spirit as *Wissen* of the absolute Idea. Subjective and objective spirit, Hegel adds, are the way in which *Realität* builds itself up. The Idea was defined initially in the section on logic as "the true in and for itself, the absolute unity of the concept and of objectivity" (213, 182). If *Realität* corresponds approximately to "objectivity," and since objective spirit is the absolute Idea in itself, then so too is the subjective spirit. In this

case, it is the concept that corresponds to the absolute Idea for itself. *The*
Absolute, i.e. absolute spirit, is then the union of absolute Idea in itself
(the union of subjective and objective spirit) and for itself (the concept as
Wissen). This proposal does not seem to correspond altogether with the
definition of the absolute spirit as "eternally self-producing *unity* of the
objectivity of spirit and of its Ideality" (385, 315). But we might try to
reconcile them as follows. The Ideality or concept, as fully developed, is
the absolute spirit for itself, and so, as not yet united with objective
reality. The self-producing and eternal activity of unification is indeed
the activity of the Absolute. The difficulty lies then in the apparently
dual location of subjectivity. And this can be resolved by pointing out
that objectivity is already a product of will; purposiveness and so subjectivity is ingredient in the Idea from the outset.

I do not regard this as a very satisfactory resolution. The difficulty can
be signalled by noting that, since the Absolute is union of the subjective
and the objective, it must already be for itself as in itself. However, I
want to state the whole issue in one last and more general manner. To my
charges of structural incoherence, Hegel might defend himself as follows. The unity of theory and practice occurs decisively in objective
spirit, and is a necessary precondition for absolute spirit, i.e. *the* Absolute: for the whole and knowledge of the whole. The unity of the
philosopher and the state is then effected by the fact that the philosopher
is a citizen, and in that guise, an element of the precondition for his
identity as thinker of the Absolute. In other words, what looks like a
dualism between citizen and philosopher is overcome at the level of the
Absolute, where the philosopher sees the necessity of his citizenship as
an ingredient in totality. In art, religion, and philosophy, the spirit rises
"above" the state, but only on the basis of the state. And the basis or
ground is contained in the grounded.

In my opinion, such a defense could work only to establish the
conclusion that, within the whole, there must be both citizens and
philosophers, and that philosophers are *also* citizens. But this serves
merely to internalize the dualism within the philosopher. Since the
philosopher, or sage, is the final manifestation of the Absolute, he
naturally "includes" all elements of that manifestation. With the proper
definition of terms, one could say that the philosopher is a tree or star, a
cow or a dog, as well as a citizen. Does it follow from this that the
difference between the philosopher and, say, his dog is overcome? My

point is not that one must first be a dog in order to be a philosopher, but that knowledge of an object is not the same as union with that object. The difficulty lies in Hegel's suppression of the "somehow" in Aristotle's assertion that the intellect becomes somehow what it knows. In the given instance, and putting the point as simply as possible, if objective spirit is the Absolute in itself, then the unity of theory and practice is unstable. Such a unity is carried out by objective spirit, which cannot be practical because it is not subjective, and cannot be objective because it is not theoretical. Still more explicitly, the state is not a philosopher, but neither is it a citizen. And the completion or fulfillment of the state depends upon a uniting of citizen and philosopher that ought to result in the *Aufhebung,* or, in Marx's term, the withering away of the state. We therefore see how critical is the inversion, in the shift from Idea to spirit, of the order of initiative in the work of subjectivity and objectivity. This inversion is necessary for Hegel, in order to "exteriorize" subjectivity in politico-historical activity. But it is accomplished at the price of a distortion in the symmetry of the structure of the system, and by failing to answer the question as to the nature of the activity of objective spirit. I realise that the answer seems to be *Sittlichkeit.* But this is defective, since there is no apparent reason why a satisfied citizen should become a philosopher. And there is every apparent reason why, once having become a philosopher, he should be a dissatisfied citizen.

We come finally to the question: what is freedom? Is it thinking, or thinking united with doing? I have suggested that if freedom is *Sittlichkeit,* then the Absolute must be beyond freedom. But if freedom is thinking, then there is no unity between theory and practice. It is by no means obvious that man can be free under any circumstances, or in accordance with any philosophical explanation. I think, however, that if freedom is to have any meaning at all, there can be no union of physics and politics, to use somewhat old-fashioned terms. Man is free, if at all, only in the interstices of the split within nature between the cosmos and the state. But whether free or not, man remains man only as "alienated" from both cosmos and state. The suppression of a *Jenseits* may be effected by an act of extraordinary genius, as in the case of Hegel, or by obtuseness and self-forgetting. In either case, it is a philosophical error of the first magnitude.

NOTES

1. Numbers in parentheses, unless otherwise indicated, are the paragraph and page number (in that order) from the Nicolin-Pöggeler edition of the *Enzyklopädie* of 1830 (Hamburg: Felix Meiner Verlag, 1969).

COMMENT ON

Rosen's "Theory and Practice in Hegel: Union or Disunion?"

HEINZ KOLAR

The more formal question which can be raised first is that regarding the location of Hegel's *Encyclopedia* within the context of his philosophical system as a whole. Can we indeed say that the *Encyclopedia of 1830* is "the one comprehensive and authoritative statement of Hegel's system," though quite a few modern interpretations take the *Encyclopedia* as their starting point and understand it as the latest authoritative work by Hegel which has been handed down to us?

I would like to make explicit the point that it was Hegel's own understanding that the *Encyclopedia* was a textbook for the students who attended his lectures.[1] Dieter Henrich is the latest to emphasize that, as seen from this particular character of the work, the *Encyclopedia* actually does not advance arguments. As Hegel himself remarks "ce livre n'est qu'une suite de thèses."[2] It could even be held that it is a summary of Hegel's own system in terms of reflective thinking (*Reflexionsphilosophie*).

But these preliminary considerations do not intend to do more than put a question mark behind all enterprises which, to my mind, conclude from the *Encyclopedia*, something which it is not meant to show and cannot serve as evidence for. Hegel says: "Näher kann das Bedürfnis der Philosophie dahin bestimmt werden, dass . . . der Geist . . . auch seiner höchsten Innerlichkeit, dem Denken, Befriedigung verschaffe und das Denken zu seinem Gegenstand gewinne" (§ 11,44). Can we infer from this statement that "spirit is satisfied in thinking," which "contains implicitly Hegel's intended union of theory and practice"? Are we not rather impelled to think that the union of theory and practice is a form of spirit, which is also thinking as the highest form of the interiority of spirit, as Hegel maintains? Insofar as thinking is my activity, it is the production of my mind as thinking mind. This thinking mind as the subject, which is *bei sich*, is the I and as this *Bei-sich-Sein* it is freedom as the self-relation of the subject to itself which has then nothing outside itself; it is the subject, which in thinking itself, is itself. Thinking which thinks itself is nothing other than the subject which is reconciled with itself or is that itself, which it is as free being—the identity of being as particular being and being as universal. Thus the thinking I is the abstract I, as it is freed from all particularity, i.e., properties, particular states, and only "does the universal" insofar as it is identical in this "acting" with the other individuals. The actualization of the self as subject is possible only by and through action as a reflective notion (self-thinking).

It was stated, following Hegel, "in thinking nature, I am thinking myself as the notion is immanent to nature" (*Encyclopedia,* § 245). Nature as such does not contain absolute teleology within itself, it is the notion which attributes teleology to nature.

The question of the relation between self-knowledge and knowledge of nature is identical to the question of theory and practice in Hegel, as it is nothing other than the relation of the One to the Other or, more precisely, the dialectical movement from the One to the Other, which can be conceived of as action. The transition from necessity to freedom or from actuality to concept is the hardest to make, because "it is independent actuality which has to be conceived of." As identity in difference in the sense of the identity in the difference of opposites, it is true substantiality. Like is the concept of the identity of opposites. Necessity as a term of reflective thinking is the dissolution of the seeming contradiction; it is the coming-together of itself with the other-than-itself in thinking. Thus thinking is the overcoming and the liberation from the opposites; it is freedom.

Hegel emphasizes that this freedom is not an abstraction (§ 159, annotation) but an actual which is bound by the power of necessity. What is the actual reflection or reflection in its actuality? It is I, free spirit, love, and the "feeling of elevation" *(Seligkeit)*, which does not necessarily mean salvation. *Seligkeit* need not be translated in religious terms and I would think that its does not have this connotation within the context.

Can we say that in the activity of *Erkennen* as practico-productive theory the opposition between subjectivity and objectivity is overcome? Would this not mean an overemphasizing of the activity of *Erkennen* in Hegel or, in other words, to give an interpretation which has been called a "transcendentalist interpretation" of Hegel? The *Aufheben* of the opposition is only *an sich*, which means *für uns*, according to Hegel's understanding, as we know. But the *Aufheben* of the opposition is *an und für sich* or fully mediated present in the absolute Idea in its notion of pure concept. In addition to what was said it can be maintained, it seems to me, that the Idea has two moments of its own, namely, *Erkennen* and *das Gute*, which are synthesized in the absolute Idea as the union of theory and practice.

The two formal definitions of theory and practice as assimilation and formation by the subject do not, to my mind, allow us to speak of the "theoretical activity of the Idea" as already practical activity, though "*Erkennen* includes the practico-productive activity of the will." I perfectly agree that according to Hegel's own understanding "the unity of the theoretical and practical idea is already implicit in the purposiveness of reason." When we say that in the *Logic* the unity of the subjective and the objective is absolute, total truth, which is not yet as the whole, we are referring, I understand, to the specific character of the *Logic,* i.e., the Idea as thinking, logical or absolute Idea.

It was stated that "the union of theory and practice is essentially the same as the union of objective and subjective . . . in the Absolute." Therefore the question was raised how the union of theory and practice can take place in the state as the domain of objective spirit.

Mr. Rosen further raises the question, whether the difference of "theory," "practice," and "production" in Aristotle would not be interpreted by Hegel into the one *energeia* as the movement of the dialectic as such. I would agree that the question of the difference in Hegel's system is obviously absorbed into the concept of Absolute. In other words, it has to be asked, whether the absolute Idea can be considered as being the actual synthesis of both, knowledge and the good. It is still a synthesis of knowledge which does not render justice to the particular character of action or the good, but is reduced to a mere moment of the dialectical process, which has its meaning in the ongoing dialectical process, but has no meaning in itself (*in sich,* but not *an sich*). Whether the union of objective and subjective in the absolute Idea is the absolute spirit in its absolute truth can still be asked, despite Hegel's seemingly similar utterances in the *Encyclopedia,* when he speaks of the arts, religion, and philosophy as the domains of absolute spirit. Therefore the question, whether the subjective and the objective are united in the objective and the absolute spirit could be misleading. The author gets into these difficulties, it appears, because he has overlooked—with good right, in his sense, if I understand him correctly, the difference between the synthesis of subjective and objective spirit as being a form (*Gestalt*) of absolute spirit. In other words, absolute spirit remains distinct from itself, even as absolute knowledge in the *Phenomenology* and the absolute Idea in the *Logic*.

Does Hegel's argument adhere to the view that the "satisfied ethical citizen" initiates a unification of subjective and objective spirit in art, religion, and philosophy? I quote the main section indicating the transition from the state to absolute spirit: "Der denkende Geist der Weltgeschichte aber (indem er zugleich jene Beschränktheiten der besonderen Volksgeister und seine eigene Weltlichkeit abgestreift) erfasst seine konkrete Allgemeinheit und erhebt sich zum Wissen des absoluten Geistes, als der ewig wirklichen Wahrheit, in welcher die wissende Vernunft frei für sich . . . " (*Encyclopedia,* § 552). Thus it is spirit itself which conceives of itself as concrete Universality, which is the knowledge of absolute spirit. It is world history as such as a domain of *Sittlichkeit,* which comprehends the essence of its own and thereby is concrete universality as absolute knowledge. In other words, art, religion, and philosophy is the particular contents of absolute spirit, which has sublated its historical content and thereby has become, what it always has been. This way absolute spirit is the consequence of *Sittlichkeit* in being spirit in its particular development. In other words, it is the dialectic as such which passes the various steps of its development. Certainly the question of the mediation of the particular steps of the dialectic cannot be answered by referring to the ongoing dialectical process as such.

The totality of "objective *Sittlichkeit*" qua unity of theory and practice is but a moment of the dialectical process. The process as such is based on spirit as unfolding actuality or, in other words, on a principle which allows for a continuing development or a substratum of the process. The last step of objective spirit is world history, which can be characterized as an objectification of spirit, which as such has to be sublated in order for spirit to become what it always has been.

Thus one could say that a terminus of the development of the dialectic can neither be conceived of in *Sittlichkeit* as such nor in a certain "concrete singular," i.e., concrete historical state. What is meant is the state qua form of appearance of the World Spirit *(Weltgeist)* or of the People's Spirit *(Volksgeist)*.

There are two concepts of absolute spirit which have to be distinguished. According to one of them absolute spirit appears as the continuing dialectical process as such or the continuity of the "historical" process qua development of self-consciousness to absolute knowledge, to put this in terms of the *Phenomenology*. The other concept of absolute spirit refers us to the domains of the arts, religion, and philosophy, as they appear in the *Encyclopedia*. But this second concept needs further interpretation. Absolute spirit in this sense thematically appears only in the *Encyclopedia*. Therefore it can be asked with good reason, I think, whether absolute spirit appears in these domains as it is in itself or whether the difference between the appearance and its being-in-itself is sublated in either the concept of the arts, of religion, or of philosophy.

The idea that "complete knowledge is not analogous to complete political satisfaction" or, differently stated, as I think Mr. Rosen would agree to formulate it and as could be inferred from the context: philosophical knowledge does not mean political satisfaction. This insight would point to the question of the relation of theoretical to practical knowledge, so it seems to me. In other words: theoretical knowledge *qua* theoretical knowledge does not provide answers in the domain of political philosophy.

Though for Hegel "free spirit" is the *Aufhebung* of the onesidedness of the theoretical and the practical and appears in the state as the free activity of objective spirit or in *Sittlichkeit,* Hegel's claim that the theoretical and the practical "are unified within the domain of objective spirit" does not seem justifiable, if I understand Mr. Rosen correctly, as we are still within the domain of theoretical thinking.

The seemingly two unifications of theory and practice or of the subjective and objective within *Sittlichkeit* and within absolute spirit take place at two different levels. As this dialectic is not a dialectic of political ideas, but of the process of philosophical knowledge as such, Hegel can maintain that absolute spirit as a cognitive entity is the highest form of dialectic; the completion of objective spirit is *Sittlichkeit,* that of absolute spirit "philosophical knowledge" as absolute knowledge in a very specific sense. The author uses a very interesting formulation when he states that spirit steps as will into actuality, as *Wissen* remains within the "foundation of the universality of the concept" (§ 469, p. 380). That freedom as concept "is essentially nothing but thinking" cannot be questioned, so it seems, but this freedom as actual freedom is beyond a solely theoretical determination of what freedom is.

In which sense is "self-conscious freedom" (§ 513) the completion of subjective and objective spirit? It is freedom which has become nature, or freedom which has overcome the difference between freedom and nature. It is the "an und für sich allgemeine vernünftige Wille" which actualizes itself as the universal of *Sitte*. Practical spirit, which occurs in Sections 469 and 379, and which Mr. Rosen quotes as being as concept "essentially nothing but thinking," is within the domain of thinking as "psychological concept" or a concept of subjective spirit. I therefore would not like to draw far-reaching conclusions regarding the relation of the practical to the theoretical from this concept of practical spirit.

The freedom we are dealing with here is the concept of freedom of subjective spirit, which has not reached its universality so far and has neither achieved its *für sich* nor its *an und für sich sein*. The "actually free will" as the unity of the theoretical and the practical is the synthesis of both in subjective spirit or the free will as reflection on the free and real will as psychologically or subjectively free will. It is "die durch sich gesetzte unmittelbare Einzelheit, welche aber ebenso zur allgemeinen Bestimmung, der Freiheit selbst, gereinigt ist" (§ 481, 387). Insofar as the will reflects on itself or thinks itself, as Hegel says, it is free intelligence (ibid). It seems illuminating that he does not say free spirit, but says free intelligence.

I think we can say the term absolute spirit has its location in the *Philosophy of Spirit,* while the term absolute Idea is a specific concept of the *Logic.* To interpret both concepts as one would indeed seem difficult to me. But one could of course speak of absolute spirit as appearing under various forms *(Gestalten)* in having reference to the system as a whole and to the question of the "continuum." If absolute spirit is to be conceived of "as eternally self-producing unity of the objectivity of spirit and of its Ideality" (§ 385, 315), we are in a position to state a difference between spirit itself and its way of self-comprehension in the sense of self-reflection. Whether Hegel's ideality or concept is to be conceived of as being the absolute spirit in its being *für sich* and thus not yet united with its objective reality, can be asked with good reason, so it would seem. Mr. Rosen accepts this argument and says that since "the Absolute is union of the subjective and the objective, it must already be for itself as in itself."

In what sense can we speak of the philosopher as being a citizen? Differently stated: what is the relation between the state as the absolute of objective spirit and the concept of absolute knowledge? In considering also Hegel's developments in the *Phenomenology,* I have reference to the often quoted "we" indicating the continuity and the identity of the dialectical process. In which sense we could say that the "philosopher or sage, is the final manifestation of the Absolute"? Is it not the "transcendental I" or the "transcendental subject" as concrete, but neither individual nor empirical historical subject?

Mr. Rosen emphasizes, with reference to Hegel's theory of knowledge, that "knowledge of an object is not the same as union with that object," and that Hegel would suppress the "the 'somehow' in Aristotle's assertion that the intellect becomes somehow, what it knows" (ibid.). I agree with Mr. Rosen, but have to raise in this context an additional systematical question regarding the relation between method and system of the dialectic, more precisely, how a specific difference between method and system could be indicated. Because, if there were no such difference to be determined, the coherence of the dialectic would be seriously questioned.

To continue with the question of the relation between philosopher and citizen, objective spirit upon its completion passes to *Sittlichkeit,* which is already a mediated position or the synthesis of the individual and the universal. The "satisfied citizen" who is no longer alienated from the state has achieved this position as a result of his reflection on the actual situation of the individual in relation to the state. Thus the "satisfied citizen" has comprehended the true character of the state which is not "exterior" to the individual, but is the actualization of its own freedom, which is never "subjective" in the proper sense, as it necessarily is in a relation to the universal.

One could even go so far as to say, if I understand Hegel correctly, that a philosopher who has become a dissatisfied citizen is an individual in subjective abstraction or a philosopher of abstract reflection. If the state is experienced as being void of meaning, Hegel would say, it is abolished by a revolution and replaced by another form of state, which better corresponds to the will of its citizens. All revolutions and reformations are conceived of by Hegel along the line of a necessary historical development, as we know.

The author raises the question whether freedom is mere thinking or whether it is united with doing. In other words: is freedom theoretical or practical or both? It seems that the Absolute as absolute spirit is beyond the freedom of objective spirit. It is the freedom of absolute spirit, which appears as absolute knowledge and annulls time. The unity of theory and practice occurs at different steps of the dialectic. But it cannot become practical in the sense of a self-actualizing production qua *praxis.*

A remaining alienation of man from both, cosmos and state, is unthinkable for Hegel, as I indicated above. Every form of alienation could only be subsumed under a concept of abstract subjectivity. Man is alienated only as long as he does not conceive of his alienation. In conceiving of it, he has already overcome it, as he knows how to meet it. The concept of production (*praxis*) is more concrete even than that of practical reflection, so it would seem. It would refer us to a concept of *praxis* as a differentiation within practical reflection. Anyway, practical in its relation to theoretical reflection passes through theoretical reflection in order to surpass it. But this is a consideration which leads us beyond Hegel. For him the union of theoretical and practical can be conceived of only in terms of a theory of the theoretical which is to be distinguished from a theory of the practical.

NOTES

1. Cf. G. W. F. Hegel, *Enzyklopädie der philosopischen Wissenschaften 1830,* ed. Pöggeler and Nicolin, 6th ed. (Hamburg: F. Meiner, 1959), Preface by the Editors, pp. xxiv, xxvii-xxx; Prefaces by Hegel to the 1st, 2nd and 3rd editions, pp. 3, 20, 23; Introduction by Hegel, sec. 16.

2. Ibid., p. xxix. In Hegel see *Briefe von und an Hegel,* Bd. I-III, ed. J. Hoffmeister (Hamburg, 1952-54), III, 169.

Hegel's Lectures on Natural Law (1802-1805/06) as an Early Counterpart to the *Philosophy of Right* (1821)

by

H. KIMMERLE

During his time as a teacher of philosophy at the University of Jena (1801-1807) Hegel gave several series of lectures, which he announced as *ius naturae*. We find them listed for the following terms:[1]

(1) Summer 1802 (together with Logic and Metaphysics)

(2) Winter 1802/03 (together with Logic and Metaphysics)

(3) Summer 1803 (together with the Outline of the Whole Philosophy)

(4) Winter 1803/04 (together with the System of Speculative Philosophy)

(5) Summer 1805 (together with the Science of the Whole Philosophy)

I want to make some short remarks in order to indicate the place of this subject in the system of philosophy of that time, and its specific content as compared with that of the *Philosophy of Right* of 1821. In the 1802 essay on "Natural Law," as is apparent from the title, Hegel asks what place it has in "practical philosophy." The system of 1801/02 distinguishes between Theoretical and Practical Philosophy, each of which has a theoretical and a practical part,[2] and "Natural Law" forms the practical part of Practical Philosophy. The precise lay-out of the whole system at that time is as follows:

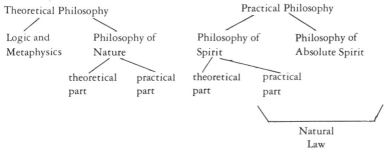

53

This means that Natural Law, as then conceived, is the prefiguration of the later philosophy of objective spirit, together with the philosophy of absolute spirit. Confirmation that this was the conception is to be found in the essay on "Natural Law"[3] and in the "System of Ethical Life," which provide us with a rather complete account of the subject.[4]

We have no documents from the following years which indicate the place of Natural Law in the system of philosophy, but we do have the Philosophy of Spirit constituting part of the System of Speculative Philosophy of 1803/04, as well as the Philosophy of Nature and Spirit of 1805/06. Although Natural Law, as a subject, is distinct from these systems, it does form part of them. Within the Philosophy of Spirit of 1803/04 it includes the following sub-sections:

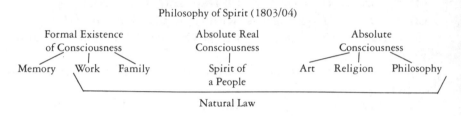

This conception was changed in 1805/06, when the Natural Law contained within the Philosophy of Spirit was sub-divided as follows:

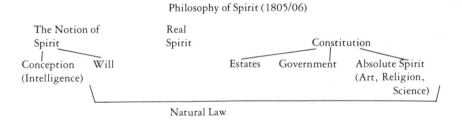

The collection of Hegel's texts edited with a commentary by G. Göhler entitled *Frühe politische Systeme,* has the merit of showing that this constitutes an important aspect of Hegel's conception of the system of philosophy during the Jena period.[5] Göhler, however, gives no precise definition of the subject, as I have attempted to do. A comparison with the *Philosophy of Right* (1821), immediately brings out one important difference:

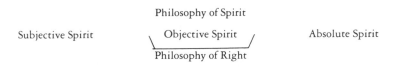

Philosophy of Spirit

Subjective Spirit   Objective Spirit   Absolute Spirit

Philosophy of Right

The exoterical treatment of inter-subjectivity, society, and the state (the former subject of "Natural Law") no longer contains the philosophy of absolute spirit. This means that: (1) in the Jena writings these topics are more closely associated with the exposition of art, religion, and philosophy. In the later work, the world is constituted as recognition and as the social and political world, and again as the purely spiritual world. Ethical life *(Sittlichkeit)* constitutes the common foundation of the two further forms. The freedom of the individual is realized externally in the forms of finite spirit, absolutely in the world of free spirit. The state in itself is not the realisation of ethical spirit. (2) The whole philosophy of spirit is to be seen in its relation to practical life. It shows how freedom in the practical sphere can be realized as external action and internal conviction. According to the later conception, the revolution of society and the state is not in fact completed, as it should be, by the reformation of consciousness.

But of course, there are important differences between the conception of 1802 and that of 1805/06. In the earlier texts, especially the "System of Ethical Life," the sphere of natural ethical life contains realistic or even materialistic aspects: work, for example, is conceived of as the satisfaction of physical needs, the foundation of all ethical life. In the conception of social and political life, however, an Aristotelian and Spinozistic notion is dominant, the state is regarded as being prior to the individual, and the individual as finding freedom through realizing himself as part of this whole. In the Philosophy of Spirit of 1805/06, however, the reality of spirit is defined as the reality of the self, while the materialistic foundation of ethical spirit loses its central systematic significance. The will is free, but its freedom is in the first instance a void, which is filled and structured by action, through work and satisfaction of physical needs.[6] The acknowledgement of the self as a spiritual being forms the basis of social and political life. The result of Göhler's comparison of the two texts is that the "preponderance of what is general" is preserved, although the tendency of the dialectical exposition of the subject matter, which is increasingly predominant at this time, is to destroy it.[7]

According to Göhler, the unity of the general and the particular in the singular is not achieved within the sphere of social and political life on account of Hegel's preoccupation with certain political objectives. He suggests, and I concur with him in this respect, that in the texts of 1802 and 1805/06 we have a counterpoint of positive and negative aspects.

1802   1805/06

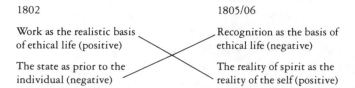

Work as the realistic basis   Recognition as the basis of
of ethical life (positive)   ethical life (negative)

The state as prior to the   The reality of spirit as the
individual (negative)   reality of the self (positive)

It is reasonable to assume that in the "Natural Law," belonging to the system of 1803/04, there is a mediation of these two positions. Chronologically, the text comes between the two others, and with regard to the problem, forms the point of intersection. Hegel himself expressed the mediating conception of this position by pointing out that so-called realism and so-called idealism constitute an inadequate opposition. In its existence, this opposition can be regarded as the opposition in the middle of "the matter known" and consciousness. These are only the abstract opposites, on which the so-called realism and the so-called idealism are based. The issue is actually the potency of the middle (of consciousness), which is at variance with itself.[8] The problem of generality, particularity, and their union in singularity finds a solution in the union of "being, sublating, and being as being sublated." Hegel said: "It is the single totality which *is,* for the other single totalities are only posited as sublated," and *"within* this it is *for itself* as a *sublatedness.*"[9]

But it is quite evident that this text is not in itself the solution to this problem, nor, as Habermas indicates,[10] "the only model that offers itself as a synthesis" of the knowledge of production and the knowledge of reflection. It provides a solution as an object of critical and discriminating interpretation. The object of the present remarks is to initiate the finding of such a solution through the study of the Jena writings as a whole.

NOTES

1. *Dokumente zu Hegels Jenaer Dozententätigkeit.* Edited by H. Kimmerle. In *Hegel-Studien,* 4 (1967), 53-55.

2. H. Kimmerle, *Das Problem der Abgeschlossenheit des Denkens. Hegels "System der Philosophie" in den Jahren 1800-1804.* Bonn, 1970, pp. 25-30.

3. G. W. F. Hegel, *Gesammelte Werke.* Vol. 4, *Jenaer Kritische Schriften,* edited by H. Buchner and O. Pöggeler. Hamburg, 1968, pp. 432-34, 453-55, 463-64.

4. G. W. F. Hegel, *System der Sittlichkeit.* Edited by G. Lasson. Hamburg, 1967; K. Rosenkranz, *Hegel's Leben.* Berlin, 1844, pp. 132-41; R. Haym, *Hegel und seine Zeit.* Berlin, 1857, pp. 164-65, 414-15, 509.

5. G. W. F. Hegel, *Frühe politische Systeme,* edited by G. Göhler (Frankfurt/M., Berlin, Wien: Ulstein Verlag, 1974). The present contribution is based on my review of Göhler's work in *Hegel-Studien,* 11 (1967), pp. 119-228.

6. G. W. F. Hegel; *Gesammelte Werke.* vol. 8, *Jenaer Systementwürde III,* edited by R. P. Horstmann, with collaboration of J. H. Trede, Hamburg, 1967, p. 202.

7. G. Göhler, *G. W. F. Hegel, Frühe politische Systeme.* Frankfurt—Berlin—Wien: Ulstein Verlag, 1974, pp. 608-09.

8. G. W. F. Hegel, *Gesammelte Werke, Vol. 6: Jenaer Systementwürfe I.* Edited by K. Düsing and H. Kimmerle. Hamburg, 1975, pp. 291-92.

9. L.c., p. 313-314.

10. J. Habermas, *Erkenntnis und Interesse.* Frankfurt, 1968, p. 77; see also J. Habermas, *Arbeit und Interaktion. Bemerkungen zu Hegels Jenaer "Philosophie des Geistes."* In *Technik und Wissenschaft als "Ideologie."* Frankfurt, 1968, pp. 9-47.

Economic and Social Integration in Hegel's Political Philosophy

by

RAYMOND PLANT

I

In this paper I want to argue that issues of political economy lie at the very centre of Hegel's particular concerns as a philosopher and that his general philosophical position so structures and governs his account of political economy that the latter cannot be understood fully or appreciated without taking his general philosophical position into account. In addition, I shall argue that Hegel's interest in problems of political economy can be traced back to his student days in Tübingen, and that an understanding of his development during this period and subsequently shows why political economy had to be for him a dominant intellectual concern. In arguing this thesis I hope to be able to say something briefly about Hegel's views, not just on political economy and its role generally but also on particular concepts drawn from this field—concepts such as need, labour, exchange, public authority, and the state. It is only right that at the very beginning of this paper I should say just how indebted I am to the researches of Professor Paul Chamley in this area, particularly his two articles in *Hegel Studien* for 1965,[1] and also his books *Economie Politique et Philosophie chez Steuart et Hegel* and *Documents relatif à Sir James Steuart*.[2]

II

The first part of this paper will be concerned with the development of Hegel's views on political economy up to 1800, and I shall have to make as assumptions certain points of view argued more fully in my book, *Hegel*.[3] Having said that I wanted to place Hegel's theory of political economy at the centre of attention, it has to be admitted that there are definite limits to the feasibility of such an enterprise. Not only did the mature Hegel hold that truth is the whole, so that an abstracted discussion of political economy would be inadequate, but the young Hegel, too, held an equally daunting view about the intricate interrelationships of social institutions and practices when he argues in his *Theologische Jugendschriften* that: "The spirit of the people, its history, its religion, the level of its political development cannot be treated in isolation either with respect to their mutual influence, or in characterising each by itself they are woven together into a single bond."[4] The same point would hold true for political economy, and the view is mirrored in the analysis of his development presented here: issues of religion, history, politics and economics are closely related in his mind.

In my *Hegel* I argued that Hegel's thought was dominated by two interrelated ideals: the restoration of some sense of wholeness and integrity to the individual personality; and the restructuring of society on a more harmonious, reciprocating basis, that is, to restore some sense of community.[5] A crucial influence here on the formation of these ideals in the mind of Hegel, and indeed the minds of others of Hegel's generation,[6] was a romanticised and idealised picture of the ancient Greek and particularly Athenian polis. In such a society, so it was believed, a real sense of community had been achieved. Social practices and institutions such as religion, morality, and politics were all closely interwoven, thus making the social system homogeneous. The individual citizen was able to develop a roundedness and wholeness to his personality by being able personally to take part in all these interwoven social activities, an integrity of the personality which has been denied to the modern man. For many, and for Hegel in particular in his early years, Greece was the ideal and, even when his enthusiasm for the Greek model had evaporated somewhat, he still extrapolated from Greek political culture a deep and abiding political conviction about the need for society to recover some sense of the harmony of Greece, albeit in its own and modified way, and to recover something of the sense of human wholeness which had been such a dominant part of Greek culture.[7]

While Hegel was preoccupied with these ideals relating both to society and the individual during this early period he does not seem to have been interested in exploring the material and economic conditions which enabled this kind of society to flourish in the ancient world and the changes in the material conditions of life which made such a form of communal life more difficult if not impossible to achieve in the modern world. On the contrary, during the period of his earliest writings in Tübingen (1789-93) Hegel seems to have seen *religion* as the key to the unified nature of Greek life and religious changes to have been the cause of the baneful structure of modern society. In Hegel's view Greek folk religion had been a unifying institution. It appealed to all the powers of the human mind, to head and heart,[8] to the cognitive, conative, and affective sides of the personality; whereas modern European religion has become too deeply rationalistic and theological, neglecting the need for religion to nourish the emotions, which Hegel regards at this time as the springs of moral life.[9] Because folk religion managed to appeal to the whole man, it encouraged a sense of personal wholeness and integration, but in addition it was a powerful force for harmony in society generally. All practices in society had a religious dimension and, as such, there were close connections between them mediated by this religious bond.[10] In its social function Greek folk religion was very different from modern Christianity, the practice of which has become a kind of specialism, reserved for special days of the week, involving specialised ceremonies and liturgical forms, with the result that it has become more and more dislocated from the forms of political life and social and moral relationships. The recapture of a sense of community, and with it the regeneration of modern life, is thus seen by Hegel at this period very much in terms of rediscovering something like Greek folk religion, largely by a fundamental reshaping of Christian beliefs and in particular by a rigorous attempt to demythologise the Gospels in order to exclude all elements of transcendence and positivity.

There is therefore very little in the Tübingen material to suggest that Hegel had an interest in the *material* conditions of life which constituted the environment within which forms of communal life could exist. However, there are two places in the Tübingen writings in which issues generally falling under the rubric of political economy are discussed: one deals with needs and labour; the other relates to the communistic tendencies of early Christianity and how these relate to the requirements of modern bourgeois life. The first passage, although long, is worth quoting in full as Chamley makes quite a good deal of it in his work on Hegel's economic beliefs:

> The father of this genius [i.e., Greek society] is Time on which he remains dependent all his life—his mother the polis, the constitution his midwife and religion his wet nurse, who took the five acts into her service to aid in his education—and the music of physical and spiritual motion—an ethereal essence—that is drawn down to earth

and held fast by a light bond which resists through a magic spell all attempts to break it for it is completely entwined in his essence. This bond whose main foundations are our needs is woven together from the manifold threads of nature; and because he [the Greek] binds himself to nature more firmly with every new thread, he is far from feeling any constraint that he finds an amplification of his enjoyment, or exclusion of his range of life in this voluntary augmentation, this multiplying variety of threads. . . . The brazen bond of his needs fetters him too to Mother Earth but he worked it over, refined it, beautified it with feeling and fancy, twining it with roses by the aid of the Graces, so that he could delight in these fetters as his own work, as part of himself.[11]

One might interpret this puzzling passage somewhat as follows: the Greek, like every other man, is tied to the earth by the material conditions of human existence, the central one being the requirement that my basic needs be satisfied. However, the form of satisfaction may seem either self-imposed or alien, depending presumably upon the system of labour prevailing. In Greek society the way in which needs were satisfied, i.e., labour, was not seen as a constraint but as part of oneself, and thus labour became in turn the basis of the cultural life of the community. Chamley sees in this passage a clear echo of Hegel's reading of Locke during this period, particularly with the idea present in the passage that man externalises himself in free labour and finds himself mixed with it and reflected in it.[12] Man binds himself more and more to nature by his multiplying needs and their satisfactions but these do not appear as a positive constraint so much as an extension and a growing richness of life, unlike in modern life where needs, he says, are "iron fetters and raw." At the same time man's natural environment is still considered benign, it is "mother earth." However, the passage is still very complex and difficult to attach any firm meaning to but certainly Chamley's reading of the passage is consistent with it.

The other passage, not noted by Chamley, is on page forty-one of the *Theologische Jugendschriften* and it is interesting because it ties in with Hegel's religious preoccupations at the time. The passage occurs during a general attack on Christianity as inimical to human existence. He argues that many of the moral injunctions of Jesus are in apposition to values which Hegel holds dear: "One also finds many commands of Christianity go against the basic presuppositions of legislation in bourgeois society, the basic propositions of the property owner's right to self defence." What Hegel does not go on to discuss until much later in his life is how such an atomistic-seeming form of social organisation can generate forms of solidarity and interrelationship. At this point he does seem to be settled in the position of seeing religious alienation as the basic cause of the fractures in social and personal relationships in the modern world and the reform of religion as a way of recapturing community.[13]

Hegel's writings during the Berne period involve a significant shift in his opinions.[14] In the Tübingen writings he has seemed to assume that religion has played the determinant role within society, forming its structure, its patterns of personal and social relationships. In Berne, however, Christianity is seen against a background of the social and political changes of the later Roman era. Far from Christianity appearing to have a determining role in the fashioning of social life and personal experiences, it is now seen very much as a projection of a malaise that has already set in in society, a malaise with political and economic roots. Hegel argues that the military might of Rome had led to the formation of a governing elite who used military power and the riches derived from conquests to maintain themselves in power. This form of economic and political domination led, in Hegel's view, to disastrous social and political consequences. The individual began to feel estranged from the state: "The picture of the State as the product of his own energies disappeared from the citizen's soul. . . . All activity and every purpose now had a bearing on something individual—activity was no longer for the sake of the whole or the ideal."[15] These socio-economic and political changes had a very profound effect upon religious life. Folk religion could not adapt to this changed situation; it was based upon and mirrored a system of reciprocity and integration. With this breakdown of social integration, folk religion had to disappear.[16] Christianity, with its emphasis upon the privacy of the individual in his personal relationship to a God who transcended the social order, fitted the gap. Christianity arose out of the unhappy consciousness left by the decline of a sense of participation and community in Rome. When men could no longer find fulfillment in the social life of the community they either projected their ideals onto a purely private world, or a world beyond the political order, namely the kingdom of heaven. By this period, the Christian religion was for Hegel not so much a cause of human estrangement as a projection or symptom of it. The separation of public and private was not produced by Christianity, making men strangers to human feeling, but rather Christianity encapsulated in a series of images the deep discords present in the Roman world, caused by changes in the economic and social structure of the society.

This move towards a more materialist-based approach to social exploration becomes more pronounced after Hegel's move to Frankfurt when we begin to see Hegel, under the influence of Sir James Steuart, beginning to reflect more systematically upon the material and economic basis of cultural forms, social values, and social structures. I will argue that Hegel derived three major insights from his reading of Sir James Steuart's *Inquiry Into The Principles of Political Economy*:[17] first, the beginnings of a philosophy of history which enabled him to take up a far more positive attitude towards the development of modern society; second, the idea that the development of the exchange economy caused an increase in human freedom and self-development, but which at the same time yields its own forms of integration; and finally, from Steuart's theory of the statesman, he derived a very distinctive theory about the role of the state *vis à vis* modern commercial society. Hegel emphatically did not turn his back on his Tübingen ideals of an integrated man in an integrated society; rather, as the result of his researches into political economy, he gradually worked his way towards seeing in the economic life of modern society the development of new forms of integration and community appropriate for the modern world. These influences are perceptible in his Frankfurt essay, *The Spirit of Christianity and Its Destiny*.

In his *Inquiry* Steuart had postulated a three-fold process of development in history from pastoral/nomadic, through agrarian to modern exchange economics. The change from one to the other he interprets as a result of the necessity to increase the food supply, as a result of the increasing growth of the population caused by the domination of the sexual impulse in human life. Steuart also correlates with these distinct economic formations particular kinds of social structures with different sets of social values.

So long as men remained unaware that the supply of food could be increased by human effort, man depended entirely upon the bounty of nature, consuming and moving on. In such a pre-agrarian society men do not labour, but live in idleness—as such the society, if such it can be called, is a system of natural liberty. If a man lives off the spontaneous fruits of the earth there can be no inducement to come under any restraint or subordination. This sort of social system could not last very long, in Steuart's view, because of the very definite limit which it set to the level of population, and life could only be maintained at subsistence level. The pressure of the population leads to labour in order to augment the food supply by human effort. This marks the transition to an agrarian economy. The effect of agriculture is that each cultivator can produce much more food than he himself requires, and this surplus allows for the population to increase.

However, natural differences in physical strength, ability, and intelligence mean that different levels of surplus are achieved by different men, and those who produce most eventually become the masters of those who produce least. An agrarian economy introduces labour, but replaces a system of natural liberty and independence by a system of servitude and slavery.

On the other hand, the exchange economy is an advance upon the agrarian system out of which it develops because it replaces compulsion by inducement. If wants are multiplied above the level of physical necessities then once the taste for what Steuart calls "luxuries" is developed a man has an inducement to produce a surplus through his labour with which he can produce luxuries in exchange. The developed commercial system is a system of freedom rather than of compulsion and servitude.

Not only this, but the exchange economy unites men into relations of functional dependence. One set of men, the farmers, concentrate upon producing a surplus of foodstuffs, another set, the free hands, a surplus of luxury goods, i.e., goods which go beyond the line of bare necessities. Each group exchanges with the other. Thus society is divided into two mutually dependent classes, having recognised wants, and the exchange economy thus produces a system of freedom and a system of mutual independence. Along with the realisation of these values goes the development of urbanisation and the political state. Members of commercial society are bound together by a cycle of activities and functions, the creation and expenditure of incomes, the production and consumption of commodities; it is a "tacit general contract from which reciprocal and proportionate services result universally between all who comprise it."

The development of a modern differentiated society is therefore seen by Steuart as a *rational* development, and one which also develops human freedom and individuality but also one which develops its own forms of solidarity and interrelationship.[18]

This typology of social development is implicit in Hegel's discussion of Jewish history in *The Spirit of Christianity and Its Destiny*, and in this essay Hegel clearly shows that he regards the development of modern commercial activity as part of the "fate" of man in the modern world. In the essay Hegel describes the development of Jewish history from *Hirtenleben* (pastoral society) to *Staat*, the political constitution, and in what follows I want to try briefly to fill in this typology.

Abraham, for Hegel, is the crucial figure in Jewish history. In Hegel's view, Abraham reversed the trend of progressive development in history.[19] Abraham left an urban society, however primitive, in Ur of the Chaldees, and reverted to a nomadic type of existence, trying to free himself from social ties. Throughout his wanderings, in his attempt to reassert the pastoral/nomadic existence, Abraham scorned social ties: "He struggled against his fate which would have offered him a stationary communal life with others."[20] The development of patterns of mutual integration including labour—surely part of what is necessarily involved in the notion of a stationary life—is thus clearly regarded by Hegel as part of the fate of modern man. This kind of simple nomadic existence could not maintain itself, as was revealed in the time of Jacob by the famine, when Jacob and his sons were forced to buy corn from Egypt, which had a highly developed agrarian system. At this point Hegel argues: "The fate against which Abraham and hitherto Jacob also had struggled, that is to say the possession of an abiding dwelling place and attachment to a notion, Jacob finally succumbed. The spirit which led them out of this slavery and then organised them into an independent nation works, and is matured from this point onward in more situations than those in which it appeared."[21] The development of urban life, mutual dependence, and a political culture is thus seen by Hegel to be a part of man's destiny against which the Jewish patriarchs struggled. Abraham sought independence, in Hegel's view and, as Steuart had shown, independence is a correlate of pastoral societies; but though Abraham may have been independent, he was not *free*, in Hegel's view, just because of the pressure of material needs in such a truncated economy: "With the Jews, the State of independence was a state of total passivity and total ugliness. Because their independence secured them only food and drink, an indigent existence, it followed that with this independence, with this little all was lost or jeopardised. There was no life left over which they could have enjoyed. This animal existence was not compatible with the more beautiful form of life which freedom would have given them."[22] Abraham was independent, but was not free. Freedom, for Hegel, was always a much more complex value than mere independence and self-maintenance. It became linked with self-realisation within a rationally comprehensible social order involving intricate forms of mutual interdependence.[23]

The influence of Steuart is very clear here. A nomadic society of this sort is passive because it does not involve labour; it maintains only a bare level of subsistence; there is nothing left over for the development of individuals or for culture. In addition it seems clear that Steuart's typology is being employed in the essay. The development of modern society with its highly differentiated forms is not an unremitting process of degeneration, as hitherto he had been prone to see it, but is rather a rational process and in some sense part of the fate or destiny of the modern world. Steuart had shown, at least in principle, that reflection on modern society could reveal that it realised certain values, such as complexity of culture and individual freedom which could not be realised in less developed forms of life. At the same the commercial structure of modern society with its system of exchange for mutual advantage throws up new less direct but still present forms of social solidarity. Hegel began to hark back to Greece and the homogeneity of Greek society far less and instead to concentrate on the structure of modern society in an attempt to describe the way in which the social, political, and economic practices of modern society themselves embody the conditions within which freedom can be realised and forms of social solidarity appropriate to the changed conditions of the modern world could be achieved. There is a rose to be discerned within the cross of the present; modern society for Hegel comes to embody within itself the seeds of community and mutuality without the sacrifice of personal liberty. There *is* a unity, a harmony, a totality to be discerned beneath the apparent arbitrary surface of bourgeois life. This developing conviction comes out in another rather abstract way in an essay of this period, "On Love." In this essay it is clear that Hegel has a far more positive attitude towards differentiation and plurality than he had in his earlier essays, which embodied his structures on the severe and unreconciled diremptions of modern life:
". . . the linking of many persons depends upon similarity of need and reveals itself in objects which can be common, in relationships assuming such objects and then in common striving for then and a common activity and enterprise. A group of similar aims, the whole range of

physical need may be the object of limited enterprise and in such an enterprise a like spirit reveals itself and this common spirit delights to make itself manifest."[24] This possibility, that forms of harmony and integration could be developed out of what seem to be forms of differentiation, in this case the striving to satisfy personal physical need, was most likely suggested to Hegel by his reading of Steuart and indeed, as we shall see, in his future discussion of political economy Hegel was very keen to show how apparently egocentric interests, the ownership of property, the labour of the individual in the satisfaction of his own needs, his use of tools, all of which seem to involve a progressive differentiation of one man from another, also generate new, less immediate but still perceptible forms of harmony and social solidarity.

Finally, at this point in the argument, I want to say something briefly about Steuart's conception of the "Statesman." By "Statesman" Steuart means merely the form of government, whatever it happens to be in any particular society, and in his *Inquiry* he argues that all economic activity requires the oversight of a statesman, whether it is a representative government of some sort overseeing the development of the modern commercial society, or the patriarch acting as the leader of a nomadic pastoral society. In a modern commercial society, Steuart suggests, the government is able to mitigate some of the more baneful aspects of the growth of commercial relationships by a policy of control over economic activity:

> It is hardly possible suddenly to introduce into the political economy of the state the smallest innovation be it ever so reasonable, nay ever so profitable without making some inconveniences. A room cannot be swept without making a dust and one cannot walk abroad without dirtying one's shoes neither can a machine which abridges the labour of men be introduced all at once into manufacture without throwing very many people into idleness. In treating every question of political economy I constantly suppose a statesman at the head of the government systematically conducting every part of it so as to prevent the vicissitudes of manners and innovations by their immediate effects from hurting any interest in the commonwealth.[25]

This conception of public intervention and control of the pace of economic development favoured by Steuart was, broadly speaking, foreign to the *laissez faire* views of Adam Smith and others, and indeed his views were very critically received in Britain. It does seem, though, that Steuart was influenced by the work of the Cameralists in Germany, and particularly by Justi.[26] As we shall see, it is possible to interpret Hegel's Jena writings, as well as a good deal of his subsequent work on political economy, as an attempt to come to a philosophical grasp of the developing relationship between economic activity, the role of the state in the economic sphere, and personal liberty.

Hegel's task, as he saw it in 1800, was rather different from how he had envisaged it ten years previously. No longer was he convinced that the redemption of modern society was to be found in the recapture of something like Greek folk religion; on the contrary, correctly understood, the mechanisms of modern bourgeois society do provide the seeds of their own redemption. Modern commercial society, beneath the surface play of alienation and diremption, does yield institutions, practices, principles, and values which generate forms of social solidarity which are no doubt very different from those of the Greek model but which, nonetheless, are more appropriate for the changed circumstances of the modern world. To detect, describe, and comprehend these latent forms of unity within differentiation was a philosophical task. As he says in his essay, *The Difference between Fichte and Schilling's System of Philosophy*, "Bifurcation is the source of the need for philosophy." In this particular case philosophy will attempt to grasp the forces at work in modern society which can, on reflection, be seen to be working for harmony and integration and produce a transfigured understanding of civil society, the system of needs, the state, and public authority.

III

In this section of the paper I shall try to illustrate how Hegel attempts this philosophical redescription with particular institutions and practices within the economic sphere. The three examples are labour, tools, and property. In each of these cases Hegel's strategy is just the same; as seen by many economists and political theorists of his day these three activities and institutions involve an increase in individuality, a growth in the differentiation of one man from another, and an undermining of the intimate bonds of communal life. Hegel endeavours to produce by reflection a dialectical reversal of this conventional picture by showing that while labour, tools, and property may well be seen to have a strongly individualistic dimension, they nonetheless fall within the public domain and are characterised by that integration which in fact they secure within that domain.

The first text in which this philosophical strategy for dealing with issues in the sphere of political economy becomes clear is in the *Jenenser Realphilosophie*, in which Hegel uses for the first time in any extended way a central thesis of his about the character of labour: that individual labour undertaken to satisfy individual needs in fact takes on an intrinsically social and universal dimension in commercial society: "The work of each person in regard to its content is universal labour, seeing the needs of all and also apt to satisfy the needs of an individual: otherwise stated, labour has a value. The labour and property of a single individual are not what they are to him, but what they are to all. The satisfaction of needs is a universal dependence of all particular individuals in their relationship to others. . . .each person though an individual having needs becomes a universal."[27] For Hegel labour is not just an individual activity but inherently social. A man produces not merely to satisfy his own needs but also on a reciprocal basis for others. The satisfaction of all my needs above their basic subsistence level is beyond the power of my own labour and depends upon the production of commodities by others. Labour plays a crucial role in the intricate system of mutual interdependence, which he calls the system of needs. At the same time he clearly argues that labour is central to the growth of individuality, self-consciousness, and self-discipline. The argument here, which has the effect of stressing the differentiating function of labour, is classically put in the *Phenomenology*:

> Desire has reserved to itself the pure negating of the object and thereby unalloyed feeling of self. This satisfaction however, just for that reason is itself only a state of evanesence for it lacks objectivity and subsistence. Labour on the other hand is desire restrained and checked, evanesence delayed, in other words labour shapes and fashions the thing. . . . the consciousness that toils and serves accordingly attains by this means the direct apprehension of that independent being as itself. . . . By the fact that the form is objectified, it does not become something other than the consciousness moulding the thing through labour; for just that form is his pure self-existence which therein becomes truly realised.[28]

Labour is therefore crucial to attaining self-consciousness and at the same time seems to sap the bonds of social solidarity just because of its role in the development of an individual's conception of himself as a free and independent being. Hegel therefore clearly recognises that the development of labour and productive activity increases individuality and self-consciousness. However, he is not willing to draw unremitting individualistic consequences from his recognition of the differentiating role of labour. On the contrary; the satisfaction of an individual's needs requires the labour of others once his needs extend beyond mere subsistence: "Need and labour are thus elevated into universality and this creates in a great nation *an immense system of communality and mutual dependence.*"[29] The close-knit *sinnliche Harmonie*[30] of the Greek polis depended upon the fact that the citizens did not labour. The growth of the commercial economy has destroyed this *sinnliche Harmonie* and replaced it with a unity in difference, a system of functional mutual interdependence, a system of interrelationships which requires a good deal of intellectual effort to grasp and to tease out. In this task, classical political economy has played a decisive role for Hegel because the economist is attempting to find " . . . reconciliation here, to discover in the sphere of needs this show of rationally lying in the thing and effective there."[31] In his account of labour, therefore, Hegel attempts to produce a philosophical redescription of the social relationships engendered by labour and to argue that a recognition of the differentiating role of labour in modern society does not require us to take up an individualistic view of society. Of course, for Hegel, this redescription, which yields a communitarian vision of society even within a recognition of the differentiation engendered in commercial relationships, is not just some kind of consoling fantasy in terms of which we come to terms with the world by veiling its real nature. Rather, the philosophical description of labour relationships, both from the individual and the social perspectives, cuts far deeper and reflects more faithfully the *real character* of the phenomena than either individualistic political theory or classical political economy from which such political theory has developed. These structures of understanding of social life remain at the level of the understanding which trades in bifurcation, abstraction, and a reductionist account of reality and social relationships. A conceptual grasp of the world as given in philosophy in Hegel's view reflects the true nature of reality just because reality is itself dialectical. To this extent the underpinning of Hegel's claim that his communitarian redescription of social life is not a consoling dream depends upon his arguments about the congruence between thought and the world developed in the various logics.

In his treatment of other facets of commercial society Hegel utilises the same kind of principles which we have seen at work in his account of labour. One of these facets, the use of tools, is closely bound up with labour and one can see again how Hegel uses this feature to draw conclusions about the degree of mutuality which exists, often unrecognised, in the heart of production and exchange systems. The invention of a new tool may seem, on the face of it, to require us to acknowledge the free creative vision of the self-conscious individual who created it, and Hegel certainly does not wish to undervalue individual human achievement in the creation of new tools. However he insists upon two points which are of great importance in seeing how even an activity such as invention has its non-contingent social dimension. First of all, the tool responds to a felt need within the labouring process, and in addition its invention requires a background of inherited skill or expertise,[32] but more than this it is a *tool* only insofar as it encapsulates a help or a solution to a productive problem which is open to anyone with the appropriate skill to take up and utilise. The invention of a tool is not, then, a private creative activity but has this double-sided social aspect: "Faced with the general level of skill the individual sets himself off from the generality and makes himself more skillful than others, invents more efficient tools. But the really universal element in his particular skill is his invention of something universal; and others acquire it from him and thereby annul his particularity and it [the tool] becomes the common immediate possession of all."[33] Invention therefore requires two sorts of social dimension: (1) a tradition of inherited skill in production against the background of which the tool is invented and (2) its nature as a *tool* as opposed to any other sort of object requires that it satisfies certain public criteria relating to the productive process within which it is to play a part and, because of this, its use is open to all. These points are nicely summed up in the *Jenenser Realphilosophie I*: "It is that wherein working has its permanence, that alone which remains of the labourer and the substances worked upon in which its contingency is externalised; it is inherited in the traditions while that which desires as well as that which is desired only subsist as individuals and individuals pass away."[34] Tool making and tool using therefore relate to a public domain of inherited skill and wisdom in productive processes and the invention of tools has to be made intelligible within the background of this type of social cooperation.

My final example of Hegel's attempt to redescribe and put into a more communitarian perspective the central features of commercial society is property. The ownership of property is very closely bound up in Hegel's view with the development of individuality, self-consciousness, and the distinctness of one person from another. It is the way in which the specific and individual character of a person's will is made objective: " . . . personality is that which struggles to lift itself above this restriction and give itself reality, or in other words to claim the external world as its own."[35] Conceived in this way property may be regarded as a decisive differentiating institution within society. But again a dialectical reversal in the argument occurs which has the result of crediting property with an equally central social dimension. Possession and appropriation are necessary, but not sufficient conditions of property. Property as a *right* has to be recognised. If property is not recognised then although an object may be appropriated entitlement to it has not been vindicated. The property has to be recognised as property by those who have been excluded by the act of appropriation. Appropriation may be an individualistic, indeed a possessive individualistic act,[36] but property requires social recognition: "The security of my possession becomes the security of the possession of all: in my property all have their property";[37] and "I hold my property not merely by means of the thing and my subjective will, but also by means of another person's will as well and so hold it in virtue of my participation in a common will."[38]

Property as embodying a claim to entitlement as opposed to a power of appropriation can exist only within a nexus of mutually recognised rights and obligations. In addition, property relationships lead to more concrete interrelationships in contractual situations. A freeman must be able to alienate his property, otherwise he would be tied to the particularity of nature. A man needs property in which to objectify his will, but he does not need *this* object as opposed to *that*. This capacity to alienate one's property, because it means transferring an entitlement, requires contractual relationships and a legal system. The appropriation of objects, therefore, may be a sheer act of will by the free subject, but the act of appropriation has to be conjoined with social recognition. So at the heart of the property relationship which seems so individualistic is a non-contingent social dimension within which entitlement is recognised.

As we have seen, Hegel does not see the modern commercial system as necessarily yielding a radically individualistic vision of society. Rather, the very activities so characteristic of the commercial system, both in production and exchange, presuppose very intricate patterns of relationship. At the heart of the system of needs, therefore, can be seen seeds of mutuality and social solidarity. Nor is this just a feature of labour, tools, invention, and property: it is true equally of other features of the system of needs, the division of labour, the generation of economic value, and membership of corporations. In all of these cases Hegel tries to show that below the surface play of rather arbitrary atomism there are generated criss-cross patterns of human interrelationships which may not be discernible in any immediate way. Modern solidarity has to be detected, exposed, and described by the philosopher. This is a philosophical task even within the sphere of political economy because although political economists have done important work in producing a sketch of the structure of the modern economy, they have done so in terms of rather one-dimensional and simplistic postulates about human nature, which has led them to undervalue precisely those social corollaries of economic activity which Hegel wishes to bring to the fore in his account. In addition they have failed to connect their accounts of, for example, labour, with any more general theory about human nature and its development which would have enabled them to have put the sphere of the economic into a broader perspective, which would have included, as it does for Hegel, putting it into the moral, political, and cultural perspective of the modern world. Hegel seeks throughout to relate economic activities both to an individual anthropological dimension— attempting to place economic activity such as labour and ownership of property into an account of the incremental development of the powers and capacities of the individual human mind—and equally to link these developments with their social effects, which he regards as being basically integration.

IV

Hegel's account of how the modern system of needs can provide a basis for mutual interdependence and social solidarity is not exhausted by his attempt to demonstrate the integrative forces at work in the activities undertaken within the system of needs. Such patterns of integration do exist: but in Hegel's view they do so in a somewhat haphazard fashion. The intricate patterns of interrelationships secured within the system of needs may be very easily disrupted by changes in the methods of production and the demand for new commodities, and by external factors such as changes in the terms of trade between one nation and another. The interrelationships produced within the system of needs are fragile: "Whole branches of industry which supported a large class of people suddenly disappear because of a change in fashion or the values of their products fall because of new inventions in other countries."[39] Hegel's conclusion is that "the system moves this way and that in a blind and elemental fashion and like a wild animal calls for permanent control and curbing." As a result of this somewhat fragile set of mutual interactions Hegel argues that there has to be some form of control over economic relationships if the patterns of dependence secured in the system of needs are to be rational, stable, and capable of being exhibited by systematic thought. Here again, we may perhaps see the influence of Steuart on Hegel. Although by the time of the Jena period (1801-1807) Hegel was aware of the work of other political economists, notably Adam Smith, these ideas about the necessary limitations of the *laissez faire* economy are less likely to have come from that particular source than they are from Steuart. Steuart's doctrine of the statesman was, as we have seen, expressly formulated in his discussion of the exchange economy as an instrument of control over that economy, with the object of preventing changes in the terms of the economy harming the commonwealth. Rosenkranz, in his discussion of Hegel's relationship with Steuart, argues among other things that Steuart influenced Hegel's thinking on the police role of the state[40] and the connexion between Hegel's preoccupations as we have seen them developing so far and Steuart's argument appears at precisely this point. By *"Polizei"*[41] is meant the general controlling function of the state over society as a whole, and in his writings of this period Hegel begins to work out a theory of public authority, or the police functions of the state, which would enable the blind system of dependence secured in the system of needs to be made more rational and secure. It is crucial to his aim to show that the modern world can secure some sense of community that he should be able to demonstrate that the modern state in fact has the structure and the will to intervene in the economic life of society if tensions within that sphere could lead to the forms of social solidarity engendered within it from breaking down. In fact, it was Hegel's view that the modern state did exhibit this feature; both in France under Napoleon, and after 1807 in Prussia, the state did take a hand in overseeing the development of the economy on progressive lines, but in such a way as to secure the basis of social solidarity within the economic sphere.[42]

However, Hegel's actual theory of the role of public authority and its relationship to the system of needs is rather different from that of Steuart. The latter's theory of the statesman did not entail any particular view about the character of the control to be exercised by the government; indeed his use of the wholly general term "statesman" would seem to indicate this. Hegel, however, wished to argue that only state intervention in the economy by a public authority of a special kind could be legitimate in the context of the modern commercial economy. Hegel was as concerned as Steuart about the general equilibrium of the exchange economy but his interest in the sort of control involved went beyond that of Steuart. We are told by Rosenkranz that Hegel fought against what was dead in Steuart's system and that he sought to save "the inner life of man within the commercial system."[43] It is in his account of public authority that we can best see the actual preoccupations of Hegel on these issues.

It seems that there are two aspects of Hegel's desire to save the inner life of man within the commercial system and both of these aspects require for their treatment a move on Hegel's part beyond the theories on *dirigism* put forward by Steuart. The first is concerned with the way in which a sense of individuality and subjective freedom are incompatible with some *dirigist* programmes; the second is concerned with the enervation of the individual within the productive processes of modern manufacturing industry and the ways in which the state can provide ways of overcoming this enervation. These two perspectives on the role of the individual and his inner life within modern society will now be discussed in turn.

In considering the police functions of the state in securing the equilibrium of the system of needs, Hegel seems to have retained in his mind the possible sense of estrangement which can exist between the individual and the state which he explored in his essay on "The Positivity of the Christian Religion": "The picture of the state as the product of his own energies disappeared from the citizen's soul. The care and oversight of the whole rested upon one man or a few."[44] Such an emphasis upon the possibly estranged character of the modern state was lacking in Steuart. Hegel, however, rejected any idea of intervention which smacked of rigidity and dictatorship. This point comes out very clearly in his criticism of Prussia in 1800-1801 in *The German Constitution:* "In recent theories, carried partly into effect, the fundamental presupposition is that a state is a machine with a single spring which imparts movement to the rest of the wheel in its infinite complexity and all the institutions of society should proceed from the supreme public authority and should be regulated, commanded and overseen by it."[45] Mere control will not suffice for Hegel. The equilibrium of the system of needs is important but the equilibrium should not be secured by the state at the risk of stifling the individual and his pursuit of subjective freedom within the market by the rigidity of its control. Hegel takes up this point again in *The German Constitution:* "This is not the place to argue at length that the centre, as the public authority, i.e. as the government must leave to its citizens whatever is not necessary for its appointed task. Nothing should be so sacrosanct to the government as facilitating and protecting the free activity of citizens in matters other than this . . . for the freedom of the individual is inherently sacrosanct."[46] The point being made here is not only a moral one, it has a metaphysical side which ties it into the previous discussion of the system of needs. Modern commercial society, based upon free labour, has seen the gradual emancipation of the individual, giving him through his labour a sense of his own worth and a sense of himself as a centre of subjective freedom. So the system of needs is a centre of subjective freedom and particularity. Consequently, any form of state control over an economic system which realises such values must be compatible with the existence of such values. Hegel is thus attempting to steer a middle course between non-intervention in the system of needs, which would be disastrous, because all that would then exist would be blind and irrational forms of mutual interdependence; on the other hand, too much control by a remote government might secure equilibrium but at the cost of producing further estrangement between the citizen and the political order. The problem of this *via media* is well put in the *Philosophy of Right:* "Two views predominate at the present time. One asserts that the superintendence of everything properly belongs to the public authority; the other that the public authority has nothing to regulate here because everyone will direct his efforts towards the needs of others."[47] The second point will not stand because of the way in which the system of needs is the sphere of particularity and no regulation would mean a system out of equilibrium; the first position outlined here is incompatible with the individual's sense of subjective freedom, which is realised in the system of needs over which control is to be exercised. Only a society without a sense of subjective freedom could justifiably use this form of social control and Hegel gives as an example the building of the pyramids in Egypt.[48] In this kind of society, in which the consciousness of subjective freedom has yet to dawn and take hold, such centralised control of the labour and economic activity of individuals is justified. However, in the modern world we are emphatically not in that position; the public authority must control the minimum necessary for the maintenance of equilibrium within the system of needs and, furthermore, as the external state, i.e., imposed upon the particularity of subjective interests in the economic sphere, it has to be under some kind of representative political control, otherwise it will appear as the state did to the Roman, an estranged institution. The kind of control which Hegel sees as being legitimately within the sphere of the public authority is the fixing of the prices for the basic necessities of life, the arbitration of disputes between producers and consumers of commodities, the dissemination of information relating to the terms of trade, and the general economic situation within which industry operates. The operation of the public authority in these sorts of spheres will enable the system of needs to operate more effectively and calculably than it otherwise would have done. At the same time, although an advocate of *dirigism*, as we have seen, Hegel is very clear that the subjective freedom of man, part of his inner life, should be considered very carefully when deciding what to oversee in the system of needs.

The second way in which Hegel goes beyond Steuart in his concern with the individual personality within the commercial system is his consideration of the enervation of human capacities and powers which goes on within the productive processes of modern society. Hegel retained a very great deal of respect for the Greek ideal of the wholeness and integrity of the personality and he was concerned with man's fate in terms of this value in the modern world, and most especially within the system of needs. Already, as we have seen, in the argument over the role of the public authority Hegel was concerned that this intervention would not

diminish subjective freedom more than necessary, but at the same time
he was well aware that this subjective freedom, which reached its zenith
in the modern world, has its own costs and in Hegel's mind these costs,
broadly speaking, were twofold. In the first place the pursuit of subjective freedom within the system of needs may result in civic ties being
lessened, even though, as we have seen, the system will yield its own
forms of *economic* interdependence; second, labouring within manufacturing industry may well lead to an enervation of the human personality.
In these two ways again the inner life of man was threatened by the
commercial system. In the first case he would be made over to entirely
subjective interests, whereas Hegel was always clear that human beings
were responsive to other values as well, to do with group or state
enterprises; in the second case the division of labour was making labour
too mechanical and abstract. Again both of these factors were absent
from Steuart, although they were present in the writings of Adam Smith
and Adam Ferguson, whom Hegel had read by the early 1800s. The first
of these problems, the dissolution of civic ties caused by the self-centred
nature of bourgeois life, was a well-known problem, discussed by Herder, Goethe, Schiller, and Hölderlin within Hegel's own cultural context; the second problem, the enervation of man within bourgeois society, was posed particularly strongly by Schiller in his *Letters on the
Aesthetic Education of Man* in which he argues: "Eternally tied to a single
fragment of the whole, man develops into nothing but a fragment.
Everlastingly in his ear is the monotonous sound of the wheel he operates. He never develops the harmony of his being and instead of stamp-
ing the imprint of humanity upon nature, he becomes no more than the
imprint of his occupation and his specialised knowledge."[49] This insight of Schiller into the enervating character of the modern labouring
process was probably backed up by Hegel's reading of Adam Smith. In
Jenenser Realphilosophie I he quotes the example of the pin factory cited by
Smith in his *Enquiry into the Wealth of Nations* in the context of some
general reflections upon the character of labour within manufacturing
industry.[50] In *Jenenser Realphilosophie II* he is very explicit about this: "A
mass of the population is condemned to the stupifying, unhealthy and
insecure labour of the factories, manufactures, mines and so on. . . .
this necessity turns into the utmost dismemberment of the will inner
rebellion and hatred."[51] The problems posed by commercial society are
not just those confined to social cohesion but also concern the inner life

of men, the social and personal cost of the emancipation of the individual, which clearly occurs, in Hegel's view, within the modern world, and reached its zenith of individuality within the system of needs. Again a political economy which is going to be philosophically adequate has to be able to come to terms with these kinds of costs incurred in economic activity. While at the same time allowing for subjective freedom we must understand the modern state as supplying institutions which go some way at least toward mitigating the worst of these costs.

In Hegel's view there are solutions to these problems both within the system of needs itself and outside it. Within the system of needs he is concerned to show that in this context belonging to a social class and to a corporation are important group ties in which individuals lost in particularity can come to a sense of group affiliation and thus some of the enervating aspects of their subjectivism can be overcome.[52] These group ties of class and, to speak more modernly, occupational community are also valuable in that they are not institutions or relationships imposed on persons from outside the economic sphere but arise out of the subjective pursuits in the economic sphere. As a member of a class and of a corporation I am able to become aware of claims upon me which restrict my self-seeking and impose upon me some natural-seeming group constraints. These constraints are not of a universal character; they are rather sectional, or, as Hegel would say, specific, but nonetheless, the claims which I represent to myself as a member of a partial community or class are an incremental advance on my unfettered subjectivism. This kind of partial community membership will not give a person a universal consciousness, a perspective on his society and the values realised in it as a *whole*, and this is true of any group affiliations within the system of needs. But this does not imply, as, for example, Rousseau thought, that such intermediate groups stood in the way of the specific individual attaining this universal, this sense of identification with society as a whole. On the contrary, in Hegel's view, such institutions act as important intermediaries between the individual with his personal desires, interests, and freedom and the universal interests of society as a whole. Without these intermediary institutions within commercial life the individual would be unable to attain the universal; he would, as Hegel sometimes puts it, "be lost in particularity." Therefore, the partial communities of class and group affiliation act as educative institutions within commercial life and lift men gradually and without apparent constraint above the purely private pursuit of personal utilities. As such these partial communities overcome some of the enervation of the person caught up in the continual striving for personal utility so characteristic of bourgeois life and at the same time again reveal that within commercial society there are autonomously engendered forms of community and ways of mediating community identity between individuals.

At the same time these communities are only partial and the perspective on life which they offer is one of sectional interest rooted within the system of needs. There is still no sense of personal identification with an overall normative order which expresses universality and impartiality—features which Hegel regards as necessary features of any rounded, total human life. This universal dimension to life is provided by the state proper and the general cultural life of the community, its art, religion, and philosophy. Only within the state and the culture of the national community can the universal be realised. Within the strictly political sphere the particular individual is related to the state *via* the specificity of his social and class position to the Assembly of Estates. Although the modern world has realised most of all, and in many divergent directions, the values of freedom and moral autonomy, Hegel thought that the French Revolution and the subsequent Terror had demonstrated the impossibility of direct democracy in the modern world; but at the same time tyranny and despotism, however enlightened, are incompatible with the values realised in the modern world generally, and which also have this central place, as we have seen, in the system of needs. A representative political system, which represents not so much individuals lost in privacy, as they are when taken on their own, but individuals related to one another in estates or classes— the basic partial communities of the system of needs. Through this form of representation the individual, however particularised his activity may be within the system of needs, does have this relationship with the specific partial communities and *via* them to the universal embodied in the interests of society as a whole. At the same time, as this rather oblique political involvement overcomes this fragmentation of his being, so the involvement also prevents the state appearing as an alienated form, as it did to the Roman. Hegel sums up his thoughts about representation *via* estates in a way which brings out this point particularly well: " . . . the Estates stand between the government in general on the one hand and the nation broken up into particulars on the other.

Their function requires them to possess a political and an administrative sense and temper, no less than a sense of the interests of individuals and particular groups. At the same time the significance of their position is that in common with the organised executive, they are the middle term preventing both the extreme isolation of the crown, which might otherwise seem a mere arbitrary tyranny and also the isolation of the particular interests of persons, societies and Corporations."[53] Through the partial communities of the system of needs and the representation of the most basic of these, the class-based community, through the Assembly of Estates in the political sphere, the enervation of the individual so characteristic of the system of needs is diminished and, in addition, civic ties are forged between individuals and the groups which within the system of needs reflect their interests. Hegel seems confident that this is how the political arrangements of the modern European state will seem to the individual citizen:

> The result is that the universal does not prevail or achieve completion except along with particular interests and through the cooperation of particular knowing and willing; and the individuals do not live as private persons for their ends alone, but in the very act of willing these they will the universal in the light of the universal and their activity is consciously aimed at none but the universal end. The principle of modern states has prodigious strength and depth because it allows the principle of subjectivity to progress to its culmination in the extreme self-subsistent particularity [in the system of needs], and yet at the same time brings it back to the substantive unity and so maintains this unity in the principle of subjectivity itself.[54]

So we can see that Hegel's early ideals—the restoration of some sense of the wholeness of man and the human personality, a restoration of some sense of community, and a redefinition of man's relationship to nature, are seen by Hegel to be realised in the structure of the modern political community, once that structure is understood. This structure is not on the surface and thus unlike the Greek the modern man does not have a sensuous experience of being at home in the world. The modern man can only be *bei sich selbst* when he has grasped the forces making for integration and communal identity in the modern world. It is Hegel's thesis that these forces are there to be found and their positing is not just a consoling fantasy projected on the world by the deracinated intellectual with something of an admiration, however ambiguous, for the com-

munitarian structure of Greek society, the individual's sense of personal
wholeness, and his sense of integration into nature, into Mother Earth.
While the Greeks' achievement of this was to be achieved by the senses
and celebrated through art, that of the modern man has to be procured
by prodigious effort, by "taking on the exertion of the concept."[55] In
the final section of the paper I shall argue that not only is it absolutely
necessary, given his philosophical aims, that Hegel should have pro-
pounded his vision of the communitarian tendencies within the political
economy of modern society, this vision applied in this field is in fact the
Achilles' heel of Hegel's work, and is capable of undercutting the whole
of his attempt to show that the modern state can provide man with a
home in the world. I shall also argue that this can be shown without
importing external considerations drawn, say, from Marxist critiques of
his account of bourgeois society, nor from analytical critiques of his
whole philosophical enterprise, but rather from his own admission that
he is unable to see how the modern state, predicated upon the kind of
production and exchange system which he outlines in his various accounts of the system of needs, can cope with the problem of poverty,
with all that poverty entails for Hegel.

V

In the *Philosophy of Right* Hegel argues that poverty is an endemic and
ineradicable feature of modern society. It is not a feature of a particular
industrial society when it is in a state of decline or disintegration but
rather when it is running smoothly, when, as he says, "civil society is in
a state of unimpeded activity."[56] Poverty, by which Hegel means both
physical deprivation and an internal sense of alienation from society on
the part of those who are poor, is thus, for Hegel, an apparently structural phenomenon, generated by the smooth running of modern society.
The mechanics of the process are a bit obscure, but the main outline of
the argument seems to be clear enough.

When industry produces goods, as it does incessantly under the
pressure of men's wants, it may well find that there are not enough
consumers for its products, as Hegel says: " . . . the evil consists precisely in an excess of production and the lack of a proportionate number
of consumers who are themselves producers. . . ."[57] In such circum-

stances the bottom will drop out of the market for a particular commod-
ity and men who, by the continuing refinement of the division of labour
within the system of needs, are entirely dependent on industry producing this or that particular product, for which there is not a market in
these circumstances, will be thrown into idleness. These sorts of consequences, he seems to think, follow from the general organisation of
manufacture in civil society, and the poverty resulting from this has two
distinct sides—the actual level of physical deprivation involved and the
consequent changes in the social attitudes of those who are deprived. In
Hegel's view the level of poverty or deprivation is not fixed by some
definite or objective standard based upon a notion of absolute or basic
need but rather by some notion of the lack of satisfaction of relative
need, need relative to what is necessary to be a functioning and integrated member of a particular society with a particular standard of living
and a particular pattern of consumption: "When the standard of living
of a large mass of the people falls below a certain subsistence level—a
level regulated automatically as the one necessary for a member of the
society . . . the result is the creation of a rabble of paupers."[58] In a
comment on this paragraph Hegel gives a pithy and practical application of his point of view: "In England, even the poorest believe that they
have rights; this is different from what satisfies the poor in other countries."[59]

Poverty is then, for Hegel, a state of relative deprivation: deprivation
relative to the normal or average standard of living in a particular
society, and in this view he is surprisingly modern in his outlook. It is
also precisely at this point that poverty as both a relative concept and a
state makes contact with Hegel's other view that there are social attitudes which are characteristic of poverty: a sense of rootlessness and
alienation, a set of social attitudes which, he considers, leads to the
formation of a rabble existing, so to speak, on the edges of society.
Because of their deprivation and poverty men become deprived of various advantages of society—acquiring skill, education, access to ju'
and even to organised religion, all of which are mediating institutions
which link men t the social system, and bereft of this link they become
estranged: "Poverty in itself does not make men into a rabble; a rabble is
created only when there is joined to poverty a disposition of mind, an
inner indignation against the rich, against society, against the government, etc."[60] The unimpeded activity of civil society therefore estab-

lishes norms relating to need and consumption. These norms are not absolute but are related to the particular pattern of economic activity in the society, but at the same time such a society is not able to satisfy the consumption needs of large groups of people in that society in terms of its own criteria of need. Consequently a group of people are pressed down to this internally posited poverty floor and within such groups there is generated a profound sense of alienation and social hostility. Modern society then renders groups of people deracinated and compels them to live both materially and spiritually on the very periphery of society. What then becomes of Hegel's claim that he can provide an account of the modern world which will enable man to be *zu Hause*, to be integrated into the modern political community and find it expressive of his own deepest desires? It is absolutely necessary for the coherence of Hegel's vision that he should be able to provide an answer to this probing question. The institutions of the modern state should be able to provide a way of overcoming this structural tendency of modern society to produce groups of social outcasts. If he could show that such institutions are present or are at least intimated within the general structure of the modern European state then the coherence of his theory would be vindicated; without it there is a gaping hole in his view that, correctly understood, the modern state can provide man with a home and a sense of belonging in the modern world.

However, it is clear that Hegel cannot do this, and he admits as much in his discussion in the *Philosophy of Right*, although he does not sufficiently attend to the consequences of his admission for the coherence of his own overall theory of modern society. In paragraph 245 of the *Philosophy of Right* Hegel discusses several possible solutions to the problem of poverty as he sees it. The first solution is that of organised charity, utilising money raised from taxes levied on the wealthier classes or money raised from private foundations of various sorts, monasteries, hospitals, etc. But the problem created by charity is that while the physical poverty of the deprived may be alleviated, it will do nothing to change those social attitudes which, as he has argued, go along with poverty. Poverty undermines self-respect, self-subsistence, and self-maintenance, but so does charity. Charity will not cure the problem because, as he had argued, these same social attitudes engendered by poverty are equally sustained by charitable activity: " . . . the needy would receive subsistence directly, not by means of their work, and this would violate the principle of civil society and the feeling of individual independence and self-respect in its individual members."[61]

Another possibility open to the modern state might be to create work by stimulating the economy. However, in Hegel's view, this would in the long run only make matters worse, because the problem of poverty has been caused by overproduction in the first place and so cannot be cured by further economic growth. Hegel, writing in 1821, did not entertain the possibility of creating work by providing for public works which do not issue in consumer goods. Bereft of the Keynesean way out Hegel was left to conclude: "It hence becomes apparent that despite an excess of wealth civil society is not rich enough, i.e. its own resources are insufficient to check excessive poverty and the creation of a penurous rabble."[62] Modern society within its own boundaries generates poverty, and the alienation which Hegel sees goes with it, and is by his own admission unable to overcome this central structural feature.

The only solution which Hegel can envisage is that of colonisation—not for the sake of raw materials but more to seek new markets for its overproduced goods and for transporting part of its population—just those who are driven to deprivation by the unimpeded activity of civil society. For Hegel, as for Rosa Luxemburg, Lenin, and Bukharin, there is an internal connexion between capitalist society and imperialism. Imperialism, for Hegel, is the only solution to the problems of poverty and as those problems are interminable so is imperialism. However, the important point to notice, so far as the argument of this paper is concerned, is that the modern state cannot *within itself* provide the answer to one of its own self-generated problems and, consequently, the modern state, however philosophically comprehended, cannot provide a home in the world for certain of its members. Hegel has delved deeply into this aspect of modern society and has in his own terms provided a conceptual grasp of it; but for the poor man faced with having to move to the colonies, to understand the inner dialectic driving civil society to push beyond its own limits is poor recompense. This seems to be a clear case where Hegel's famous assertion, made within the *Philosophy of Right*, "*Ich ist in der Welt zu Hause wenn es sie kennt, noch mehr wenn es sie begriffen hat*" sounds very hollow. At the heart of this claim there lies a deep contradiction and one which strikes at the heart of the Hegelian theory of reconciliation. As a recent commentator has argued, "Does not Hegel's manifest inability to find a solution to the problem of poverty indicate his failure as a social philosopher in the terms of his own philosophy which has as its purpose the systematic inclusion of the totality which would mean the overcoming of all contradiction and alienation."[63] Perhaps in certain moments Hegel was aware of this. Certainly he was concerned with the problem of poverty from a very early period and it was a concern which with all the problems it poses for his own system stayed with him for the rest of his life. In Rosenkranz, we find Hegel reported as being concerned sufficiently with the problem prior to 1800 to have made excerpts from English newspapers which reported Poor Law debates in Parliament: " . . . Hegel followed with great excitement the Parliamentary debates on the poor law and the alms by which the nobility and the aristocracy of wealth attempted to appease the rage of indigent masses."[64] Rosenkranz also argues that it was in the no longer extant commentary on Steuart's *Inquiry* that Hegel concentrated his ideas on poverty, and there are discussions of the problem in *System der Sittlichkeit*, in *Realphilosophie I* and *II*, and in the *Philosophy of Right*. It was thus a problem which goes all the way through Hegel's writings and which in his very last works on the subject he came no nearer to solving. Hegel was always concerned with the inner life of man and the quality of human relations, yet here, in the heart of his theory of society, which represents virtually the culmination of his attempts to produce this transfigured grasp of the modern world in the interests of just these values, there is this deep discrepancy between what is required by the character of the theory and the actual structure of society.[65]

NOTES

1. "La Doctrine Economique de Hegel et la Conception Hegelienne Travail" in *Hegel Studien*, Beiheft 4(Bouvier Verlag: Bonn, 1965). "Les Origines de la Pensée Economique de Hegel" in *Hegel Studien*, Band 3 (Bouvier Verlag: Bonn, 1965).
2. Libraire Dalloz: Paris, 1963; Libraire Dalloz, 1965.
3. George Allen and Unwin: London, 1973 and Indiana University Press: Indiana, 1973.
4. J. C. B. Mohr: Tübingen, 1907.
5. F. G. Nauen, *Revolution, Idealism and Human Freedom* (M. Nijhoff: The Hague, 1971).
6. J. Taminiaux, *La Nostalgie de la Grece dans l'Idealism Allemand* (Gallimard: Paris, 1968).

7. Even in 1805 in *Jenaer Realphilosophie*, II, ed. J. Hoffmeister (F. Meiner: Hamburg, 1969) he is still able to write as follows about the Greek city state: "In der alten Zeit war das Schöne öffentliche Leben die Sitte aller, Schönheit (als) unmittelbare Einheit des Allgemeinen und Einzelnen, ein Kunstwerk, worin kein Teil sich absondert vom Ganzen, sondern diese genialische Einheit des sich wissenden Selbsts und seiner Darstellung" (p. 251).

8. Nohl, op. cit., p. 9.

9. Ibid., p. 16.

10. Vide Schiller's poem, "Die Götter Griechenlands," written in 1787-88 in Schiller, *National Ausgabe*, ed. Blumenthal and von Weise (Bohlau: Weimar, 1943), Vol. 1, pp. 190ff.

11. Nohl, op. cit., p. 28.

12. Paul Chamley, "Les Origines de la Pensée Economique de Hegel," op. cit., pp. 226-27 and particularly: "En depit de leur artifice, les besoins ne present pas comme une contrainte: il ne cessent pas de faire partie de la nature humaine."

13. Ibid., p. 227.

14. Particularly in "The Positivity of the Christian Religion," in Nohl, op. cit., pp. 139ff.

15. Ibid., p. 251.

16. This sociological account of the decline of folk religion is given in Nohl, op. cit., pp. 220-21.

17. London, 1767. Reprinted in an edition edited by A. Skinner (Oliver and Boyd: London, 1966). Hegel read and made a commentary on this book between 19th Feb. and 16th May, 1799; vide Rosenkranz, *Hegels Leben* (Wiss. Buchges: Berlin, 1969), p. 86. Unfortunately this commentary is no longer extant. Manfred Riedel is one of the few commentators to have discussed Steuart's influence on Hegel in his *Studien zu Hegels Rechtsphilosophie* (Suhrkamp: Frankfurt, 1969), pp. 75ff. G. Lukacs, in *The Young Hegel*, trans. R. Livingstone (Merlin Press: London, 1975), argues that it is useless to estimate the influence of Steuart's particular economic principles on Hegel (p. 71). I have no general defence to offer to this charge other than suggesting to the reader that he pay careful attention to the points made in the body of the paper.

18. As Chamley rightly says: "L'Inquiry est avant tout une theorie de l'evolution," in *Economie Politique chez Steuart et Hegel*, op. cit., p. 59.

19. This comes out particularly clearly in the unpublished text by Nohl, which begins *Zu Abrahams Zeiten. . . .* Vide H. S. Harris, *Hegel's Development 1770-1801* (The Clarendon Press: Oxford, 1972), p. 285.

20. Nohl, op. cit., p. 246.

21. Ibid., p. 245.

22. Ibid., p. 253. Cf. H. Marcuse, *Studies in Critical Philosophy* (New Left Books: London, 1972), p. 162.

23. Leszek Kolakowski helped me a good deal to clear my mind on this point. On all of this cf. *The Philosophy of Right*, trans. T. M. Knox (Oxford: The Clarendon Press, 1952), para. 194.

24. Nohl, op. cit., pp. 322-23.

25. *An Inquiry into the Principles of Political Economy*, ed. A. Skinner, op. cit., p. 122.

26. The *Inquiry* was written in Tübingen where, as a Jacobite, Steuart lived in exile after the abortive 1845 rebellion.

27. *Jenenser Realphilosophie*, I, ed. Lasson (F. Meiner: Leipzig, 1932), p. 328.

28. *The Phenomenology of Mind*, trans. J. Baillie, 2nd ed. (George Allen and Unwin: London, 1931), pp. 238-39.
29. *Jenenser Realphilosophie*, I, op. cit., pp. 239-40; cf. *The Phenomenology of Mind*, op. cit., p. 377.
30. I borrow this term from Schiller.
31. *The Philosophy of Right*, op. cit., para. 189.
32. Compare the account given of invention by a latter-day Idealist, Michael Oakeshott, in *Rationalism in Politics* (Methuen: London, 1962).
33. *Jenenser Realphilosophie*, II, op. cit., p. 197.
34. Ibid., I, p. 221.
35. *The Philosophy of Right*, op. cit., para. 39.
36. Vide C. B. Macpherson, *The Political Theory of Possessive Individualism* (The Clarendon Press: Oxford, 1962).
37. *Jenenser Realphilosophie*, I, p. 240.
38. *The Philosophy of Right*, op. cit., para. 71.
39. *Jenenser Realphilosophie*, II, op. cit., pp. 232-33.
40. Rosenkranz, *Hegels Leben*, op. cit., p. 86.
41. Vide *The Philosophy of Right*, op. cit., para. 231 and Brian Chapman, *Police State* (Pall Mall Press: London, 1970).
42. Vide W. H. Bruford, *Germany in the Eighteenth Century* (Cambridge University Press: Cambridge, 1965).
43. Rosenkranz, *Hegels Leben*, p. 86.
44. Nohl, ed., *Hegels theologische Jugendschriften*, op. cit. p. 223.
45. *Schriften zur Politik und Rechtsphilosophie*, ed. Lasson (F. Meiner: Leipzig, 1923), p. 28. Cf. *Dokumente zu Hegels Entwicklung*, ed. J. Hoffmeister (Frommann Verlag: Stuttgart, 1936). This view of the state was certainly held by Justi, one of Steuart's mentors, in almost identical language; vide Justi, *Gesammelte Politische und Finanzschriften* (Leipzig, 1761), Vol. 3, pp. 86-87. There is some discussion of Cameralism in M. Oakeshott, *Human Conduct* (The Clarendon Press: Oxford, 1975), p. 300, and in G. B. Parry, "Enlightened Government and Its Critics," in *The Historical Journal*, 6, no. 2 (1963).
46. Lasson, ed., *Schriften zur Politik und Rechtsphilosophie*, op. cit., pp. 28-29.
47. *The Philosophy of Right*, op. cit., addition to para. 236; cf. para. 124.
48. Ibid., para. 236.
49. Schiller, *National Ausgabe*, op. cit., Vol. 20, p. 322. Hegel thought that these letters were a masterpiece; vide the letter from Hegel to Schelling, 16th April, 1795, in *Briefe von und an Hegel*, Vol. 1, ed. Hoffmeister (F. Meiner: Hamburg, 1952).
50. *Jenenser Realphilosophie*, I, op. cit., p. 238.
51. Ibid., II, p. 232.
52. This has a good deal in common with modern theories of occupational communities. For further discussion of these themes vide my forthcoming paper, "Community: Concept, Conception and Ideology," to be published in *Politics and Society*, Fall 1977.
53. *The Philosophy of Right*, para. 302.
54. Ibid., para. 260. The additions to this paragraph are also well worth reading on this point.
55. G. A. Kelly, "Notes on Hegel's Lordship and Bondage," *The Review of Metaphysics*, June 1966.

56. *The Philosophy of Right*, para. 243.

57. Ibid., para. 245.

58. Ibid., para. 244.

59. Ibid., para. 244 addition.

60. Ibid.

61. Ibid., para. 245. This problem very much exercised the British Hegelians such as Bosan-quet and Green. They argued that charity could be part of the answer to poverty if charitable donations could be given to those who, on investigation, could be shown to be in a position to use if effectively to improve their position. To be effective and to avoid Hegel's difficulty charity must be organised and given only to the deserving poor. Bosanquet was active in the Charity Organisation Society which had just this aim.

62. Ibid., para. 245.

63. R. L. Perkins, "Remarks on the Papers of Avineri and Pöggeler" in *The Legacy of Hegel*, ed. O'Malley (Nijhoff, 1970), p. 220.

64. Rosenkranz, *Hegels Leben*, p. 85.

65. This paper has been read in the Universities of Glasgow, Hull, Manchester, and Oxford. I am particularly grateful for the comments of the following: in Glasgow, Professor G. B. Parry and Dr. A. Skinner; in Manchester, Professor I. Steedman and Dr. H. Steiner; in Oxford, Professor L. Kolakowski and Dr. Z. Pelczynski, and in Hull, Dr. R. Berki.

Relation Between Economics and Politics in Hegel

by

W. VER EECKE

In this paper I will restrict myself to an analysis of the relation between economics and politics as it appears in the *Phenomenology, The Philosophy of Right*, and *The Encyclopedia*.

The thesis I want to defend is that some of the most valuable insights of Hegel can be reduced to Hegel's stubborn realism expressed in the insight that the universal must be represented by a particular and that a particular does not cease to be a particular by the mere fact of assuming a role which is related to the universal.

This anti-utopian vision of political man is the basis for Hegel's rejection of two cherished ideals: the Rousseau type of direct democracy and the classical theory of representative democracy based upon universal suffrage. The first is rejected in the *Phenomenology;* the second is rejected in the *Philosophy of Right.*

It is in the light of this thesis that we can understand the crucial function of a free market economy.

A. *The Rejection of the Rousseau type of direct democracy*

The passage in *The Phenomenology of Mind* which analyses the Rousseau type of democratic ideal has the title: "Absolute Freedom and Terror."[1] This passage is preceded by an analysis of the Enlightenment. It is followed by an analysis of the moral vision of the world. Attention will first be drawn to how Hegel connects his analysis of "Absolute Freedom" with these two other moments in the culture of the West. Then the specific argument will be analysed which according to Hegel shows the necessary failure of the ideal of "absolute freedom."

(1) *The Enlightenment period, absolute freedom, the moral vision of the world.* The Enlightenment period produced a very critical intellectual attitude towards the political institutions of its time. However, few political institutions were changed during that period. The Enlightenment created an intellectual climate whereby the actual political institu-

tions were deprived of their traditional theocentric justification. Instead it was thought that political institutions could find justification and legitimation only by what they meant for the people.

Hegel relates this dual relationship between the Enlightenment and the political reality to the new image (notion) that consciousness developed about itself. The Enlightenment period is part of the section on *Spirit*. In this section consciousness has already reached the insight that as a self, the ego gets its form from the social institutions. Then social institutions are not a dead reality. They are a living reality. This can be explained, Hegel thinks, because social institutions (objective spirit) have three interdependent aspects. First, the social institutions have objective reality. They exist. Second, the social institutions have a meaning for the people. It is this meaning to which the people appeal; it is this meaning too, which is transformed into an ongoing project of improvement and defense of the existing institutions. Third, as a result of the continuous projects related to social institutions, these institutions are at any time also a human product.[2]

The Enlightenment period concentrates its efforts on the second aspect of the social institutions. This period affirms that the meaning of these institutions is to be found in the service they can render to the individuals as they live together in a historical community. Institutions are to be responsive to individuals. Individuals are not supposed to be required to live by blind faith in the validity of institutions. Responsiveness, or in Hegelian terms, *utility* is the concept (notion) by which the individual in the Enlightenment period reconciles himself with the fact that his self is formed by social institutions. The possible alienating dimension of the influence of social institutions upon the self is overcome by consciousness affirming the principle that those social institutions have to be *useful* for the self.

The Enlightenment does not address itself to the first aspect of social institutions, i.e., that they have objective reality. Such restraint does not allow consciousness to claim that it is fully in control of the self it is. The substance of the self as it is produced by the social institutions is not the product of consciousness itself. Subject and substance therefore do not yet coincide. On the other hand, the substance is not fully alien to the subject either. The subject is capable of imposing a predicate upon the substance: it must be *useful for the subject.*

The willingness of consciousness to require nothing more from social institutions than their utility in order for consciousness to be at peace with itself as a social being is a fact that Hegel expresses as follows: "Consciousness has found its notion in the principle of utility."[3]

The ideals behind the French revolution are a move made by consciousness. In order to be at peace with itself as a social being, consciousness requires that the social reality be *not just useful* but *its own product*. If this can be achieved, the ego as a social self would be a product of its own enterprise. Such a requirement means that consciousness aims at "absolute freedom"—self determination of the self even as a social self—as a prerequisite for being at peace with itself.

But the social self is not independent of the social self of others. When consciousness insists upon self determination of the social self, it is unavoidable that consciousness will get into conflict with other consciousnesses for the determination of the social reality.

Hegel sees the solution to this problem in the willingness of consciousness to withdraw from the social reality but still maintaining that the ego determines itself as a self. For this to be possible, consciousness must not define itself any longer as a social self, but as a moral self. Indeed moral self determination allows for the self determination of the self without having to impose upon others—as automatically binding—the content of the moral self that one accepts as unconditionally binding for oneself.

Thus it is the lack of full self determination as a social self which forces consciousness to move from the Enlightenment attitude to the hopes of the French revolution. It is the insight in the unavoidable deadly fight required for the self determination of the self as a social self which forces consciousness to move from the disillusioned hopes of the French revolution to the moral vision of the world.

(2) *The Rousseau type of direct democracy.* For Hegel it is not enough to show that a particular self image (a notion) of consciousness is unsatisfactory, he also looks for indications that consciousness is de facto already further than its own notion.

Hegel makes precisely this move, when he comments that the autonomy of the social reality in the Enlightenment period is but an empty semblance, because consciousness takes itself to be the legitimising ground for any social organization.[4] If there is still an in-itself dimension to the social reality, it exists legitimately only as a reality *for somebody else,* for consciousness.

The consciousness that serves as the legitimising ground for the social reality is individual consciousness. It is however, in function of being the representative of all consciousness that individual consciousness is the legitimising ground of social reality. Consciousness must conceive of itself as universal subject in order to conceive of itself legitimately as the legitimising ground of all social reality.

Consciousness is not just thought. Consciousness is also will.[5] The social reality is not just something that exists. It is also something that is constantly produced. Now, in order that consciousness as will be the ground of social reality—itself seen as a product—it is necessary that this consciousness participates in the making of this social reality. Inasmuch as consciousness considers itself to be the universal subject—and not a particular universal, an incarnated universal—each particular must require that the social self be its own product. This can occur only if the existing distinctions in social groups, social classes, or governmental functions are abolished.

This results in the *legitimate* social reality being reduced to what an individual (as self-conceived universal) actually wills. Nothing that is not actually *willed* by an individual is acceptable or legitimate.

This consequence permits a first refutation of the Rousseau type of direct democracy. Indeed, if only that which is *actually* willed is legitimised, then what was willed in the past remains legitimised only if the particular still wills it now. Something that exists objectively has no legitimation independent of the actual will of the individual as a representative of universal consciousness.[6] But the ground for legitimation is the way particular consciousness conceives of itself as a representative of universal consciousness. This conception (notion) of consciousness, conceived to be in the interest of the universal yesterday, cannot be normative for consciousness the next day.

Hegel's argument is thus essentially an anthropological argument. The social-political argument is a derivative argument. Indeed, Hegel argues that a consciousness—who requires that only its actual will is the legitimising ground for commitment, submission or obedience to an objective reality—such a consciousness has created a legitimatisation requirement that is so strong that consciousness is *not even obliged to loyalty to the commitments made to himself.* Indeed, nothing objective is legitimate. Only the actual will produces legitimacy.

If consciousness is not bound to the commitments made to himself, how can it be bound to commitments made to others? This destroys both the *contract theory* and *representative democracy*.

Hegel applies this anthropological argument in two ways to the social reality. The first is at the level of thought. The second is at the level of action. In concrete terms, one could say that the Rousseau type of anthropology first does not allow the creation of a constitution, i.e., the production of a binding thought, and second does not allow the organisation of an effective government.

Hegel develops this last argument at somewhat more length. Hegel's argument is built on the assertion that the universal, in order to be able to act, must incarnate itself in a particular. Indeed, to act is to do something determinate, particular. Only the particular can do so. For the universal to be effective, it is necessary that a particular takes it upon himself to represent *effectively* the universal. But the Rousseau type of anthropology does not possess a theory of mediation. Thus, if one particular performs the tasks of the universal, the others are excluded necessarily. Even worse, the grounds by which other particulars are excluded from participating in the determination of the universal are precisely also the reasons by which each particular can claim to have a right to be the head of the government. Thus the government must be seen necessarily and automatically by the other particulars as a faction. The other individual in turn must be seen by the head of the government as a necessary threat to his claim of being the universal.[7]

The problem can be formulated as follows: as the effectiveness of the universal requires that the universal be tied to a particular, the only way by which other particulars can still participate in the universal is when all particulars—the particular tied to the universal included—adhere to a theory of mediation between particular and universal, i.e., a theory that imposes a distance between the universal and the particular that happens to represent one universal.

B. *Rejection of universal suffrage*

In his *Philosophy of Right*, Hegel rejects universal suffrage as a satisfactory mediation between the universal and the individual. The reason is that the particular remains particular even when performing this act of universal significance, i.e., casting his vote. Indeed, Hegel argues that the act of casting one's vote makes so little difference in the outcome that the individual might be logical in not going to the ballot box.[8]

The content of Hegel's argument allows the formulation of two reasons for the indifference of the individual towards his civic duty or civic right to vote. The first argument has it that universal suffrage is inefficient in large countries, since the influence of the individual when he performs the act by which the universal is determined remains a particular, the act pertaining to the universal must have meaning for the particular who performs this act. This is clearly not the case in universal suffrage in large countries. Thus, the particular acts rationally by not participating in the elections.

The second argument runs as follows: Universal suffrage does not guarantee proportional representation of the different spheres of interests in the parliament. Thus participating in universal suffrage might legitimate a parliament—the instrument of the universal—which does not represent fairly the different spheres of interests. Thus universal suffrage is reduced to a formal ritual that produces a formal legitimation of the universal, without guaranteeing that the universal is tied to the particular as particular. Such a universal is for Hegel a farce. Such a legitimation is but an abstract legitimation.

Thus Hegel's rejection of universal suffrage rests on his insistence that the particular have an effective and guaranteed interest and participation in the universal. Any arrangement that forgets that the particular remains a particular even when he performs a universal act is for Hegel unacceptable. The Rousseau type of governmental theory is rejected because it forgets that the acting universal is a particular and thus excludes other particulars. Universal suffrage is rejected because even the voting citizen remains a particular and might find it in his interest as a particular not to participate in the universal. Thus the universal becomes a farce.

C. Hegel's own solution

Hegel's solution must be built on mediation, since his rejection of other solutions rests upon their lack of mediation between particular and universal.

In the previous analysis two dangers emerged. The first danger is that the particular who incarnates the universal leaves no place for other particulars; this danger becomes obvious when this particular takes care of his own interests under the cloak of the universal. The second danger is that the particular is given such an insignificant participation in the universal that the particular does not bother to participate, and that he thereby becomes a mere particular and the universal an empty universal. Hegel's solution—even if it may not be acceptable for practical or theoretical reasons—attacks both problems.

(1) *The particular representing the universal* In his political theory, Hegel takes care of not restricting the universal to one particular. He does it by limiting the function of the particular representing the universal. Indeed, the king is almost but figurehead, someone who is allowed to set the dots on the "i's."[9]

Furthermore, Hegel subscribes to the theory of separation of powers. He would divide the functions of the state between the legislature, the executive, and the crown.[10] This is an institutional guarantee against total identification of one particular with the universal.

Third, the executive itself is restricted by the imposition upon the government employees of a hierarchal structure of answerability and, more importantly, by the barriers erected to protect lower societal units (e.g., corporations, associations) from lower interference by the executive.[11]

Fourth, the legislature, too, is restricted and made answerable. Indeed, the legislature is to be composed of representatives of the different estates (the word used by Hegel for interest group being "estates").[12] Furthermore, these representatives must mediate the interests of their interest group with the representatives of other interest groups.

Finally, Hegel restricts even the domain of the universal itself, i.e., the rights of the state. This restriction occurs in two directions. The first is by affirming that the state is transcended by art, religion, and philosophy. These are all values which require freedom of thought and expression for the particular.[13] The second restriction is the restriction of the state in the objective domain of spirit itself. Hegel remarks that the freedom of the particular within the state is ultimately not guaranteed institutionally if the economic order does not contain economic centers of decisions independent of the state. Thus a form of free market economy is here seen to be the long-term institutional guarantor of the freedom of the individual.[14]

(2) *The universal made available to the particular.* Hegel defends a second form of mediation between the particular and the universal. This second argument is built upon Hegel's insight that the universal can be reached in degrees. Reaching the universal is for the particular not an all or nothing proposition. The economic order is credited by Hegel for providing several levels of universality to an individual. The economic order creates the possibility of reaching a minimal form of universality to those particulars who do not participate in the universality of the state. Furthermore, the economic order *educates* all particulars towards universality, as will be seen in the analysis of the different levels of universality offered by the economic order.

The first and best-known form of universality connected with the economic order is the universality that an individual gives himself through his work. This idea is already present in the *Phenomenology*'s analysis of the slave and of stoicism. The universality produced in work is a double one. It is the objectivity of the result of my work (remember Horace saying about his poems: *"Exegi monumentum aere perennius"*). [15] It is also the objectivity of the skill connected with producing these works (poems made Horace a poet for the Roman community). [16]

The second form of universality is the one achieved by the particular when he invests his labour into the system of social needs. [17] Thus he is willing to produce what is demanded by others for the purpose of satisfying his own needs. This idea comes from the economists of Hegel's time. It is among economists often referred to as the theory of "the invisible hand." Again there are two aspects to this form of universality, the one produced by the invisible hand. The first is the *guaranteed production* of those goods that are demanded by the individuals. [18] The second is the willingness of the individual to choose a kind of work, to acquire *a skill that is socially demanded.* Thus the individual ties himself actively to or accepts passively that he is tied to the vicissitudes of the economic order. [19]

The third form of universality is the one which results from the insertion of the particular into a subgroup of the economic order. Hegel hits on this form of universality in different places. He hits on it when he talks about professional groupings, about corporations, and about pressure groups. [20] He naturally talks about them in his own terminology, but this does not alter the substance of the argument.

What a professional group, a corporation, or a pressure group does is to provide a *particularized universal* that an individual can identify with and work for.[21] In the case of professional groups, Hegel distinguishes between the agricultural, commercial, and bureaucratic professions. Each has its own difficulties, rewards, aspirations, and virtues. It is the acquisition of the special skills and the special ethics to overcome the difficulties related to the particular profession which is the measuring rod of social recognition. It is the capability of the particular to *be content with the recognition and the rewards* of the chosen profession which transforms the particular into a universal. Instead of Mister X, he is now either farmer, merchant, or government official.

A similar argument is developed by Hegel for the case of an individual willing and capable of identifying with his corporation or his union (indeed, Hegel talks about the place where one earns one's income, and about the guilts).[22]

(3) *The transition from economics to the state.* The previous forms of universality present cases where the particular inserts himself into the universal. Hegel also mentions, however, two cases where the universal is imposed upon the particular, but the imposition is justified not by the requirement of the universal but by the self-interest of the individual. The two cases are the judicial system and the police.

The particular in the economic order has the will to acquire the goods he needs through his participation in the economic order. This requires the protection of the goods he acquires against claims of others. This is what the judicial system does.[23]

The term "police" has for Hegel a broader meaning than it has now. It covers the law enforcement area, but it also covers the area of welfare provision. The argument used by Hegel is that the act of an individual has influence upon other individuals. This can be good or bad. The police have a right and a duty to restrain individual acts which harm other individuals too much intentionally or accidentally. The exact delimination of legitimate police interference is a matter that cannot be determined philosophically, according to Hegel.

Similarly, those goods that benefit many individuals or that are necessary for the private activity of individuals should be available whether or not individuals have a private incentive to produce it. If private incentive is failing, the police should provide it, according to Hegel.[24]

This argument is similar to the justification of the economists' justification of the *minimum function of the state,* i.e., the state should perform those services which in total benefit individuals more than it costs to produce the services.

As it is in the interest of an individual to get the services of the state without contributing towards its costs, it is necessary for the state to make taxes obligatory. Thus what Hegel describes under the heading "judicial system" and "police" requires an enforcing agency. This is in our society the state. We therefore want to separate these latter two universals from the economic order even if Hegel discussed them as part of the civic society. It is clear, though, that they too present forms of universals that are different from the universal that Hegel identifies with the function of the state.

Conclusion

The economic order provides Hegel an opportunity to provide a solution to the political problem of reconciling, the particular with the universal, without having to adhere to utopian political ideals.[25]

Alternatively, one could conclude that Hegel lacks the trust in individuals required for allowing a fully conflictual political society to work out its problems. A fully conflictual political society would be a society in which the politician is not constrained by organic structures, by which he can compete for votes to realize his ideas of the good society.[26]

NOTes

1. Hegel, *Phenomenology of Mind,* pp. 599-610.
2. Boey, *L'aliénation,* pp. 57ff.
3. Hegel, *Phenomenology,* p. 599.
4. Ibid., p. 601: "individual consciousness conceives the object as having no other nature than that of self-consciousness itself."
5. Ibid., pp. 600-601: "this will is not the empty thought of will."
6. Ibid., pp. 602-603: "in which it [consciousness] lets nothing break away and assume the shape of a detached object standing over against it."

7. Ibid., pp. 604-605.
8. Hegel, *Philosophy of Right,* Comment to Par. 311, pp. 202-203. This passage in Hegel has drawn enthusiastic attention from public choice theoreticians. Buchanan, J.M., "Hegel on the Calculus of Voting," *Public Choice,* XVII, 1974, pp. 99-101.
9. Ibid., Addition to Par. 280, p. 289.
10. Ibid., Par. 273.
11. Ibid., Par. 295.
12. Ibid., Pars. 301, 302.
13. This kind of limitation to the function of the state is made quite explicitly in Hegel's *Enzyklopädie,* where the state is said to be transcended by absolute Spirit, which includes art, religion, and philosophy.
14. Unfortunately, I cannot find in Hegel's texts the best quotation. I must therefore substitute a less convincing quotation. "If the state is represented as a unity of different persons . . . then what is really meant is only civil society. . . . In civil society each member is his own end, everything else is nothing to him" (addition to Par. 182). See also Hegel's criticism of Plato's conception of the state in Par. 185.
15. "I erected a monument that is more durable than bronze" (Horace, Carm. 3, 30, 1). The monument to which Horace is referring is his poems. This aspect of work is referred to in Hegel, *Phenomenology,* p. 238.
16. Hegel, *Philosophy of Right*, Pars. 187, 197.
18. Ibid., Par. 199: the idea of a "universal permanent capital."
19. Ibid., Par. 200.
20. The words used by Hegel are: *"Korporation"* and *"Stand."*
21. Hegel, *Philosophy of Right,* Pars. 206, 207, and additions to Pars. 201, 206, 207.
22. Ibid., Pars. 251, 253, and addition to Par. 255.
23. Ibid., Pars. 209, 230.
24. Ibid., addition to Par. 236
25. We should notice that Rousseau's ideas are more complex than Hegel makes us believe. Indeed, Rousseau allows for a legislator—a man of genius—who is able to see what is in the public interest and who also is able to suppress his own self-interests. But as Lionel Gossman argues in "Rousseau's Idealism" (*Romanic Review,* 1961), Rousseau involves himself in a contradiction. He holds that on the one hand the people have the fundamental right to legislate by enacting the laws proposed by the legislator. On the other hand, the legislator was needed because Rousseau believes that the people—a blind multitude—were unable to discern what is best for the public interest. How is this ignorance lifted by the legislator? Thus Hegel's basic objection to Rousseau remains valid. (This note was suggested by W. Desan and R. Parise).
26. This paper is an outgrowth of research done with an A. von Humboldt grant in Bonn, West Germany on philosophy and economics, 1975-76.

Person, Property, and Civil Society in the *Philosophy of Right*

by

PETER G. STILLMAN

(1) Hegel discusses property in greatest detail at the beginning of the *Philosophy of Right*,[1] in the part entitled "Abstract Right." The actors in "Abstract Right" are persons. Logical abstractions from individuals, persons have their arbitrary free will (to "do or forebear doing"[2] as they wish), lack a developed moral and ethical will, and regard particular characteristics (like age and heights, desires and passions) as inessential (35, 37). Persons face a world of things—natural objects and animals, lacking free will and incapable of rights (42). Property comes into existence when a person puts his will into a thing and makes it his own (44). Property thus results from a mental act; the person simply decides that he wishes the thing: "I want it," "this is mine." Hegel's person claims property in a way different from the claimant of many other modern theorists who, like Hegel, rely on a pre-political condition: Locke's natural man must mix his labor with the natural object, Blackstone's pre-historical man must occupy the object.[3]

Because it is a single person who puts his will into the thing, property for Hegel is inherently private property (46). Because property derives from the will, Hegel sharply distinguishes property from possession, which is related to the person's needs and interests:

> The particular aspect of the matter, the fact that I make something my own as a result of my natural need, impulse, and caprice, is the particular interest satisfied by possession. But I as free will am an object to myself in what I possess and thereby also for the first time am an actual will, and this is the aspect which constitutes the category of property, the true and right factor in possession [45].

In other words, possession is the particular and external act; property is the underlying right. Because possession is not the essence of property, "what and how much I possess, therefore, is a matter of indifference so far as rights are concerned" (49), and thus the distribution of property can be (and is) unequal, so long as each person has at least some property (Enc. 486) in order that his free will have actuality.

While willing is the essence of property, the person must

"occupy"—by grasping or marking—his property in order that others may recognize it as his (51). These persons then relate to each other by making contracts. In a contract, persons freely exchange "single external things," of equivalent value, deciding which properties to exchange according to their own arbitrary wills (75, 77). So persons relate through the medium of things, and recognize each other as persons through recognizing each other's property and through the free and equal contract relationship.

(2) The content of the *Philosophy of Right* is the science of objective spirit. In the circle that is Hegel's philosophy (2), it follows the science of subjective spirit, in which the free will develops itself fully, but in abstraction from the objective external world (27). Faced with that world which is so different from itself, the free will seeks to grasp and comprehend it, to transform the objective world into a world of freedom (29) and into a world penetrated and permeated by the free will (33). Property is thus "the first embodiment of freedom" (45R)—from Hegel, a multifaceted statement.

Property is freedom because it is the first actualization of the free will (and its freedom) in objectivity. The free will thereby overcomes "the pure subjectivity of personality" (41A) and attains an objective existence for itself. Thus, property is a necessary and substantive end and right of the free will (45R).

For Hegel, property is not primarily a means to the attainment of other ends. In many labor theories of property, where "emphasis is placed on my needs, then . . . property appears as a means of their satisfaction" (45R). If property is justified primarily by social convention, as in Hume and Rousseau,[4] then property is merely a means to whatever ends the society determines. Because Hegel's political philosophy begins with the person's right to property, and actualizes that right in civil society (208), it is marked by the attempt to recognize, generate, and maintain individuality.[5]

In a strict logical sense, property is the precondition for all other freedoms in the objective world, since it is the first and essential externalization of the subjective will. Concurrently, property is the precondition for freedom because the property right—the will in the thing—is the basis for the rights of the person to life and liberty. Hegel sees the person as claiming himself through his willing to own, to occupy, and to modify himself: "it is only through the development of his own body and mind, essentially through his self-consciousness's apprehension of itself as free, that he takes possession of himself and becomes his own property and no one else's" (57). Once a person gains property in himself, his rights are inalienable. Since a person can alienate only "single external things" (75, 65),

> therefore those goods, or rather substantive characteristics, which constitute my own private personality and the universal essence of my self-consciousness are inalienable and my right to them is imprescriptable. Such characteristics are my personality as such, my universal freedom of will, my ethical life, my religion [66; see 66R].

The right to property is the original of the rights to life and liberty.

For Hegel, property is paradigmatic; using the claim to property as a model, the person claims his right to life and liberty. Hegel's approach differs from, for instance, Locke's. Where Hegel treats property in things first, Locke postulates the individual's property in himself, i.e., his right to life, as the original: "every Man has a *Property* in his own *Person*. . . . The *Labour* of his Body, and the *Work* of his Hands, we may say, are properly his."[6] Locke assumes that the individual owns himself as property, and derives property in things from property in self.

From this difference in paradigmatic rights flows a difference in emphasis generally between Locke and Hegel. Since Locke begins with the assertion that individuals own their minds and bodies, he regards that property as a given, not as a task for the individual nor as a problem for his political philosophy. But Hegel sees that the individual's appropriation of himself as his own property—his self-conscious apprehension of himself as free—is neither automatic nor easy. Thus, much of Hegel's political philosophy is devoted to developing and discussing the means whereby the individual can gain possession of and property in himself. Hegel defines rights broadly, including not only rights to "life, liberty, and estates" (57, 44) but also, for instance, rights to formal education (174), public services (242R), and subsistence (241), i.e., to all that is necessary for the individual fully to appropriate and own himself. Similarly (Hoffmeister, 338), Hegel sees education (*Bildung*) as crucial for an individual to attain his rights to life and liberty, and to "translate into actuality what one is according to one's concept" (57), a free and rational being. The lessons the person learns in wrong, the subjective willing of morality, and the rational institutions of ethical life are all directed in part towards the education of the individual into all facets of ethical life and reason (187R). Freedom must "be first sought out and won; and that through an unending mediating discipline and cultivation [*Zucht*] of the intellectual and moral powers."[7] Because Hegel sees and allows for the possibilities of variation and development in the individual's appropriation of himself, he defines rights broadly and sees education (*Bildung*) as of central importance.[8]

Property is freedom also because it gives the individual a scope for action and makes possible his extending and expanding his personality. In the most obvious sense, the person gains a locus for action by his will just in putting his will in the thing and then by occupying it. The further relations of the will to the thing that Hegel spells out—taking possession, use, and alienation (53)—indicate that the person's scope for activity is broad: he can do almost whatever he wishes to do (and can effect) to the property, including to use it whatever way he pleases (62) and, in contract, exchange it for any other property. In civil society, the individual's property allows him to pursue his own idea of satisfaction in whatever way he wishes, subject to the constraints of his resources and of the interactions of society. To guarantee that property and thus the individual's freedom, the administration of justice exists (208).

Property is also an essential condition for the possibility of moral action. Without property, i.e., without a locus for the independence of the individual will, the individual cannot be independent of, for instance, the purely substantive life like Greek ethical life, or the strict and immoral legalism that pervaded both China and Rome.[9] In a society without property, the restraint imposed upon an individual by his membership in society is not, and has not the opportunity of becoming a self-imposed restraint, a free obedience, to which—though he can do otherwise—the individual voluntarily submits because he sees it as his true good.[10]

The person develops his own personal characteristics through property ownership as well. Through the exercise of his arbitrary will, the person attaches to himself various properties that express his will. By appropriating as his property his mind and body, the person is in a position to create his own characteristics, aims, and intentions. In his private property, the person as a unit has privacy, in that he can enclose himself within that property and exclude others (46). Thus, he has a space in which he can produce his own achievements, and define his own substantial being, without being swamped by the external world. Finally, in occupancy and especially in contract, the person gains explicit recognition from other persons that he is a person with rights. Through his property, the individual creates himself in society and is recognized therein by others as a full member.

(3) At the same time, however, it is clear that the person must go beyond being a property-owner—and that man must be more than economic man—if he is to develop his personal characteristics and his scope for action. Property, while a form of freedom and necessary for individuality, is limited, in part because in property the will has "its freedom *immediately* in reality, in something external, therefore, in a thing" (Enc. 513). For instance, the characteristics of the abstract person are not very appealing:

> To have no interest except in one's formal right may be pure obstinacy, often a fitting accompaniment of a cold heart and restricted sympathies. It is uncultured people who insist most on their rights, while noble minds look on other aspects of the thing [37A].

Similarly, in the system of needs the individual need look only after himself and his own desires (182A), ignoring "other aspects" of himself, others, and the situation. The will that is content to find its freedom in property, the individual for whom his property is the highest concern, the isolated individual concerned only with his own desires—all are defective, unable fully to participate in the education and development of ethical life.

Not being in a construct of pure freedom the will in property is limited by the external characteristics of the thing. What the person can and cannot do with his property, for instance, is partially determined from the outside, by nature and society, i.e., by the particular characteristics of the thing he owns as property and the social context in which he owns it. Similarly, by putting his will in such a thing, the person makes himself vulnerable; his will "becomes liable to the lot and chances that external things suffer."[11] Hegel, in short, sees that property, while necessary to individuality and freedom, may also be in tension or conflict with them.

To mitigate the tension and conflict between property and individuality, Hegel sees that it is necessary that the person come to be concerned not solely with rights but also with what is moral, not solely with his own self and its property but also with what lies beyond himself and his property. Thus, the person must be educated in ways of living that are not exclusively tied to rights and to property. The education limited to rights and property—and thus to contractual interactions in civil society—is an education that need make the individual only "Industrious and Rational,"[12] with a cold heart and restricted sympathies (37A). So, for Hegel (although not, for instance, for Locke),[13] it is necessary for education to include morality and a variety of types of social interactions. Through the understanding of morality, and through the social institutions of the family, the state, and civil society (187R), the individual comes to be more than merely a property-owning person and more than narrow economic man; he has a concrete set of characteristics and attitudes which shape and express, indeed which are, his life.[14]

In other words, property contributes to individuality only by being both posited and transcended. Hegel's political philosophy is founded on property; but it is founded on property only so that it can transcend property. This transcending, of course, is an *Aufhebung*; property is not only overcome, it is also preserved. The individual who has developed himself by education and non-contractual social interactions, while he has surpassed the limiting characteristics of the property-owning person and the economic man of contract, nonetheless still needs and uses his right to property. To the fully developed individual, property is a permanent apparatus for carrying out a life-plan, an effort to give reality to a conception of his own good, his further development, and his self-satisfaction.[15] Because the individual is more than the person, property is valuable not because it provides the means for the realization of the arbitrary or selfish whims of the person, but because it is an essential for the full life of reason of the individual.

(4) Property represents freedom in a further way. The prevalence of property manifests man's liberation from and dominance over nature, and man's liberation from the direct domination of other men. Property is the proof of man's control of nature. As Joachim Ritter has argued well and at length, behind the apparent objective immobility of property as a thing is hidden, for Hegel, the historical activity that has led to the domestication of nature, that has transformed nature into things and thus, as thing, into that which can be appropriated by man.[16] For instance, the freedom of the Egyptians, Greeks, and Romans was limited by their worship of and reverence for some animals and other parts of nature, which were, in effect, regarded as having rights which could

not be infringed.[17] Only by transforming nature into things—objects without rights—has man, historically, made possible property and its concomitant rights, of life and liberty; the freedom of man is thus directly related to the reification (*Versachlichung*) of nature.

Nature is reified; and things are also humanized. Contract is the manifestation of this humanization; for, in a contract, things (properties) that are very different from each other are exchanged by persons. What makes the contract an equal and valid contract is not the particular differences the individual properties possess, but rather the underlying commonality that they share:

> what thus remains identical throughout as the property implicit in the contract is distinct from the external things whose owners alter when the exchange is made. What remains identical is the value [77].

Since value is defined in terms of satisfying human needs (63), the universal and common element in things (properties) is value, i.e., human needs.[18] Things and property are humanized.

The historical activities that transform nature into humanized things are work and (conscious) social interaction.[19] It is work in a social context by which historically man has transformed nature from being a terrible force alien to and oppressing him into being controlled by, manipulated by, and at the service of man. What the slave performed in the pre-political condition described in the "Phenomenology" is transformed and regularized in civilized civil society (Enc. 432A) (and the dichotomy between the work of the slave and the desires of the master is healed by the union of work and need in civil society [192]), where man continues to dominate nature and to liberate himself through the social context of needs and through work (194, 195). Property and contract, the continuing manifestations of the reification and humanization of nature, are thus the continual proof that the external world is a world of things to be dominated; and property and contract are also, in civil society, one set of means by which the external world is transformed into a world for man. Nature, humanized, does not dominate but rather serves man.

Through property, the individual is also liberated from natural, direct, or full domination by other men, in all relations of ethical life and especially in economic relations and in civil society. The master-slave relationship cannot exist in ethical life, in which the ownership of property by all makes each independent of the other. But one precondition for this independence is the ability of men to transform themselves—or limited portions of themselves—into things, i.e., the *Versachlichung* of human beings.

At the beginning of the section "Property," things that can be property are strictly defined, as external natural objects. When the person appropriates his own mind and body as his property, he gains the inalienable rights of life and liberty (66). Thus, no person can be the slave to another. But, for those whose labor on their own property does not produce enough of what they desire (or need), the definition of alienable things is expanded:

> Single products of my particular physical and mental skills and of my power to act I can alienate to someone else and I can give him the use of my abilities for a restricted period, because, on the strength of this restriction, my abilities acquire an external relation to the totality and universality of my being [67].

Thus, a person can work for another, without becoming a slave, by contracting for a limited portion of time.

Further, persons in a contract situation "really exist for each other" "only as owners" (40), only through the mediation of each person's private property. The baker relates to his customer not directly, but through the media of the baker's bread which the customer wishes and the customer's money, which the baker wishes in exchange for the bread. By retaining and legalizing contract, civil society makes concrete the reification of individual relations.[20]

In civil society the reification of humans and of human relations increases individual freedom and equality. First, because of the universal possibility for the laborer to alienate part of his labor time while nonetheless maintaining his freedom, "for the first time, liberty becomes, without any limitation, the principle of a society,"[21] as all unfree forms of subordinate work relationships—slavery, serfdom, indentures—are abolished as unright (57R).

Second, since human relations are mediated through things and property, an individual's occupation, social interactions, and status are not determined by feudal hierarchies, noble (or non-noble) birth, caste systems, or other rigid hierarchies. While the unpredictable chances of birth and the marketplace exist in civil society, these chances can be overcome by individuals; in many previous societies, on the other hand, the chance of birth was determining and unconquerable, the will of the ruling group unchangeable (200, 201A, 206).

Third, because human relations are reified in contract, men relate to each other as equals—for the contract relation is an equal one, in terms of the substance (i.e., value) of the property exchanged (77). Fourth, the freedom from direct dependence of one person on another is increased by money. For Hegel, money is the abstraction that represents value, or utility in satisfying need (63). Money frees men from the direct dependence on others. In the modern state, services owed can be paid with money, earned or obtained as the individual chooses to or can earn it, and need not be paid in kind, i.e., by one specific type of labor. There is, for instance, no more corvée (299A), nor payment of land rent in kind. In sum, the reification of humans and their relations liberates man from other men, develops freedom, and guarantees equality.

(5) But Hegel also perceives the drawbacks of reification that critics of civil society, like Burke and Marx, stress.[22] Since persons in a contract relate to each other through the mediation of the properties being exchanged, persons tend to define other persons—and also themselves—in terms of things. Thus, it is not surprising that, in civil society, individuals are concerned with what others have. Hegel raises the idea of "keeping up with the Joneses" to a philosophical level: the "demand for equality of satisfaction with others" involves "emulation, which is the equalizing of oneself with others" (193). While this emulation is, for Hegel, essential because it is related to the liberation in social needs (194), nonetheless it in large measure involves copying appearances and thus frequently material objects; so that others are frequently copied, not as individuals, but as the sum of their material possessions.

The reification of human relations also explains the morality of interactions of civil society, especially what has been labelled "wage slavery" and the like. The interactions of civil society do not (immorally) involve using other men as means, because of the prevalence of contract. All contract relations about property are voluntary, not coerced; moreover, they do not use other men as means, they only involve using property (defined as "single external things" [75]) as means, and thus wage labor is the using as a means not the other person (that would be slavery) but a restricted and limited thing, e.g., an hour's labor.

But the results of these not-immoral interactions are interactions that are amoral: "in civil society each member is his own end, everything else is nothing to him" (182A). Thus, the reification of relations tends to lead man in the system of needs to be self-centered and impersonal, and to depersonalize his interactions. Further, the escape from slavery to wage labor has its disadvantages. As Hegel lectured,

> The Athenian slave perhaps had an easier occupation and more intellectual work than is usually the case with our servants [and day laborers], but he was still a slave, because he had alienated to his master the whole range of his activity [67A].

The expansion of individual freedom that derives from the reification of men is purchased at a price.

(6) The extensions of personal freedom that derive from property have yet more serious costs: the chaos, and the poverty and misery, of civil society. The working of the system of needs, in the context of private property and wage labor, leads to capital (*Kapital*). While Hegel does not explicitly distinguish nor explain capital separately from property (*Eigentum*) or resources (*Vermögen*), he does introduce the term *"Kapital"* in his discussion of classes *(Stände)* (200) and then of the highly developed, ongoing, and active system of needs where the police intervene (237).

The workings of the (capitalist) economic order are frequently chaotic, especially "in the case of the larger branches of industry" which are dependent on foreign trade and thus on distant and uncontrollable events (236). There is also continually "the danger of upheavals arising from clashing interests" and from the working of economic laws of which the participants in the economy "themselves know nothing" (236R). Hegel does think that "on the whole" "a fair balance between [conflicting interests] . . . may be brought about automatically" (236), and that, where adjustments were necessary, the public authority (*Polizei*) could intervene as a control standing above the competing parties and conscious of economic laws and necessities.[23] But, despite the general harmony of interests, and despite the police, civil society is subject to upheavals.

Another serious cost is that "civil society affords a spectacle of extravagance and want as well as of the physical and ethical degeneration common to them both" (185). The rich—both the "leisure class" and those intensely and narrowly concerned with their own interests—suffer. The leisured, non-working rich are like the master in the master-slave dialectic in the "Phenomenology," who does not liberate himself either from external nature through work (194R) or from his naturally given desires through social needs (194). The rich person who remains solely concerned with his own interest also suffers, since he too misses out on the liberation of needs and work, and does not participate in the recognition that derives from membership in a corporation (254, 255).

The poor also suffer. Unlike the rich, the poor suffer physically. They also participate little if at all in the liberation of social needs and of work. Furthermore, when poverty becomes grinding enough (a level that varies from country to country),

> and when there is a consequent loss of the sense of right and wrong, of honesty and the self-respect which makes a man insist on maintaining himself by his own work and effort, the result is the creation of a rabble of paupers [244].

For Hegel, there is eventually a relationship between poverty and *misère*. And this poverty is necessary, not avoidable (245). It is "one of the most disturbing problems which agitate modern society" (244A).

Hegel's discussion of poverty, misery, and the rabble suggests that he is aware of the problem of the worker's lack of property in anything other than his own labor. For Hegel as for T. H. Green lecturing sixty years later,

> a man who possesses nothing but his powers of labour and who has to sell these to a capitalist for bare daily maintenance, might as well, in respect of the ethical purposes which the possession of property should serve, be denied rights of property altogether.[24]

Like T. H. Green, although for slightly different explicit reasons,[25] Hegel sees no way out of this dilemma. In a purely formal sense, the laborer is free by virtue of having property in his powers of labor; he may also benefit to some extent from some of the liberation implicit in property. But in terms of most of the benefits, of freedom and education, for which property is valued, the laborer himself gains nothing.[26] And there is no way—for T. H. Green or for Hegel—to change or to conceptualize a possible change in that situation.

Finally, while in property and civil society the individual is liberated from his dependence on nature and on other men, in civil society he is also made dependent on an economic order which, while rational overall, contains much that is natural, external, and contingent—and these aspects greatly influence the individual's final status in society. "A

particular man's . . . opportunity of sharing in the general resources
. . . are . . . dependent . . . [in part] on accidental circumstances
whose multiplicity introduces differences in the development of
natural, bodily, and mental characteristics" (200). Since the goal of the
individual in Hegel's civil society is not wealth but education (187) and
recognition (254; 255A), these differences in status would be irrelevant
(on Hegel's terms) if all occupations and classes had education and
recognition available equally. But clearly at least the very rich and the
very poor fail here (185).

In part because Hegel delves at such length into the uses of property
and thus discerns and explicates the workings of civil society, he presents the ambiguities inherent in property as freedom for individuals.
Property is the manifestation of and locus for individual free will; it is
the result and continuing condition for the liberation of man from the
domination of nature and of other men; it is the basis of the expanded
equality, opportunity, *Bildung,* and freedom for individuals in the
modern world. But civil society, where these ethical aspects of property
are developed, is not unambiguous.[27] It contains ethical degradations,
in its extremes of wealth and poverty and the results of those extremes,
and in the inequalities of education and recognition by others. Property
is and produces freedom for the person in abstract right; for the men who
inhabit civil society, it produces ethical benefits for many, but ethical
degradation for a few.

(7) While civil society fortifies, protects, and manifests many aspects of property apparent in "Abstract Right," the family and the
state—the other two major moments of ethical life—generally are outside the realm of property and contract. Since contracts can only be
about "single external things" and not, for instance, about the whole of
one's life, neither marriage nor the citizen's relation to the state can be
matters of contract (75R). Similarly, private property is subordinated
and transformed in the family and the state. In the family, property
ought to be treated as the family capital or resources (*Vermögen*), not as
individual property (171). In the state, the influence of property-
owning burghers on the monarch and legislature is limited (281,
301R); the property of the agricultural class is entailed to help make
them good legislators (305); and the state sometimes causes the destruction of property in war (324R).

This demarcation means that the freedoms and the costs, the liberations and the degenerations, of civil society do not exist in the family and the state. Hegel places property and contract in civil society in order to limit their costs to civil society and to allow other spheres to have other types of human relations with other benefits. For instance, Hegel's state can seek the common good, the universal, because it does not have as its prime aim the protection of property. Equally, Hegel places property and contract in civil society because, despite their costs, they are essential for freedom; property and contract liberate man from nature and other men, and produce personal freedom and equality. Property must be posited and developed for individuals to be free; but property alone is inadequate for a full life of freedom, and so property and its relations must be transcended, by institutions not based on property, by the family and especially by the state.[28]

NOTES

1. G. W. F. Hegel, *Philosophy of Right* [1821], trans. with notes by T. M. Knox (Oxford: Oxford University Press, 1945); Hegel, *Grundlinien der Philosophie des Rechts*, ed. Johannes Hoffmeister (Fifth edition; Hamburg: Felix Meiner, 1955). In conformity to the sensible continental practice, citations to the *Philosophy of Right* are placed in parentheses in the text, and are according to section (not page) number; where the material cited is from the main text of the section, the section number alone is given; where it is from the "remarks" Hegel added to the text, the section number is followed by "R"; where it is from the "additions" which later editors appended to posthumous editions by collating student lecture notes, the section number is followed by "A." Hegel wrote marginal comments in his own copy; these, untranslated by Knox, are cited by the page number of the German edition, preceded by Hoffmeister's name. The material in the *Philosophy of Right* is presented, in briefer compass, in G. W. F. Hegel, *Philosophy of Mind* [1830], trans. William Wallace (Oxford: Clarendon Press, 1894), which is Part Three of G. W. F. Hegel, *Enzyklopädie der philosophischen Wissenschaften (1830)*, ed. Friedhelm Nicolin and Otto Pöggeler (Seventh edition; Hamburg: Felix Meiner, 1969), cited in parentheses in the text, with the section number preceded by the abbreviation "Enc."

    The best treatment of Hegel's discussion of property is Joachim Ritter, "Person und Eigentum," in his *Metaphysik und Politik* (Frankfurt am Main: Suhrkamp, 1969) and (in French) as "Personne et Propriété selon Hegel," *Archives de Philosophie*, XXXI, no. 2 (Apr.-June 1968), 179-201. In addition, Hugh A. Reyburn, *The Ethical Theory of Hegel* (Oxford: Oxford University Press, 1967 [1921]), is always helpful on the *Philosophy of Right;* and T. H. Green, *Lectures on the Principles of Political Obligation*, presents a sophisticated neo-Hegelianism. Unfortunately, most recent full-length treatments of Hegel's political philosophy devote little space to property.

For other discussions of "Abstract Right," see Peter G. Stillman, "Hegel's Critique of Liberal Theories of Right," *American Political Science Review,* LXVIII, no. 3 (Sept. 1974), 1086-92; David E. Cooper, "Hegel's Theory of Punishment," in Z. A. Pelczynski, ed., *Hegel's Political Philosophy* (Cambridge: Cambridge University Press, 1971); and Peter G. Stillman, "Hegel's Idea of Punishment," *Journal of the History of Philosophy,* XIV, no. 2 (April 1976), 169-182.

Since this chapter was presented as a paper, Hegel's treatment of property has been discussed by Richard Teichgraeber, "Hegel on Property and Poverty," *Journal of the History of Ideas,* XXXVIII, no. 1 (Jan.-March 1977), 47-64. There is little overlap in Teichgraeber's article and this chapter; but Teichgraeber's article is defective in a number of ways, including his unwillingness to see that reason in the realm of objective spirit is not yet unencumbered, perfect reason.

2. John Locke, *An Essay Concerning Human Understanding,* Book II, Chap. XXI, sec. 15. See also, e.g., Thomas Hobbes, *Leviathan,* Chap. 6.

3. See John Locke, *Two Treatises of Government, Second Treatise,* Chap. V, and Blackstone, *Commentaries,* Book II, opening section on "Property in General."

4. Jean-Jacques Rousseau, *The Social Contract,* Book I, Chap. 9, and David Hume, *A Treatise of Human Nature,* Book III, Part II, secs. ii and iii.

5. Whereas Marx's property-less vision aims to make man a universal, not an individual, being; see Karl Marx, "Estranged [or "Alienated"] Labour."

6. Locke, *Second Treatise,* sec. 27.

7. G. W. F. Hegel, *Die Vernunft in der Geschichte,* ed. J. Hoffmeister (Fifth edition; Hamburg: Felix Meiner, 1955), p. 116; G. W. F. Hegel, *Philosophy of History,* trans. J. Sibree (New York: Dover, 1955 [1858]), pp. 40-41.

8. For this argument developed at greater length, though with different terms and in a different context, see Stillman, "Hegel's Critique," pp. 1087-89.

9. On Greece, see Hegel, *Philosophy of Right,* sec. 185, and *Phenomenology of Spirit,* VI-A; on China, see Hegel, *Vorlesungen über die Philosophie der Weltgeschichte,* ed. Georg Lasson (second edition; Hamburg: Felix Meiner, 1923), II, 306-308, and *Philosophy of History,* pp. 128-29 (and see Stillman, "Hegel's Idea of Punishment," sec. II and note 14); on Rome, see any of the references scattered through the *Philosophy of Right,* and esp. secs. 2R, 40R, and 180R.

10. The will in the thing that is property, thus, is both a result and a manifestation of reason's complete penetration of the external world, including the world of natural (i.e., not self-conscious) myths and customs; reason in the world in property both manifests and maintains the rationality of the world. When Hegel asserts (in the "Preface" to the *Philosophy of Right*) that "to comprehend what is, this is the task of philosophy, because what is, is reason," he can know that "what is, is reason" because the will has fully penetrated the world, in property as in other ways, and thus made the world rational.

11. Reyburn, *Ethical Theory of Hegel,* p. 126.

12. Locke, *Second Treatise,* sec. 34.

13. Ibid., and Stillman, "Hegel's Critique," p. 1086 and notes 7 and 8.

14. The assertions in this sentence are developed in Peter G. Stillman, "Hegel's Civil Society: A Locus of Freedom," *Polity* (forthcoming, 1979).

15. See T. H. Green, *Principles of Political Obligation,* secs. 213-20.
16. See Ritter, "Person und Eigentum," sec. 6.
17. G. W. F. Hegel, *Vorlesungen über die Philosophie der Weltgeschichte,* II, 479-80; Hegel, *Philosophy of History,* p. 212.
18. Or what Marx would call "use value"; see *Capital,* vol. I, Bk. I, sec. i.
19. While Ritter stresses only work (and thus on this point follows Marx's view of the proper interpretation of Hegel), it is clear that both work and interaction make up the process. Historically, interaction (in the form of the recognition of the other) is the goal—as both cause and result—of the master-slave struggle and thus of the work of the slave. Looked at from another perspective, work without interaction would clearly be inadequate in the context of Hegel's "Phenomenology": without interaction (and the self-consciousness and recognition that it gives), human labor would be purely natural and unselfconscious, i.e., human labor would be like the labor of animals. But, with interaction and its resulting recognition and self-consciousness (*Phenomenology,* Chap. IV-A; Enc. 430-35), labor becomes human, and humans develop out of their natural condition towards a more spiritual and rational condition. In civil society, the modern manifestation of the historical struggle, liberation occurs both through work (195R) and interaction (194). See Jürgen Habermas, *Towards a Rational Society* (Boston; Beacon, 1971), Chap. 6, for a contemporary restatement of Hegel's view here.
20. For Hegel, since the family and the state are not in essence contracts (75R), the family-member and the citizen are not subject to the reification of human relations; see Stillman, "Hegel's Critique," p. 1090, and see sec. 7, below.
21. Ritter, "Person und Eigentum," sec. 9.
22. Thus for instance Marx: "The bourgeoisie . . . has left remaining no other nexus between man and man than naked self-interest, than callous cash payment. . . . It has resolved personal worth into exchange value" (*Communist Manifesto,* Part I); and Burke: "But the age of chivalry is gone. That of sophisters, economists, and calculators has succeeded, and the glory of Europe is extinguished forever" (*Reflections on the Revolution in France* [New York: Library of Liberal Arts, 1955], p. 86). See especially Hegel, *Philosophy of Right,* sec. 182A.
23. Hegel's *Polizei* at least have the good of all as their goal when they intervene, since Hegel's state, of which the police are an arm in civil society, aims at the good of all, not at the protection of the property of each. Where the goal of the state is the protection of property, police intervention may not be intended to adjust interests into a fair balance.
24. T. H. Green, *Principles of Political Obligation,* sec. 220.
25. Ibid., secs. 220-32; Hegel, *Philosophy of Right,* sec. 245. Hegel does suggest imperialism as a short-run solution that has obvious geographical limits (246).
26. Similarly, Hegel regards corporate (as opposed to personal) property as deficient (279R), because an artificial person cannot participate in the ethical benefits of property.
27. See Stillman, "Hegel's Civil Society: A Locus of Freedom."
28. I should like to thank the American Philosophical Society and Vassar College for research grants that greatly assisted the preparation of this paper. I am grateful to those who raised questions and made suggestions when earlier versions of this chapter were presented to the Hegel Society of America meeting and to Professor Z. A. Pelczynski's graduate seminar on Hegel at Pembroke College, Oxford.

Of Human Bondage: Labour, Bondage, and Freedom in the *Phenomenology*

by

HOWARD ADELMAN

I. Introduction

"The easiest thing of all is to pass judgements on what has a solid substantial content; it is more difficult to grasp it, and most of all difficult to do both together and produce the systematic exposition of it." [1]

It is easy to become absorbed in judging Hegel and his interpreters. It is harder to grasp the development of non-rational self-consciousness. This paper concentrates on "grasping" that development rather than the even harder task of providing a systematic exposition of it. [2] The latter is facilitated by translating the language of religious myth into thought. In order to grasp that thought in the fullness of living, in the specific acts of individuals it is appropriate in dealing with the middle section of the *Phenomenology* to translate thought back into myth. This is particularly true since the non-rational development discussed is, for Hegel, archetypically Jewish and Hegel realized how little of that "Jewish" spirit could be rendered by an intellectual analysis. [3]

These three aspects: (1) classifying and judging, (2) grasping the material at hand and expressing it, and (3) producing a systematic exposition are also ways of differentiating the three different aspects of the spirit depicted in the most basic divisions of the *Phenomenology of Mind:* consciousness (naming, classifying, and subsuming under general laws), self-consciousness (which leaves the lifeless universals for the fullness of experience), and the third section of rational self-consciousness including reason, spirit, religion and absolute knowledge. Since our subject matter falls within the middle section in the fullness of living experience and not its abstract corpse, it is appropriate to plunge directly in and dwell within the section.

But before we dive note the lifeless corpse which is our diving board. What began as a world full of sensations of which consciousness was certain, a dynamic world of flux and change in which one sought stability, ends up in understanding as a stable system of mechanical forces in equilibrium in which, instead of certainty, everything is the

opposite of what it appears and things are defined by what they lack.
Life has been reduced to a system of forces in equilibrium within a
self-moving world system. Life has become lifeless without movement
and development.[4] Man has become master of the knowledge of nature,
subsuming everything under his laws and categories, but he has not
grasped life in the living of it for he has not faced the fact that life ends in
the experience of death. The world is a projection of man's categories
and laws and thereby his self has become other; man cannot find himself
in that otherness. He cannot say who he is in what is projected. He is a
lonely, empty "I." Adam in the Garden of Eden with all his powers of
naming everything in nature is alone and needs a helpmeet.

II. The Truth of Self-Certainty

(A) *Desire:* To be conscious of himself as a self, there must be another
self-consciousness. This is generally agreed. However, it is also generally believed that the other self-consciousness does not appear in Hegel
until the Lordship and Bondage section. What Hegel says, however, is
that an independent self-consciousness does not appear as a *fact* for
self-consciousness until then. But it does appear before this as an object
which is not yet recognized as an independent self-consciousness. A
helpmeet appears as a *physical* projection of myself, as "bone of my bone
and flesh of my flesh." The other self-consciousness at this stage is not
an intellectual projection. It has the physical shape of an independent
self-consciousness but it has not yet expressed the essential independent
spirit. As Hegel says, "When for self-consciousness the distinction does
not also have the shape of *being,* it is *not* self-consciousness" (*P.M.,* p.
219). Of course, everything is the opposite of what it appears, as has
been learned from consciousness, and this fantasy is in reality the fact
that I am born as a projection of another body into the world and project
this in my isolated dream world as if everything out there were merely a
projection of my own body.

If the infant thinks he is the center of the world, he feels he is nothing,
that he is merely an extension of the mother. But he doesn't yet recognize that feeling. The consciousness of that feeling as the first stage of
self-consciousness, of consciousness as an inward state, emerges in an
inverted way distorted by the prism of consciousness which experiences
the world as a projection of self. The mother is an extension of self, but

not merely any extension. The mother is a physical extension with whom one desires to be physically reunited.

The three moments of Desire remain an abstraction. Desire has not yet become a vital experience. Adam is conscious of himself as the centre of the universe. His consciousness tells him that he is not allowed to eat of the Tree of Knowledge of Good and Evil, that is, to eat of that which will destroy that consciousness of himself as the centre of the world, and his consciousness as the essence of that self. Knowledge of his bodily self will destroy both the illusion that the self is the centre of a self-moving cosmic system and the illusion that the essence of that system is simply thought. At this stage, however, Adam merely knows himself as one who names objects in nature and does not know his own body or govern its conduct. Adam is defined by what he lacks *in knowledge,* the knowledge of his body. Further, Adam is alone; he has no body in the world with whom he can be. It is a duality in which Adam has a body which he cannot know and has no body with whom he can be.

In the second moment, unknown to Adam's conscious experience, while Adam is sleeping another body appears which in consciousness must necessarily be a projection of his own body. Eve is made as a projection of Adam's flesh. Further, there is something in the ego, which is other than thought, which is rooted in the body, and which, when raised into thought, is interpreted as a projection of the body. One might say that, for Hegel, the superego is conscious thought when it addresses itself towards the body; responsibility for the body is reciprocally projected onto the thought of the world. The unconscious is in turn the body as a thing which makes other things; when raised into consciousness the responsibility for making things is projected onto the world as a unity of thought.

But if consciousness is this refusal to take responsibility for the body while at the same time insisting that the self is the centre of a self-moving world, then it is imperative for consciousness that the self reincorporate that physical projection of itself as part of itself, even if again the responsibility for this instruction is also projected into the thought of the world as a whole. In the third moment of Desire, God *tells* Adam and Eve that they shall be one flesh. What was actualized without reflection in the second moment is now posited as a unity in consciousness without actualization. What was a mere abstraction without realization becomes in the third moment a recognition of a duality, internal and external, with an imperative to achieve unity.

(B) *Life:* Nevertheless, Desire, as the first moment of learning the truth about oneself, is still an abstraction. It has not yet been experienced in Life. In the first moment of self-recognition, the meaning that the self is not-other has been given substantive meaning, but only in thought. The meaning of the self as that which identifies objects has not yet been dealt with. Since that self already exists in consciousness, what it needs is actualization in life.

If Desire is the inversion of consciousness of self as a non-other, a bare ego, so that one becomes conscious that one is ignorant of one's own identity at the same time as the other is experienced, although only in the abstract, Life is the inversion of the other aspect of consciousness, the consciousness of the object which receives its identity from the I. In the inversion, the object becomes an object for experience rather than for consciousness and thereby loses *its* identity. The only unity is the unity of the self in contrast to Desire in General in which a duality exists in the ego between one's ignorance of who the self is and one's self as a concrete other; from an infantile perspective, we feel the mother is our self as other while we are curious about our own body as if it were another of which we are ignorant.

In the first moment of Life, the self is experienced as extension. Thus there is a negation in experience, as it appears to the self, of the negativity of the first moment as we reach out to make the other part of the self. There are objects independent of the self but the subject does not regard objects as having any continuity independent of the self. When an infant watches an adult come in one door and leave through another, it looks back to the first door to see that adult reappear. There is no extension except as a projection from the subject; there is no continuity in time except as a continuity within that spatial extension. The existence of *independent* objects in experience is not yet recognized.

> The essential element (Wesen) is infinitude as the supersession of all distinctions, the pure rotation on its own axis, itself at rest while being absolutely restless infinitude, the very self-dependence in which the differences brought out in the process are all dissolved, the simple reality of time, which in this self-identity has the solid form and shape of space (*P.M.*, p. 221).

This is, of course, Life as the self-moving world system described at the end of consciousness, but the solar system is no longer an object for consciousness here; rather, I experience myself as a solar system. Life, which, in general, is the *experience* of unity of the self, in its first moment is a duality in the unity, for though independence of all objects is sublated in the existence of the self, the objects are still sublated as independent objects. The independence of objects is itself broken up in the second moment of Life when there are no objects, as such, but only an infinitude of distinctions in experience. For the first moment is but an abstraction; its actualization in experience results in the immediate grabbing for the infinite number of objects presented among which no distinctions can be made. The mother's breast and the corner of the child's blanket are sucked as if they were the same.

In the third moment of Life, the self posits itself by separating out objects as extensions of the self and then denying the separateness of the object by consuming it. In the process, stability is consumed. At the same time the self experiences objects as food for the body; the self is posited as a body to consume objects, as the continuity of the self in relationship to an undifferentiated continuity.

Life as Living has become the process of defining oneself as the eater of fruit in a Garden of Eden in which no distinctions are made. There is no evaluation of what is good or bad for the body. Life, the reunion of the object world and the subject, is no longer a mere Idea. Nor is it a natural instinct to guide us to the breast which provides sustenance. It has become universalized.

In Life as Spirit, *all* things are seen to exist for consumption by Man's body. Man lives obsessed with the Tree of Life in the Garden of Eden. In the first moment of Life, objects exist for Man but are not yet in Man. In the second moment, the existence of objects themselves is negated in favour of undifferentiated experience. In the final moment, the mother, Eve, is opposed to the self since she is not simply an object which exists only for consumption by the self; the Individual, Adam, in turn exists, but only lives to feed his body. "Life as such is partly the Means of Spirit, and as such opposed to it; and partly it is the Living Individual, and Life is its Body."[5] Note that it is Eve who is the Means of Spirit. Adam has become his body, has become the solar system and ignores his body as other.

(C) *Desire in Life:* The third stage following Desire and Life is the experience of Desire in Life. It is not an abstraction of which we learn. Nor is it experience without consciousness. It is Desire directed towards the Consciousness for which we hunger, the lack of knowledge of our own bodies both in ourselves and as other.

In Desire in General one is torn between the feeling of one's body projecting into the world as an object, and the consciousness of ignorance of one's body. In Desire in Life, an inversion takes place. The self wants to "make" an object in the world, that body which is already projected in the world as ourselves, while at the same time being an independent Life, a self which exists in its own right, which experiences all the fruit of the Garden as objects to be consumed. The self wants both to consume that object and be consumed by it.

However, Eve wants to be one flesh with Adam, not just as an Idea but as a concrete reality. It is Eve, the second moment in human creation, consciousness which maintains itself as an immediate unity, who gives substance and acts out her will through her feelings as a concrete individual. Adam is hung up on his own duality—as the one given dominion over all of nature but who has no dominion or command over his own body, as the one who knows that he shall be one flesh with Eve but who knows he must not eat of the Tree of Knowledge of Good and Evil. His thoughts and feelings are internally torn apart.

> Thus one sex is mind in its self-diremption into explicit personal self-subsistence and the knowledge and volition of free universality, i.e. the self-consciousness of conceptual thought and the volition of the objective final end. The other sex is mind maintaining itself in unity as knowledge and volition of the substantive, but knowledge and volition in the form of concrete individuality and feeling. In relation to externality, the former is powerful and active, the latter passive and subjective.[6]

Adam and Eve ate of the Tree of Knowledge of Good and Evil and Adam knew Eve and Eve knew Adam.

> And self-consciousness is thus only assured of itself through sublating this other, which is presented to self-consciousness as an independent life; self-consciousness is *Desire*. Convinced of the nothingness of this other, it definitely affirms this nothingness to be for itself the truth of this other, negates the independent object, and thereby acquires the certainty of its own self, as *true* certainty, a certainty which it has become aware of in objective form.
>
> In this state of satisfaction, however, it has experience of the independence of its object. Desire and the certainty of its self obtained in the gratification of desire, are conditioned by the object; for the cer-

tainty exists through cancelling this other; in order that this cancelling may be effected, there must be this other. Self-consciousness is thus unable by its negative relation to the object to abolish it; because of that relation it rather produces it again, as well as the desire (*P.M.*, p. 225).

But, of course, this whole section leading to Desire in Life is itself an abstraction *in feeling,* a fantasy which is not yet recognized as such by the self-conscious individual. Because these feelings are filtered through the prism of consciousness, where the child is the self-moving centre of a world he controls, and since the child does not yet know who he himself is and cannot yet make distinctions between feelings, thoughts, and actions, he thinks that what he feels is real. In experience the other is an independent self-consciousness which is not sublated into the self. They do not become one flesh. The child comes to the shocking recognition of a truth, that the other is an *independent* object.

But if the self only knows and recognizes itself as the centre of the *whole* world excluding nothing, then it experiences frustration. The self finds new satisfaction only when it projects onto the other the desire to negate itself, to become one with the first self; this is seen as the essence of the other. It is Eve who seduces Adam, who negates herself as other, who is seduced by "force" of desire which Adam *"controls."*

On account of the independence of the object, therefore, it can only attain satisfaction when this object itself effectually brings about negation within itself. The object must *per se* effect this negation of itself, for it is inherently (*an sich*) something negative, and must be for the other what it is (*P.M.*, pp. 225-26).

To ensure *satisfaction,* self-consciousness has had to come to recognize another self-consciousness who is not merely oneself objectified, while retaining the illusion that it is oneself "subjectified," as it were, oneself out there but as an independent source of action.

When God discovers that Adam and Eve have eaten of the fruit of the Tree of Knowledge of Good and Evil and have become conscious of their mortality, Consciousness, which saw the world out there as the objectification of self, now must take account of the self as an actor. Man has set out on the path of history; thought operates through that which is acted out by passion. Emotions and thoughts are sundered so that feeling ignores thought and thought distorts feeling.

III. Lordship and Bondage

"Self-consciousness exists in itself and for itself, in that, and by the fact that it exists for another self-consciousness; that is to say that it is only by being acknowledged or 'recognized'." (P.M., p. 229)

This is how the section "Lordship and Bondage" begins. And Hegel warns us immediately after making this assertion that in the distinction of the moments of self-consciousness, these moments must be taken as *not* distinguished. They must always be understood and accepted in their *opposite* sense. To interpret the above to mean that a self-consciousness is truly other takes Hegel's meaning in the introduction not in its *opposite* sense but in its literal sense. The latter self-consciousness is not a self-consciousness which also is said to exist in and for itself.

Hegel is *not* simply talking about two self-conscious beings in relationship to one another. He is talking about the *nature* of self-consciousness itself where double meaning is rooted; it is the nature of self-consciousness to see double meaning even when reflecting on its own nature. Self-consciousness at this stage is still narcissistic, seeing the other as the extension of self at the same time as it experiences the self as other than itself, and, as such, wanting the same reunion with itself as it wants with the other.

Seeking recognition by another self-consciousness is *acting out* the process of self-recognition. How does narcissistic thought, which considers the world as an extension of itself, come to recognize the self, which experiences the world as alien and other?

(A) *Self-Consciousness Doubled:* To understand this question we must clarify the sense in which one self-consciousness appears to itself as another self-consciousness outside itself. Hegel says that self-consciousness has "outered itself," has come outside itself when self-consciousness has before it another self-consciousness. To see this simply as a depiction of two selves in relationship makes no sense of how one self-consciousness is outered. At the end of "Truth of self-certainty" we were left with a self which had not abandoned thought, which had taken the other self as an extension of its own body; feeling, however, reveals the self as other, as a subject with an independent source of will. The development is now carried forward but on the level of the immediacy of feeling, and, since we are dealing with the phenomenology of experience, we are concerned with feelings as they first appear in development. And when they first appear they are still accompanied by thought. The rest of the middle section of the *Phenomenology* has as one of its themes the increasing effort of feeling to jettison thought.

The first moment (of Lordship and Bondage) is concerned with sexual feelings as an experience (not the experience of sex), and the first moment of that moment is concerned with the thoughts that accompany these sexual feelings. In the negative moment (particularly if masculine imagery is utilized) the self experiences itself as split. The self is *not* itself but is lost in the other. On the other hand, the self is not other, since that self was projected into the other. This moment of negation is itself negated; in the immediacy of feeling, the self experiences itself as a unity (since the self experiences itself by sublating the other, an other which is itself, and therefore the self sublates itself). Sublating itself and sublating the other are then one and the same experience. But, upon reflection on this experience, the self recognizes itself as only one with itself by cancelling itself as other and cancelling being in the other. The other goes free; the pair split.

The second moment of the development of sexual feeling negates the consciousness, negates thought, and considers the relationship strictly as an *act*. As consciousness, one self-consciousness is active and the other merely passive, continuing the subject-object dichotomy. But as an action, it is mutual. Therefore, the consciousness of the first moment is reflected in the mutual immediate feelings of the partners in the second moment.

As a result, in the third moment, when recognition comes, one begins with a double consciousness both in relationship to oneself and to the other. One is conscious of restrictions at the same time as one has risked oneself by projection outwards towards the other. One also assumes that, in one sense, one is the other; but one is also not the other. No wonder lovers are all mixed up. Unity can only be experienced by repetition, by cancelling itself as existing for itself, which is identical with experiencing one's self-existence only in the self-existence of the other. Upon reflection, "they recognize themselves as mutually recognizing one another" (*P.M.*, p. 231). "And the eyes of them both were opened, and they knew that they were naked" (Genesis, III, 7). Each recognizes his own body and the body of the other; each also recognizes that the other recognizes both his own body and the body of the other.

(B) *The Battle:* In the first moment of Lordship and Bondage, the sexual appetite, the desire to be one flesh, is acted out in fantasy, and thereby experienced, but only in consciousness as the enactment of Living Desire. In the second moment of Lordship and Bondage, two bodies, self-conscious of themselves as bodies, experience the body itself *in actuality.*

Each individual now experiences himself as the unity of his own body.

> Self-consciousness is primarily simple existence for self, self-identity by exclusion of every other from itself. It takes its essential nature and absolute object to be Ego; and in this immediacy, in this bare fact of its self-existence, it is individual (*P.M.,* p. 231).

The second moment of the Lordship and Bondage section is the antithesis of two individuals as bodies and not spirits; for each the other is only an unessential object. Each is *not* thought and *not* other. Each tries to be only his or her body. This is the battle.

Each experiences itself as a body and not as other. Then each acts out that experience. For Eve, in the immediate unity of feeling, Adam becomes unessential, although she is servant to him and he is her master. Her essence is the experience of her body as a mode of reproduction. In the bringing forth of children, she suffers in pain and *labour.* Eve is enslaved within her body; she is as an object over which her husband has mastery; she is a slave to natural reproduction. Both are experienced as one and the same. Sex is experienced merely as reproduction. Adam at this time *names* her Eve for she no longer lives in herself but is the mother of all that lives.

Adam experiences his body in his labour on the soil and becomes a slave to that soil. Eve experiences her body in the labour to bring forth future life and, therefore, as the means for life's continuity. But Adam experiences the unity of his body as a duality. For the body not only performs, but Adam recognizes that it will cease performing. Adam becomes conscious that he will die.

In this, each achieves an *abstraction* of existence, Eve as the mother of all living, and Adam as the bare struggle for survival, *knowing* that he will die. This is the first moment of the Struggle (which is the second moment in the development of Lordship and Bondage). Lordship has appeared in Adam's mastery over Eve, and in Death's mastery over Adam, and Bondage is experienced in Eve's labour pains and Adam's labour and toil, but neither lordship nor bondage have been brought into reflection, into *self*-consciousness.

In the second moment of the Struggle the battle is acted out. For Adam and Eve experience their submission only in consciousness which has not yet become actualized (the precondition of its becoming self-conscious). And it is acted out by that which embodies the first moment as a unity of feeling. Their unity is embodied in their children—Cain and Abel.

Adam and Eve are conscious of their individuality as a body, but their bodies are fettered to one another, and to life, Eve as the mother of all living and Adam as the one who earns a living and knows he will die. The acting out of the independence of the body is left to their children.

Cain, as the first born, is akin to his father and tills the ground. Abel, as the second born, is akin to his mother and is a keeper of sheep just as his mother tended her babes. They express their independence from the objects produced by their labour, by the "pure negation of its objective form"—Cain sacrifices some of his produce and Abel one of his lambs. Action entailed the death of the objects of their own labour, thereby risking that which is their own life objectified. They are prepared to alienate the products of their labour, for their bodies as labouring devices are still felt to be alien. The immediacy of feeling follows this split in consciousness. Only the animal offering receives recognition as a sacrifice. Cain becomes *angry* and *crestfallen,* for he had *not* been *recognized* as an individual independent of the objects of his labour. Cain kills Abel.

In the second moment of the Struggle (Cain and Abel) a *second* action is involved in the attempt to bring to recognition the body as individual and independent of that on which it labours. In the action of the other, Abel, the shepherd, gains recognition from God (the world as thought), and not Cain. Yet, in fact, shepherding becomes obsolete and is succeeded by agriculture. Only one economic form of life can survive as primary; one must die. Though each economic form of life aspires to primacy and the death of the other, the one that dies both projects responsibility for its death onto the subsequent form and views the succeeding form as living everafter, but as empty meaningless existence. There is thus a double action and death involved, the death of one's body in an objective form as the sacrifice of the products of one's labour, and the death of a competing form of economic life.

> The process of bringing all this out involves a twofold action—action on the part of the other and action on the part of itself. Insofar as it is the other's action, each aims at the destruction and death of the other. But

> in this there is implicated also the second kind of action, self-activity;
> for the former implies that it risks its own life (*P.M.*, p. 232).

The life and death struggle involved is *not* one between two warriors but between two embodiments of different forms of economic life. The struggle is to gain recognition for their bodily independence. In so doing, they "risk life," their own life objectified into otherness through labour, though this has not yet come into consciousness. They literally "stake their life"; one sacrifices his agricultural produce and the other an animal. Each takes the risk in order to be recognized as unfettered to themselves as other.

> The individual who has not staked his life, may, no doubt, be recog-
> nized as a Person; but he has not attained the truth of this recognition
> as an independent self-consciousness. In the same way each must
> aim at the death of the other, as it risks its own life thereby . . . (*P.M.*, p.
> 233).

In the second moment of the Struggle (which is the second moment in the development of Lordship and Bondage), Cain, who fails to gain recognition for his independence, slays Abel. The truth of the independence of the self as a body is cancelled. "Death is the natural 'negation' of consciousness, negation without independence, which thus remains without the requisite significance of actual recognition" (*P.M.*, p. 233).

The lack of independence is itself negated as a fact; the negation is negated. Abel is dead. Cain is evicted from the soil and loses his source of sustenance. He becomes a fugitive and wanderer, one of the living dead who cannot even be put to death. In the second moment of the Struggle, unity and independence of the self is realized but as a "lifeless existence," "merely existent and not opposed."

And the meaning must be taken in its opposite sense, for it is Abel's feeling projected into Cain. This is how consciousness translates the feelings engendered by the experience of being suckled as an infant and shepherded about. The self projects itself as the Shepherd, but in order to grow into independence the Shepherd must be killed off. But, of course, there is a double inversion. Since in consciousness the other is a projection of the self, the thought of killing the other is also projected onto otherness. It is the other that wants to snuff out the life of the self. The mother becomes the monster of the crib who wants to devour her own children.

But after destroying itself in fantasy, the self feels itself as not only alone but cut off from its own body as well. For feeling projected into fantasy through the prism of consciousness, which insists that the self exist in and for itself, reveals again that in the Struggle between feeling and thought thought is victorious and cuts feeling off from the body and the reality of death. If the first stage in the acceptance of death is total denial (Eve), the second stage involves denying that consciousness will die while accepting the death of the body. But *I* don't die; the real I lives on. But in being cut off from the body and feelings, its living is lifeless.

(C) *Independence and Dependence of Self-Consciousness:* In the first moment of Lordship and Bondage, the moment of immediate self-consciousness, the self becomes conscious of itself as having substantial bodily independence. In the experience of the second moment, the consciousness of oneself as an independent body seems to dissolve, for survival seems to depend on thought in general. In the third moment the negation of the negation is inverted and self-consciousness is posited as existing not only for itself but for another, which at this stage is regarded as a thing. The third moment entails the inversion of lifeless existence in the recognition that life is essential to existence and is not to be sacrificed.

In the first moment of this third moment, self-consciousness for itself and for another exists as a duality without unity, but for the first time they exist *in consciousness* as Master or Lord, thought in general, which is independent, and the essential nature of which is to be for itself, and as Bondsman, as a body which is dependent for its *existence* on another and whose essence is life for another.

Noah is an artisan, unlike Cain, the agriculturalist, or Abel the shepherd.[7] He designs a boat. Noah is the descendant of Seth, the third-born son of Adam and Eve, through whom the third moment could be realized. And it is only when Seth's son is born that man began "to call upon the name of the Lord" (Genesis IV, 26). The Lordship of God emerges only at this stage. God is the only one who is independent and whose *essential* nature is to be for itself. Noah is dependent for his existence on the soil which the Lord hath cursed. Further, the essence of Noah's existence is to live for another; his name means comforter, from the Hebrew *na hen,* "to comfort."

Now God as the Lord exists for itself in *consciousness* but not in actuality. Actualization is mediated through another, man as a body—

or Noah in particular—whose existence is bound up with the existence of all things. For it is upon Noah's shoulders that his own salvation and the salvation of everything else depends. Further, Noah's existence is to live for an other—God; Noah walks with God. Feeling for another is ultimately in the service of thought which is for itself.

In the description following the introduction of the master or Lord and the bondsman, what is depicted is not primarily the relationship of the master to the slave but of the master (a) to self-existence, to existing in and for himself, and (b) to the fact that the realization of self-existence requires that the master's existence be experienced through that which is other, to an existence which is an object in the world. As a projection in the physical world the master is related to his self-existence only through mediation in a two-fold sense. The master has a relationship to an independent self-existing being only because he controls the life of the bondsman and has power over that self-existence; that is, it is the self-existence as other over which the master has control. Second, the master has a relationship to his self-existence only because the bondsman obeys the master, believing that what he too wants, independent self-existence, is possessed by the master. The body feeling as filtered through the prism of consciousness comes to think that only the mind or thought possesses independence.

If the master is related to his self-existence mediately in a two-fold sense, in the bondsman (a) seen as an existence independent of the master, and (b) seen as cognizing the master as possessing an independent self-existence, there is also a two-fold sense in which the master is related to himself as other, as a thing in the world. Insofar as it is through the bondsman's work on the things in the world that the master relates to otherness, his immediate relationship to the external world is mediated by the bondsman. Insofar as he alone has the pure enjoyment of the thing, he is immediately related to self-existence as other, and mediation is negated. The master, since he doesn't work on the world, is indifferent to the independence of the object.

The relationship must now be considered from the point of view of the bondsman. Noah does not work in forced labour for the Lord. He freely gives himself in the service of the Lord. Slaves and bondsmen have a common characteristic in that both give service without pay, but only the servant of the Lord gives it freely. As opposed to forced slavery, the bondsman is also one who is bound, in the sense that he gives security for the other. Noah is the archetypal bondsman freely giving himself in the service of the Lord doing all that God commands.[8] "We have thus here the moment of recognition, viz. that the other consciousness cancels itself as self-existent, and, *ipso facto,* itself does what the first does to it" (*P.M.*, p. 236). In a second sense of bondsman, Noah is the one who builds the ark and provides security for *all* that is other. But giving security to the world is properly God's role.

> In the same way we have the other moment, that this action on the part of the second is the action proper of the first; for what is done by the bondsman is properly an action on the part of the master. The latter exists only for himself, that is his essential nature; he is the negative power without qualification, a power to which the thing is naught. And he is thus the absolutely essential act in the situation, while the bondsman is not so, he is an unessential activity. But for recognition proper there is needed the moment that what the master does to the other he should also do to himself, and what the bondsman does to himself, he should do to the other also. On that account a form of recognition has arisen that is one sided and unequal (*P.M.*, p. 236).

What does the Lord do to the other that he should also do to himself? He commands the other who is good but does not command himself. He destroys that which he considers evil but does not yet self-destruct. What does the bondsman do to himself that he should do to the other as well? He gives himself freely but he should get others (including his Lord) to give freely without *quid pro quo*'s. The bondsman must bind the other to give security for himself.

God as master is again Lord and master of all he surveys and returns to Noah the dominion that he took away from Adam, a dominion over the birds and the beasts and all life on earth; but Noah does not have dominion over man. Noah does not appear to have the power to do to others what he does to himself. God as Lord and Master does have the power to do to himself what he does to others. The Lord commands himself neither to curse the ground anymore nor to smite everything living, and in so doing voluntarily begins to self-destruct, to destroy his own power.

Noah not only lacks the power to do to others what he does to himself, he is also, even though made in the image of God, not a very good representation of the Lord. This is true in a double sense. For considered from the "thought-side," from the point of view of consciousness, the bondsman is totally dependent on the Lord to tell him what to do. He is dependent on the Lord for his consciousness as practical reason, as conscience. The truth of God is found only in an unessential consciousness which needs to reveal itself as an independent self-consciousness.

The external, however, is only the acting out of the internal, and the inner side of Noah as the archetypal bondsman is the reflection of the external bondage to the Lord and must be unveiled. God as Master and Lord is taken to be an independent consciousness, but this is an illusion of thought, for the Lord depends on man for his realization. The mind depends on the body for expression. But if this is an illusion of feeling reflected in thought, the truth exists in feeling itself. For Noah felt the fear of death, of total destruction, fear for the entire being of the world, and as such knew in his gut that death was the sovereign master, that the Lord and Master was absolute negativity. The illusory thought which takes the Lord to be the embodiment of all independent self-consciousness and the feeling that the Lord is absolute negativity come together *in* Noah, in his work. For, in work, self-sacrifice rather than sacrifice of the other, he cancels out his dependence and attachment to natural existence, thereby establishing himself as an independent consciousness, and at the same time negates that existence through work. But they have not yet come together in his self-consciousness.

Thus, labour makes man free but man has still to come to the recognition of this. For it is the worker who experiences natural existence and his body as essential and does not suffer the illusion of consciousness desiring to be freed from external existence. Instead of the world existing as objects which are projections of the self, the self projects itself into the world with its labour to create a world of objects. The desire to negate the object and assert the independence of the self becomes the negation of the self as consciousness detached from feelings to create and fabricate a world of independent objects. In giving form to objects, the freedom is made substantive and given permanence. It is when the self works in voluntary bondage in labour that the self first externalizes itself as an objectified individual self-consciousness. And it must be work impelled by the fear of death, not simply of the death of one's own self, for that would only mean working in the anxiety of loss of contingent existence, but in the fear of the death of existence in general. Further, that work must express itself not merely in contingent forms but in forms which are permanent and therefore resist death, forms in which the sacrifice of the body expresses the spirit in a true objective immortality.

NOTES

1. *Phenomenology of Mind,* trans. J. B. Baillie (London, New York, 1931), pp. 69-70. Hereinafter cited as *P.M.*

2. Cf. Howard Adelman, "Labour and Freedom" in John O'Neill and Lionel Rubinoff, eds., *Lordship and Bondage in Hegel and Marx* (to be published).

3. Cf. H. S. Harris, *Hegel's Development: Toward the Sunlight 1770-1781* (Oxford: Clarendon Press, 1972), p. 278.

4. Piaget has noted in child development as well that "the elimination of life leads to a mechanization of force." *The Child's Conception of Physical Causality* (Totawa, N.J.: Littlefield, Adams & Co.), p. 246.

5. Hegel's *Science of Logic,* Vol. II, (London, 1929), 403.

6. Hegel's *Philosophy of Right,* trans. T. M. Knox (Oxford, 1942), p. 114.

7. Cf. H. S. Harris (1972), pp. 273-79 for a clear discussion of Hegel's earlier explicit references to Noah.

8. Lawrence of Arabia captures the essence of the experience of giving oneself freely into bondage in service of an idea.

   Willy-nilly it [the ideal] became a faith. We had sold ourselves into its slavery, manacled ourselves together in its chain-gang, bowed ourselves to serve its holiness with all our good and ill content. The mentality of ordinary human slaves is terrible—they have lost the world—and we had surrendered, not body alone, but soul to the overmastering greed of victory. By our own act we were drained of morality, of volition, of responsibility, like dead leaves in the wind.

   T. E. Lawrence, *Seven Pillars of Wisdom* (New York: Doubleday, 1926, 1962), p. 28.

Hegel's Theory of Sovereignty, International Relations, and War

by
ERROL E. HARRIS

I. Sovereignty

"l'Etat c'est moi" declared Louis XIV, and on his canon he had inscribed the legend: *"ultima ratio regum."* Hegel appears, at any rate *prima facie,* to endorse both doctrines. "Sovereignty," he says, . . . *"exists* only as subjectivity certain of itself, as the abstract (and to that extent groundless) self-determination of will in which the finality of decision lies. It is this, the individual aspect of the state as such, in which alone it is *one.* Subjectivity, however, exists in its true form only as subject, personality only as person. . . . This absolute decisive moment of the whole is, therefore, not just individuality in general, but an individual, the Monarch."[1] Further, Hegel maintains that because the relations between states has as its fundamental principle their respective sovereignties, "they are to that extent opposed to one another in the state of nature,"[2] and "The conflict of states, for that reason so far as their particular wills find no agreement, can only be settled by war."

By quoting passages from Hegel in isolation from their context is as unscholarly as it is fruitful of misunderstanding and misinterpretation, the outstanding example of which is Sir Karl Popper's critique in *The Open Society and Its Enemies.*[3] In the first place, any careful reader will be aware that Hegel, despite what is quoted above, does not identify sovereignty with the monarch. The monarch personifies the state and embodies its individuality. Hegel protests that the state is no merely legal or fictitious person but is a genuine individual personal in the monarch. To that extent *l'Etat c'est le Roi.* But the king is not the government, he is but one moment of the total unity, while, as ever in the sphere of the Notion (to which the State corresponds), each moment is at the same time the whole. The government or constitution of the state, however, is a system of functions, legislative, executive and judicial, sublating all the functions and institutions of *die bürgerliche Gesellschaft* and the family, and constituting an organic whole, the members of which are each and all as integral to it as are its limbs to a living body.[4] Monarchy is thus constitutional monarchy, and is neither despotic nor feudal[5]—to that extent, Louis XIV's assertion is un-Hegelian. He represents, perhaps, the historical transition from the feudal to the modern form of state, its centralization prior to its liberalization.

How far is Hegel justified in this contention of the personal character of the will of the sovereign and its embodiment in the monarch? Those who allege that he is advocating a personal despotism or tyranny are profoundly mistaken, as I shall presently show. Strictly, the *Rechtsphilosophie* is not the advocacy of any political form, but is a philosophical analysis of political forms in general, or, more properly, of the political form in principle. If Lord Bryce's description is hardly justified of Hobbes' *Leviathan* as a gigantic political pamphlet[6] a similar imputation to Hegel's *Philosophie des Rechts* is even less so. When Hegel insists that the individuality of the state is, and must be, embodied in a person he is doing no more than pointing to the undoubted fact that the representative of the sovereign will is always a particular individual, whom today we identify as "the Head of State," be it Queen Elizabeth, the President of the United States, Chairman Mao, or Secretary Brezhnev. But for Hegel this is no mere empirical (and so contingent) fact; it is in principle necessary to the actualization of a politically sovereign will. Every sovereign act must, to be sovereign, bear the seal and signature of the Head of State.

The key to the conception of sovereignty is the organic unity of the society as a whole, which essentially *is* the state and its sovereignty. The will of the state, what Rousseau would have identified as the General Will, is not the individual will of any particular magistrate, nor that of any citizen or body of citizens, nor that of any particular institution or function of government, regarded as independent, but is the expression of the commonalty in which any or all of these are but moments and in which they are all sublated.

A unity self-differentiating into mutually inter-dependent moments is, for Hegel, a "being-for-self," or an ideal unity. This unity of the moments, immanent in each of them yet actual only in the whole, is their "ideality." By that Hegel is far from meaning that the unity is not real. On the contrary, it is the truth and actuality (*Wirklichkeit*) of the moments and of the prior dialectical phases which it sublates. Consequently, Hegel says that sovereignty is "in the first instance only the general thought of this ideality" (*Rechtsphilosophie*, § 279). It operates in actual fact in (at least) three forms:

(1) First through the quasi-independent pursuit of individual (or family) concerns in civil society. These concerns though *prima facie* they appear separate and independent, at times even conflicting, are in principle facets of a common interest, so far as they are all interests in and subject to the *organization* of activities which constitutes the economic and social order. It follows that they all contribute to that order not only, as Hegel puts it, "by way of the unconscious *necessity* of the matter, in accordance with which their self-seeking is transformed into a contribution to reciprocal support and the support of the whole" (ibid., § 278); but also through their undisputed and presumed interest in the general order which their activity upholds. This could be demonstrated and exemplified in detail, but for our present purpose let one or two examples suffice.

The farmer, the tradesman, the craftsman, and the contractor, each following his own vocation and pursuing his own interest in apparent independence, is nevertheless providing goods and services to all the others and is contributing to the supply of common needs. The litigants in a civil suit, each maintaining his own interest against the other, are, by taking their case to court, serving the common interest in the legal maintenance of rights and the orderly settlement of civil disputes. The common benefit is not consciously or deliberately sought by any of these parties individually, but it is served in consequence of the prevailing system of social order, and necessarily so inasmuch as individual ends are deliberately sought according to customary practice and within the recognized framework of social relations.

(2) The second way in which the ideality of sovereignty manifests itself is closely related to the first and is coupled with it in Hegel's exposition. It is the direct control of private professional and business activities by government regulation in those respects required by the public welfare. The common interest, here again, impinges upon and adjusts individual conduct to conform to the requirements of general unity of purpose.

(3) Third, in contrast with the relative individualism of the two preceding manifestations, in times of emergency and crisis when the safety and independence of the whole community is in peril, personal

pursuits are consciously subordinated to national requirements, private interests are sacrificed to common needs and the diverse pursuits of all citizens are unified in the service and defence of the realm. Thus, Hegel assures us, the ideality of sovereignty comes to its own proper actuality.

Karl Marx accuses Hegel of idealizing sovereignty and then "in a mystical way" infusing it into the person of the monarch. Had he started with real subjects, he avers, as the bases of the state, he would not have found this mystification necessary.[7] But such criticism is rooted in misunderstanding of Hegel's use of the term "ideality" and the exegesis given above is sufficient to lay bare Marx's profound misconception. For as we have seen Hegel is not identifying sovereignty with the monarch absolutely, as Marx and Popper imagine,[8] nor is he "idealizing" it in any sense that involves denying its substantial actualization in the persons of both citizens and magistrates, as well as in the functions of government and the Head of State.

Still more gross is the distortion of Hegel's meaning which represents his theory as approving despotism and providing theoretical grounds for totalitarianism. The former he explicitly repudiates, and he does so in a passage which reveals beyond doubt his conception of the state as a system of rights and liberties:

> Thus oriental despotism may, on account of its similarity in that the will of one individual stands at the head of the state, be included under the vague name of monarchy, as also feudal monarchy, to which even the favoured name of 'constitutional monarchy' can not be refused. The true difference of these forms from genuine monarchy rests on the content of valid principles of right which the power of the state actualizes and guarantees. These principles are those, of freedom of property and, over and above that, personal freedom, the civil society, its industry and communities, and the regulated efficiency of official functions dependent on the laws.[9]

What Hegel is propounding is the theory of the rule of law under a constitutional monarchy which, as he himself says, despotism equally with the anarchy of mob rule, abolishes and destroys

> Because the sovereignty is the ideality of all particular authority, the misunderstanding easily arises, and is very common, of taking it for mere might and sheer arbitrary will, giving sovereignty the same meaning as despotism. But despotism means any state of lawlessness, where the particular will as such, be it of a monarch or of a people (ochlocracy) counts as law, or rather replaces law, while, on

the contrary, it is precisely in legal, constitutional systems that sovereignty is the ideality of the particular spheres and functions. . . . [10]

From these passages it is obvious that criticisms of popular government and of the "talk of 'sovereignty of the people' " that appear in the
Rechtsphilosophie (§ 279, § 301, § 308) and in the *Geistesphilosophie* (loc.
cit.) are not directed against constitutional democracy. In the context of
these very criticisms Hegel makes it clear that his objection is to unor-
ganized popular intrusion into the governmental process and not to the
constitutional structures of democratic rule. It is the aggregate of people
as *vulgus* and not the political unity of the people as *populus* that he
excludes. In the *Encyclopaedia* (§ 544) his criticism of the English system
for giving private persons a predominant share in public affairs, whether
merited or not, is immediately followed by the affirmation of the benefits of participation by private citizens in public transactions. Essentially "it is the right of the collective spirit to appear as an overt general
will acting in orderly and express efficacy for the public concern."

The use here of the phrase *allgemeine Wille* is (I suspect deliberately)
reminiscent of Rousseau, and it is precisely Rousseau's distinction between a General Will and a Will of All on which Hegel is anxious to
insist. In his comment on Rousseau in the *Lectures on The History of
Philosophy* he is quite explicit: "The universal will is not to be looked on
as compounded of definitively individual wills, so that these remain
absolute; otherwise the saying would be correct: 'Where the minority
obey the majority, there is no freedom.' The universal will must really
be the rational will, even if we are not conscious of the fact; the state is
therefore not an association that is decreed by the arbitrary will of
individuals."[11] One cannot reasonably doubt, in the light of these
statements, that Hegel's critique is not directed against the conception
of sovereignty of the people as that is advocated by Rousseau, but only
against loose and confused uses of the phrase which identify the people
with a casual association or aggregate, or fail to distinguish such an
aggregate from a genuine community.

Popper's typically wild allegation that Hegel voiced his criticism of
popular sovereignty in order to please the Prussian king, to whom he
was beholden for his academic position,[12] is stultified by the fact that
the last installment of the posthumous essay on the English Reform Bill,
despite its critical character, was suppressed by the Prussian censorship,
because it approved of the genuinely democratic aspect of the advocated

reforms and criticized the Bill for failing to attack the root cause of the former abuses.[13]

The supremacy of the sovereign power of the state, as the highest mundane authority in the nation's internal affairs, in legislating, administering and adjudicating the law, is a patent fact of modern history. There can be no right of defiance or revolt, for right is what the law recognizes and protects. Unrecognized rights may be claimed, but become rights only when legally enforced; and no right of rebellion can be claimed because revolt is itself the abrogation of law and order which, if it succeeds, becomes revolution, the dissolution of the state, and the substitution of a new political authority. For Hegel, if he ever considers its possibility, rebellion is just a rampant political disease and is justifiable in a conquered province because directed against an authority which is strictly illegitimate.[14] In form such rebellion belongs more properly to the sphere of external affairs and comes under the concept of war. To that sphere I shall now turn your attention.

II. International Relations and International Law

In external relations the state is sovereign or it is not a state, and its sovereign status has to be recognized. What is thus recognized is its independence and consequent freedom from subjection to any higher power or political authority. It is *sui juris* and, as sovereign, cannot be made subject to any law. It follows that its relation with other states are limited in form to either agreement, or treaty, entered into by its own will and determined solely by its own interest, or, where agreement fails, enmity and war. It is here that ordnance becomes *ultima ratio regum* and Louis XIV is vindicated. To say this is not to glorify or romanticize war, it is simply to state what is inevitably true so long as states are sovereign. For, as Hegel, in company with Hobbes, quite clearly saw, where no superior authority regulates, the state of nature prevails.[15]

Treaties are observed, therefore, as they are entered into, only subject to the will and interest of the parties. Observance cannot be enforced, and the only sanction against breach is war. About all this Hegel was perfectly clear, and its truth is copiously illustrated in the facts of history.[16] For the sovereign state its own interests are paramount; hence there can be no community of sovereigns because community implies a common interest which takes precedence over the particular interests of members. It is this common interest within the state that makes its sovereign authority supreme and is precisely what Hegel means by its ideality. If states were to become members of an international community, therefore, their sovereignty would be dissolved and some higher sovereignty would take its place. A community of states is thus strictly a contradiction in terms.[17]

International law is not and cannot be the law of a community and it is therefore not properly law, in the political sense of that word. It is not positive law, for it cannot be imposed; it is not effective law because it cannot be enforced. It rests simply on treaty and agreement, subject to the particular wills of the participants, so it cannot regulate treaties or ensure their observance. Its primary principle, *"pacta sunt servanda,"* as Hegel puts it, "goes no further than the ought to be"—it is an empty aspiration. The principle cannot be an article of law because the law is itself treaty which can hardly be the source of its own obligatoriness. In consequence the actual situation, as Hegel tells us alternates between the maintenance of treaty relations and their abrogation.[18]

In actual historical fact treaties are as often broken as observed, if not more often, and no less frequently are they denounced or ignored, as the interests of one party or another dictate. Moreover, the worthiest and most respected of statesmen have pronounced that no obligation to keep a treaty can extend beyond the national interest. Among them were W. E. Gladstone, Theodore Roosevelt, and even Woodrow Wilson, chief architect of the League of Nations Covenant—ostensibly a treaty to end all violations. But that no treaty could serve such a purpose Hegel had been well aware.

Above states (he reminds us) there is no judge or Praetor, no power that can enforce a law or ensure the bond of contract. Enforcement upon a sovereign state is and can but be war; and where agreement fails the settlement of disputes can only be by force. It follows, therefore, as the night the day, that no league or confederation of states can secure peace, for every such association presupposes agreement which itself depends on the particular sovereign wills and national interests. If that agreement fails the alternative is war, to try to prevent which forcibly is no less than to wage it.

The experience of half a century has borne this out in our own age, when the reasons for preventing war and the desirability of maintaining

peace have been immeasurably greater than could have been conceived
in Hegel's time. His analysis still holds good and the mutual conduct of
nations conforms to it to this day.

Kant's vision of perpetual peace involved the establishment of a world
federation, which is precisely the transference of sovereignty from the
nation-state to an international body. But Kant was confused on this
point, for while he clearly understood that states as sovereign cannot
combine into a super-state without contradiction, he contemplated a
"federation (*Föderalismus*) of free states," and he speaks of the federation
as "a compact of the nations with each other," but one of a special kind,
apparently more universal, seeking to put an end to all wars forever, not
just to one. But if such a compact were more universal, Kant shows us no
way in which it is to be made more binding or enforceable. It is to be
called a pacific federation (*Friedensbund*) but will not aim (he says) at
acquiring any of the political powers of a state. It will only be concerned
with the maintenance and guarantee of the freedom of states without
subjecting them to promulgated law and coercion.[19] If that were so,
it could at best be a kind of confederation or league of nations the futility
of which for its avowed purpose we, in our day, know only too well.

Because Hegel refers to the "pacific federation" as a *Staatenbund,*
Popper accuses him of misrepresenting Kant.[20] But the misrepresenta-
tion is Popper's, for Hegel laboured under no misapprehension. He saw
that no such arbitrating authority could have more effect than would be
allowed by the particular wills of sovereigns, the prior agreement of
which it must presuppose, and that it would therefore "remain infected
with contingency."

His insight was corroborated a century later when between the two
world wars of the twentieth century the League of Nations not only
failed in the final outcome, but never genuinely conducted itself as a law
enforcing authority and in no particular instance succeeded in converting
international relations into anything other than power politics. The
same has since been true of the United Nations which, as originally
conceived, was to have been provided with "teeth" to remedy the impo-
tence of the League. The teeth would not have been its own, but those
voluntarily provided by its members and remaining under their control.
Even that, however, was more than the sovereign nations could
stomach, and the organization remains toothless to this day. These bald
statements have been provided with supporting evidence and argument,

not only by myself,[21] but by more authoritative authors. Georg Schwartzenberger has shown that under the aegis of the League and the United Nations relations between the nations have been no other than power politics in disguise.[22] E. H. Carr develops essentially the same thesis in *The Twenty Years' Crisis*,[23] and a similar doctrine is put forward by Bertrand de Jouvenel.[24]

III. War

That power politics is the inevitable character of the intercourse between states is not only shown by the historical record, it is inherent in the nature of sovereignty. The paramount concern of a sovereign state is to maintain its power, for without means of defence its independence is in perpetual jeopardy. Because its neighbors are obsessed with a like concern, because each acts in accordance only with its own will and interest, and because further no state can be trusted indefinitely to keep a treaty, each must regard potential rivals with constant suspicion and vigilance. As one augments its power so must the others keep pace. That national interests in such circumstances inevitably come into conflict is not surprising, and the very existence of a powerful neighbour may be regarded as a threat. Hegel understood all this unerringly.

> A state through its subjects has widespread and many-sided interests and these may be readily and considerably injured; but it remains inherently indeterminable which of these injuries is to be regarded as a specific breach of a treaty or as an injury to the honour and autonomy of the state. The reason for this is that the state may regard its infinity and honour as at stake in each of its concerns . . . and it is all the more inclined to susceptibility the more its strong individuality is impelled as a result of long domestic peace to seek and create a sphere of activity abroad (§ 334, Knox's translation).

Every state, in consequence, seeks to increase its power and to prevent its rivals from gaining an advantage. It becomes, with its rivals and potential enemies, involved in an uncontrollable arms race. All its policies, when carefully investigated, will be found to rest upon and to subserve this fundamental interest in power. All its external activities are power manoeuvres, in one form or another; and the peace while it lasts, is always and only a precarious balance. Today, our political leaders acknowledge this fact in their constant pronouncements of the need to maintain the world balance of power, and their expressions of fear for the maintenance of peace should that balance be unduly disturbed.

A state lacking power has no effectual voice in negotiations with others. "In the world as we find it today," said Prime Minister Neville Chamberlain in 1939, "an unarmed nation has little chance of making its voice heard." And the methods of negotiation involve the persistent use of threats, whether veiled or open usually described euphemistically as "pressure" and necessarily backed by the potential use of force, without which no pressure can be exerted. The result is a continual series of intermittent crises threatening the peace, and the eventual outcome can hardly fail to be open warfare. In short, Clausewitz' dictum in reverse is true of international relations, for here politics is war carried on by other means. Today this is no less true than it was when either Hobbes or Hegel wrote, and both of them understood perfectly the inevitable character of relationships between sovereign states.

To see things as they are is not, however, necessarily to approve of their being so, and to realize the inevitability of war in inter-state relations is not the same as to advocate it. There is nothing in Hegel's doctrine that actually glorifies war and what he writes in its favour is consolation for an unavoidable evil, rather than eulogy.

War, he says, is not to be regarded as an absolute evil, which is far from saying that it is to be welcomed as a positive good. It has an ethical aspect, which even today few would wish to deny, especially those who, in Britain, during the perilous months of 1940 and 1941, experienced precisely what Hegel, in this connexion, perspicaciously describes. When the existence and independence of the nation is endangered, the loyalty and devotion of its citizens are most readily called forth, the sacrifice of private interests to the preservation of the nation is most complete, and the solidarity of the people is most fully realized and most intensely felt. All industrial and professional functions are subordinated to the public need and life itself is held expendable in the national cause. The ethical aspect that Hegel stresses is the aspect of sacrifice and service. He never glorifies (as did Mussolini and Hitler) the destructive and disruptive aspects of aggression. Nor does he hold, with Spengler, that man is by nature a beast of prey, or attempt to condone the element of hate and ferocity that war encourages. He seeks only to insist upon the altruistic virtues and patriotic loyalties that it requires and excites.

That war also involves harsh and undesirable aspects is not denied. It is the negative aspect of the state's external life, the incidence upon it of the Other which must be overcome and somehow reconciled. But as the state, for Hegel, was the ultimate unity of a nation's organized life, the only sublation of this negativity he could contemplate was that provided by world history. Here alone could the ultimate resolution of conflict be achieved in the hegemony of a nation embodying the dialectical phase of development of the *Weltgeist* appropriate to the age. It is for this reason that he saw *die Weltgeschichte als das Weltgericht*.

But in the early nineteenth century war was a very different phenomenon from what it has become in the twentieth. In the eighteenth it had been little more than a dangerous but gentlemanly blood sport. With Napoleon it became more generally destructive, but not until our own time has it developed into a universal disaster. Hegel could still point to mitigating advantages, the stiffening of the national moral fibre, regeneration of the national spirit, and the revitalizing of cooperative solidarity. Today even these by-products are liable to be obliterated by the universality of the holocaust that war occasions.

Hegel knew nothing of atomic bombs and intercontinental ballistics; and, short of these, could he have foreseen high explosives, aerial bombardment, fragmentation bombs, napalm, chemical and bacterial warfare, he might well have concluded, as we should, that the patriotic virtues could be no countervailing advantages. So far as they encouraged bellicosity, they might even themselves become part of the general menace. Could Hegel have foreseen the character of nuclear war as envisaged today by such prognosticators as Herman Khan and Tom Stonier, he would have seen that the very enormity of the terror of modern warfare undermines and corrodes these very virtues—as, for instance, when citizens preparing to protect themselves against nuclear fallout contemplate shooting compatriots who seek to share their forlorn and dubious shelter.[25]

Hegel's general theory of international politics is sound and his insights are penetrating. Contemporary events still exemplify the principles he set out. His doctrine is not, therefore, in this respect obsolete, but the development of nuclear weapons has rendered obsolete the whole structure of politics, national and international, a structure which, nevertheless, the practice of the nations preserves. What is obsolete is not the theory, for sovereignty is still sought, maintained, and recognized, and power politics continue. What has become a self-contradiction is the idea of nuclear war, even as a threat or as a putative means of self-defence, and its use as an instrument of policy.

That it is so used at the present time is patent in the feverish competition among the great powers to develop vaster and more devastating war-heads and more widespread and efficient systems of delivery. "When we deter the Soviets," writes Herman Khan, "by the threat that if they provoke us in a limited war, subsequent reprisals may blow up into an all-out thermonuclear war, we are deliberately or inadvertently using the threat, and therefore the possibility, of nuclear war. When we tell our allies that our Strategic Air Command protects them from Soviet aggression, we are in a sense *using* nuclear war."[26] Yet it is generally admitted that the actual use of these weapons would destroy both attacker and defender, both potential victor and potential vanquished. *Ultima ratio regum* has become *ultimum exitium nationum.* Nevertheless, sovereign states remain in a state of nature, and the practice of power politics, with its debilitation of international law, continues. The eventual outcome is as inevitable as if written by the moving finger upon Belshazzar's wall.

If contemporary mankind could pay closer attention to Hegel's teaching a salutary lesson might still be learned, a lesson that would after all send us back to Kant for salvation and for the solution of international problems. A pacific federation is indeed what is required, but one that will not shrink from acquiring sovereign power and authority. The difficulties in the path of such a project may be formidable and the obstacles to its establishment enormous, but they cannot match the enormity of the alternative. If that fact could be indelibly imprinted on the consciousness of men they would make determined and persistent efforts to overcome those obstacles. This is not the place to suggest ways in which it might be done and I have made the attempt elsewhere.[27] If it were done, and if the efforts reached their goal, *die Weltgeschichte* might indeed produce *ein Weltgericht* with some hope of genuine adjudication and the maintenance of rights. Morality would no longer be irrelevant to world-historical figures operating in an anarchical state of nature where no *Sittlichkeit* prevails, and the rationality of mankind—or, perhaps, no more than the cunning of the universal reason, working through human fear and the instinct of self-preservation—would give a new significance to the pronouncement that the real is rational and the rational real.

NOTES

1. *Grundlinien der Philosophie des Rechts,* para. 279.
2. Ibid., para. 333.
3. London, 1949.
4. Ibid., para. 278.
5. Cf. ibid.: "In former times of feudal monarchy, the state was certainly sovereign in external affairs, but internally neither the monarch nor the state was sovereign." Cf. also *Philosophie des Geistes, Enzyklopädie,* para. 544.
6. *Studies in History and Jurisprudence,* Vol. II (Oxford, 1901), p. 86.
7. Cf. *Critique of Hegel's Philosophy of Right,* trans. Annette John and Joseph O'Malley (Cambridge University Press, 1970), p. 23.
8. Cf. *The Open Society and Its Enemies* (London, 1949), p. 54.
9. *Enz.,* para. 544.
10. *Rechtsphilosophie,* para. 278.
11. E. S. Haldane and F. H. Simpson's trans. (London, 1896) (reprinted, 1968), Vol. III, p. 402.
12. Cf. *The Open Society,* Vol. II, p. 54.
13. Cf. Shlomo Avineri, *Hegel's Theory of the Modern State* (Cambridge University Press), Ch. 11.
14. Cf. *Rechtsphilosophie,* note to para. 281.
15. Cf. Hobbes, *Leviathan,* Ch. 13, and Hegel, *Rechtsphilosophie,* para. 333.
16. Cf. my *Survival of Political Man* (Johannesburg, 1950), Chs. III and IV, and *Annihilation and Utopia* (London, 1966), Chs. V and VI.
17. Cf. idem.
18. *Rechtsphilosophie.*
19. *Zum Ewigen Frieden,* Sec. II, Art. 2.
20. Popper quotes Hegel in Knox's translation, which advisedly uses the phrase "League of Nations," and Popper was writing at a time when the League of Nations set up after World War I had signally failed to prevent World War II.
21. Cf. *The Survival of Political Man,* Ch. V; *Annihilation and Utopia,* Ch. X.
22. Cf. *Power Politics* (London, 1951).
23. London, 1939, 1946.
24. *On Power* (Geneva, 1945; Boston, 1962).
25. "In Las Vegas, J. Carlton Adair, the head of the local civil defence agency announced that a militia of 5000 volunteers would be necessary to protect residents in the event of thermonuclear war against an invasion, not by a foreign enemy, but by refugees from Southern California, who, he said, would come into Nevada like a swarm of locusts. In Hartford, Connecticut, at a private meeting of citizens to consider civil defence, one man maintained that firearms were standard equipment for shelters as a means of repulsing the inroads of people maddened by the effects of wounds or radiation. One's own family, so it was argued, must be protected because there would be only sufficient food and water for them.

Neighbours caught in the open by warning of the attack, who might rush to friends for shelter and assistance must, therefore, be shot down" (*Annihilation and Utopia,* pp. 121f.).

26. *Thinking about the Unthinkable* (London and Princeton, 1962), p. 101.
27. In both of the works cited above. Cf. especially *Annihilation and Utopia,* Pts. II and III.

Hegel and the Nation-State System of International Relations

by
HENRY PAOLUCCI

. . . to bear all naked truths,
And to envisage circumstance, all calm,
That is the top of sovereignty.
John Keats, *Hyperion*

To give my exposition of the Hegelian nation-state doctrine a distinctly Bicentenary focus, I take for its text three sentences of the Declaration of Independence, signed and issued not far from here some 200 years ago—which is to say, almost half a century before Hegel developed the doctrine in his *Philosophy of Right* and lectures on the *Philosophy of History.*

The first sentence of that Declaration, vaguely familiar to everyone, leads us with epic directness into the very midst of the wrongs and rights and counter-rights of international relations. It reads: "When in the course of human events, it becomes necessary for one people to dissolve the political bands which have connected them with another, and to assume among the powers of the earth the separate and equal station to which the laws of nature and of nature's God entitle them, a decent respect to the opinions of mankind requires that they should declare the causes which impel them to the separation." Thus, in the very act of displaying the *might* required for independence, the rebellious colonists also make a bid for recognition of an alleged *right of belligerency* to secure independence.

The penultimate sentence specifies what the signers understand to be the prerogatives of a separate and equal station, on the evident assumption that, with the end of belligerency, *de facto* recognition of independence will rapidly give way to *de jure* recognition, even on the part of Great Britain herself. The long sentence reads:

> We, therefore, the representatives of the united states of America, in general congress, assembled, appealing to the Supreme Judge of the world for the rectitude of our intentions, do, in the name, and by the authority of the good people of these colonies, solemnly publish and declare, that these united colonies are, and of right ought to be free and independent states; that they are absolved from all allegiance to the British Crown, and that all political connection between them and the state of Great Britain, is and ought to be totally dissolved; and that

as free and independent states, they have full power to levy war,
conclude peace, contract alliances, establish commerce, and do all
the other acts and things which independent states of right may do.

That is a fairly complete list of the elements of right that are presumed to
obtain, by mutual recognition, in the nation-state system as Hegel
represents it.

But it is with the final sentence of the Declaration that its claims of
objective right acquire the sanction of what Hegel calls subjective
morality. The sentence reads: "And for the support of this Declaration,
with a firm reliance on the protection of Divine Providence, we mutually pledge to each other our lives, our fortunes and our sacred honor."
With that pledge, the signers acknowledge that they have ceased to be
mere burghers in England's colonial civil society; they have ceased to be
merely private enterprisers pursuing the satisfaction of private needs by
private means; they have become, instead, citizens in the full sense,
prepared to sacrifice their private individuality so that their new union,
in independence, might attain and enjoy a higher individuality of its
own.

According to President Lincoln, the Union which he was to save for
the American people by the sacrifice of 500,000 lives had in fact been
originally formed two years before the Declaration of Independence, by
the Articles of Association in 1774. The pledge of 1776 had confirmed
and matured that union and proclaimed it to the world. "It was further
matured," Lincoln specified, "and the faith of the then thirteen states
expressly plighted and engaged that it should be perpetual, by the
Articles of Confederation in 1778. And, finally, in 1787, one of the
declared objects of ordaining and establishing the Constitution was 'to
form a more perfect Union.' "[1] Perfecting a political union is obviously
a gradual process. A common will professing an abstract right to assume
a separate and equal station is the beginning, but that common will
must be exercised to *produce* a commonwealth of such value that citizens
will willingly sacrifice themselves to *protect* it, with a sense that they
share personally in its life, past, present, and future, as they *direct*
themselves in it toward realization of the highest potencies of human
spiritual freedom.

In Hegel's view, the American people as late as 1820 were still far
from having adequately redeemed, in an external sense, their pledges of
1776 and 1787. On the strength of historical example, he predicted that

the seemingly unbounded Western frontier would have to close before the Americans, pushed back upon themselves, would feel the necessity for a genuine statecraft. Within a generation of Hegel's death, the dialectic of American civil society, of competing economies based on industrial wage-labor and agricultural slave-labor, had plunged the country into a civil war that has since come to be recognized as the forge of true nationhood. But in strictly Hegelian terms, we may presume to say that it was not until the end of the century, with the overseas war against Spain, that the people of the United States assumed in fact the separate and equal station among the powers of the earth which they had abstractly claimed for themselves, as a mere warrant, in 1776.

The war with Spain, it has been said, was a turning point in American history that parallels the fateful decision of Republican Rome to send its armies overseas for the first time—across the Straits of Messina—to confront the colonial power of Carthage in Sicily. Hegel's pre-Hobson analysis of the dialectic that impels a people to pursue material interests beyond its borders—his dialectic of economic imperialism—accounts adequately for both the American and the Roman initiatives. In his doctrine of the nation-state system he stresses, moreover, that there is a direct correspondence between a people's internal development and the pattern of its external relations. Thucydides, Aristotle, and Polybius in antiquity had traced such a correspondence. The internal development of most peoples, they had noted, exhibits a downward pull on the center of governing power that takes it almost inevitably from the one, through the few, to the many, with occasional upward restorations, or balances of separated powers, that may delay, but never completely halt, the devolutionary process. The corresponding discernible pattern of external relations, it was also noted, takes a people through phases of deliberate isolation (no foreign entanglements) and full intercourse with all powers (in peace as well as war) before a time comes, as it came for the Romans after the Third Punic War and for the Russians and Americans after World War II, to decide whether to preserve a balance or seek to bring all international affairs under a single system of enforceable law, as if foreign relations were but an extension of domestic relations.

Such patterned phenomena of internal development and of external relations make up the empirical materials of political history. The task of political science, according to Hegel, is—like that of mathematical astronomy—to trace what rationality there may be in the recurring patterns, and thereby "save" the phenomena with maximum consistency and economy of thought. Yet to succeed in such a task, we cannot presume to approach it with a blank mind. It is not a task for that happily ignorant *tabula rasa* of naive empiricism. "The science of right," Hegel says in the Introduction to the *Philosophy of Right,* "is a section of philosophy. . . . As a section, it has a definite starting-point, i.e., the result and truth of what has preceded, and it is what has preceded which constitutes the so-called 'proof' of the starting-point. Thus the concept of right itself, as it comes to be, falls outside the science of right; it is to be taken up here as given and its deduction is presupposed."[2]

The basis of right is the will, Hegel explains, and "the will is free, so that freedom is both the substance of right and its goal, while the system of right is the realm of freedom made actual, the world of mind brought out of itself like a second nature." But it is not from empirical study of politics and history that we come to know what the will in its essential freedom is. Hegel writes:

> The proof that the will is free, and the proof of the nature of the will and freedom can be established only as a link in the whole chain. The fundamental premises of this proof are that the mind to start with is intelligence, that the phases through which it passes in its development from feeling, through representative thinking, to thinking proper, are the road along which it produces itself as will, and that will, as practical mind in general, is the truth of intelligence, the stage next above it. These premises I have expounded in my *Encyclopedia of the Philosophical Sciences.* . . .[3]

It is thus with his logic, philosophy of nature, and philosophy of subjective spirit in mind—not a *tabula rasa*—that Hegel approaches the objective sphere of right which culminates in the right of nation-states in international relations. The entire substance of the *Philosophy of Right* is presupposed in turn for the philosophic study of history, though here, if our study is not to remain abstract, we must come *prepared* culturally also to recognize the objective characteristics of nationhood in their particularity. "That such or such a specific quality constitutes the peculiar genius of a people," Hegel says, "is the element of our inquiry which must be derived from experience, and historically proved." He then supplies a classic statement, with a very modern stamp upon it, of how objective experience and subjective intellectual preparation are to be linked in an adequate "ratio" of truth. To accomplish this adequation of *intellectus et res,* he says,

presupposes not only a disciplined faculty of abstraction, but an intimate acquaintance with the idea. The investigator must be familiar *a
priori* (if we like to call it so), with the whole circle of conceptions to
which the principles in question belong—just as Kepler (to name an
illustrious example) must have been familiar *a priori* with ellipses, with
cubes and squares, and with ideas of their relations, before he could
discover, from the empirical data, those eternal laws of his, which are
none other than forms of thought pertaining to those classes of conceptions. He who is unfamiliar with the science that embraces those
abstract elementary conceptions, is as little capable—though he may
have gazed on the firmament and the motions of the stars for a
lifetime—of *understanding* those laws, as of *discovering* them.

What are the presuppositions for a philosophical study of history? If the
rationality of history is to be discerned, Hegel specifies, the inquiring
mind must bring to it a "consciousness of freedom and of the phases
which this consciousness assumes in developing itself." Knowing what
freedom is serves to "order" the phenomena of the rise and fall of
history-making peoples in the same way, according to Hegel, that
disciplined knowledge of conic sections and principles of mechanics
serves to order the recurring phenomena of the starry heavens.[4]

Ironically, the two powers that dominate international relations today, the Soviet Union and the United States, seem bent on pursuing
their inter-relations with a manifestly inadequate consciousness of freedom. Their chief ideologues have come by diverse ways to share an
aspiration for enforceable world peace that condemns the traditional
course of international relations as inherently irrational. The Soviet
ideologues, of course, look back to Hegel's great leftist-revolutionary
disciple, Karl Marx, for their case against the nation-state system, while
their American counterparts generally look beyond Marx to Immanuel
Kant and his evolutionary design for perpetual peace. Hegel's non-
prescriptive doctrine, we should note, *accounts* for a periodic surfacing of
all-out drives for peace. It shows, indeed, that by its own inner dialectic
pursuit of an enforceable world peace has in the past led its champions,
in bitter frustration, to recognize the civilized rationality.

Reviewing, from the perspective of inter-state relations, Hegel's account of the course of Western history, with its consciousness of freedom, we began by noting that the ancient Greeks, knowing themselves
to be free, early recognized the value for free men of maintaining a
system of independent states. Their best thinkers saw that, contrary to
oriental preferences for extended rule, a plurality of states is the best

means for actualizing the full potencies of human reason in its practical and productive as well as theoretic spheres of free activity. The trouble with the plurality of Greek states was, of course, that they were all fragments of a single and not very numerous nationality, and therefore no match militarily for a large state like Macedon, once that state came to enjoy the advantages of Greek practical thought through the education of its rulers by Aristotle himself. In his Eastern conquests, moreover, Aristotle's pupil, Alexander, adapted his statecraft to the character of the conquered peoples. Despite his teacher's demonstration of the rationality of a pluri-state system, Alexander pursued the oriental ideal of "one world," graced, however, with at least a veneer of the once-free city-state culture of Greece. But death soon ended Alexander's ambitions, reducing his empire to fragments that proved durable because they defined themselves largely on lines of ancient ethnic differences.

Rome's rise thus took place in a Mediterranean world—a post-Alexandrian world—made up of many states. In its internal development, the city whose first king was believed to be a fratricidal twin nurtured by a wolf underwent most conspicuously a devolution of power from the one to the few to the many. While it was still in progress, the Greek military hostage Polybius was able to predict that Rome's first cycle of devolution would end in mob-rule or absolute democracy at home, sustained by a vast overseas effort to bring the entire world under the exploitive peace or discipline of the Republic's insatiably democratized armies. Great statesmen warned in vain against the demagoguery of fanning populist appetites for an enforceable world peace. Domestic devolution of power needed to be checked, they cautioned, to secure individual freedom against the mob; and similarly abroad, Carthage ought to be preserved at all cost, they advised, so that, fearing foreign conquest, the Roman people might exercise restraint in their factional struggles. But Carthage was destroyed and power at home devolved to the very bottom.

Thereafter, Hegel notes, the relation of Rome "to other nations was purely a relation of force." Under Stoic influence, the Romans became globalists in theory as well as practice. What little "consciousness of freedom" had already manifested itself anywhere was soon sacrificed to the exigencies of an anti-nationalist peace which could be enforced with a *show of right,* as Hegel observes, because the "national individuality of peoples did not, as early as the time of the Romans, excite respect, as is the case in modern times. The various states were not yet recognized as 'legitimated' in the sense of acknowledging each other as real essential existences."[5]

The most freedom-loving people of antiquity were the Jews and Greeks. But even they, Hegel notes, never looked upon themselves as occupying a separate and equal station with respect to other peoples. For the Jews, other people were simply that: *other* people, *gentes,* whose only real distinction, from a Jewish perspective, was that they were non-Jews. Of the Greeks, Hegel says that their very morality "made Hellas unfit to form a common state."[6] Stressing what distinguished one Greek city-state from another, the Greeks abandoned all other peoples indistinguishably to the absolute difference of barbarism. The Romans, on the other hand, with their *jus gentium* derived from close study of the laws of other peoples (to facilitate trade, alliances, war, and imperial assimilation), were initially more respectful of alien cultures. There was lacking, however, any reciprocated sense of equality of station. "Equal right to existence," Hegel says, "entails a union of states, such as exists in modern Europe, or a condition like that of Greece, in which the states had an equal right to existence under the protection of the Delphic oracle."[7]

Though the Romans always professed to respect "Greek independence" and often accorded rights of dual citizenship to Jews of the diaspora, their cosmopolitan peace inevitably hardened into the routine of a vast prisonhouse where inmates and jailors ceased to be distinguishable. It was such a prisonhouse population of Greeks and Romans that finally gave its faith to the Judaic preaching of Christ Crucified. With Christian faith, especially under imperial persecution, came an insightful conviction that pursuit of peace on a global scale, whether in the Assyrian-Persian, or Macedonian, or Roman, or Judaic-Messianic fashion, was essentially demonic; that, in fact, the kingdom of true peace is not of this world. But in time that conviction was lost. Rulers arose in Christendom, first among the Romans and then among their Germanic conquerors, who yearned to enforce a lasting peace at least for the Body of Christ, which is the Church, if not for any merely natural human community. Holy Roman emperors who were often neither holy nor Roman claimed that priestly annointment raised them in temporal authority, as vicars of God the Father on earth, high above the annointers themselves, even as a bishop's election to the See of Peter in Rome raises him in spiritual authority as vicar of God the Son, high above those who elect him. Papal resistence to that claim of imperial divine right without priestly interposition beyond annointment set off a centuries-long struggle to determine who would have the last word in Christendom. In the end, both sides lost. But first it was the imperial statecraft that suffered an almost total fragmentation until, with lines of communication disrupted by incursions of marauding Norsemen, Magyars, and Moors, the only surviving organized power was that of the household or manorial units of feudalism.

"Feudal sovereignty," says Hegel, "is a polyarchy; we see nothing but lords and serfs." Men in virtual isolation, "are reduced to a dependence on their individual power and might, so that every point in the world on which a human being can maintain his ground becomes an *energetic* one." Yet here too a dialectic is at work. Powerful lords, heading large households, subject smaller neighboring households to their management in pursuit of a monopoly of control over the means of securing local independence; but when that measure of control is achieved, economics or household management gives way to politics, in Aristotle's sense of the term. As Hegel sums it up:

> By the arbitrary will of an individual exerting itself so as to subjugate a whole body of men, a community is formed; and comparing this state of things with that in which every point is a center of capricious violence, we find a much smaller number of points exposed to such violence. The great extent of such sovereignty necessitates general arrangements for the purpose of organization, and those who govern in accordance with those arrangements are at the same time, in virtue of their office itself, obedient to the state: vassals become officers of the state, whose duty it is to execute the laws by which the state is regulated.[8]

The unified states that result from this re-integrative process retain in this way the stamp of their feudal origin. The pressure of individualized concern for one's own safety, which is to say, the motive force of feudalism, remains enormous everywhere; and the emergent unified governments must satisfy that concern at the same time that they secure for themselves a local monopoly of coercive power. They must have the consent of the very classes whose independent authority they are in the process of suppressing, for lacking that consent, they risk being overwhelmed by neighbors who have it. What occurs, therefore, is an almost simultaneous crystalization, so to speak, of feudal units into a multiplicity of more or less well-integrated states, ranging from vestigial cities or communes, through duchies and principalities, to vast kingdoms, each manifestly capable of sustaining itself, with respect to the others, in the sort of separate and equal station which the signers of the Declaration of Independence were to claim for the American people in 1776.

The members of this new European "interconnected *system of states*," as Hegel calls it, were not—like the Greeks of the city-states or the Italians of the medieval communes—politically organized fragments of essentially *one* people. Yet they tended to act as if they were, and in relations of war as well as peace. Indeed, out of their wars especially, says Hegel, "there arose common interests," or rather, a "community of interest," the chief object of which was soon determined to be, in his words, the "maintenance of severalty—the preservation to the several states of their independence—in fact the 'balance of power.' " The motive was practical in the feudal sense, with standards of chivalry to be applied now on the political level. In Hegel's words:

> The union of the states of Europe as the means of shielding individual states from the violence of the powerful—the preservation of the balance of power—had now taken the place of that general aim of the elder time, the defence of Christendom, whose center was the papacy. This new political motive was necessarily accompanied by a diplomatic condition—one in which all the members of the great European system, however distant, felt an interest in that which happened to any one of them. Diplomatic policy had been brought to the greatest refinement in [politically divided] Italy, and was thence transmitted to Europe at large.[9]

Challenges to the system came from the imperial designs of Charles V of Spain and Louis XIV of France. They raised great storms; but through it all, Hegel observes, "the nations of Europe succeeded in maintaining their individuality and independence." When Turkish hordes threatened the heart of Europe, there was indeed defensive cooperation, but not a collapse into unity as an end in itself. The system was further strengthened, Hegel adds, by the "struggle of the Protestant Church for political independence," a struggle that culminated in the Thirty Years' War. In that war, the powers of Europe "precipitated themselves on Germany," Hegel writes, "flowing back towards it as to the fountain from which they had originally issued." It is there that the longing for a politically united Christendom is finally shattered. All contending parties in that war emerge from it exhausted. First comes embittered, only tacit acceptance of its chief lesson, which is that the multiplicity of European states has a *de facto* legitimacy that manages somehow to enforce itself. But then comes explicit acceptance of that lesson as validated by the force of history itself, and serious men labor strenuously thereafter to define descriptively the pragmatic balance of rights and responsibilities required to sustain, in conditions of war, as well as peace, such a voluntary association of independent states.[10]

The period of the Thirty Years' War was also the time of the modern scientific awakening. The method of empirical science, with its self-evident organizing principles, its geometric logic, and laboratory models that simplify access to power, was soon applied in the sphere of right, particularly for study of the phenomena of international relations where no one government could claim ultimate jurisdiction. It was a time, says Hegel, when "right and morality came to be looked upon as having their foundation in the actual present will of man," and when "what the nations acknowledged as international right was deduced empirically from observation, as in the work of Grotius."[11] But empirical science is hardly satisfied with merely marshalling facts for induction. It craves to demonstrate that all its marshalled facts, and all other facts of the same order that might yet be marshalled, are really deducible from simple common-sense principles. Thus Newton himself, for instance (as Hegel repeatedly points out), offered to deduce the complexities of terrestrial and celestial motions summed up in the observational laws of Galileo and Kepler from three highly abstract, non-empirical principles of motion. Similarly, one political theorists after another offered to deduce all the complex observable patterns of social behavior from a few allegedly self-evident principles of biological, economic, or moral motivation. But for deducing facts from principles, imaginative or laboratory models with the principles *pre*-built into them (so that the facts *are* as they *ought to be*) inevitably prove to be more serviceable than the uncontrollable complexity of "things as they are." The actuality of the past especially, having no immediate empirical claim on our senses, is particularly disadvantaged when contrasted with a rationalized model of it, fashioned to illustrate a rationalist theory of human conduct. Empiricism and rationalism thus easily demolish the authority of the past and all in the present that demonstrably depends on the past. Together empiricism and rationalism constitute the *force* of enlightenment, which confidently employs itself to sweep the present clean.

In Germany, says Hegel, "enlightenment created a new world of ideas." But in the sphere of human conduct, guided by Kant's rational critiques, the enlightened Germans, in his words, "contented themselves with theoretical abstraction," affirming the principle that the "will making itself its own object is the basis of all right and obligation." Yet the French, guided by substantially the same principle as formulated by Rousseau, "immediately passed over from the theoretical to the practical."[12] What Rousseau defined, Robespierre institutionalized, and Napoleon attempted to impose on all the peoples of Europe. But against Napoleon's armies of global revolutionary enlightenment, the strength of nations in their severalty again asserted itself. The reign of reductionist, abstract reason against history "became bankrupt everywhere," says Hegel; "first, the grand firm in France, then its branches in Spain and Italy." England, Austria, Prussia, the Low Countries, and the peoples of Eastern Europe, as well as Italy, Spain, and France, come out of the experience with a reinforced sense of national identity.[13]

That is the moment when Hegel's *Philosophy of Right* comes to be written. Reason is indeed to be the articulator of truth, but it is to be reason *in* history, not *against* history. Not an abstract laboratory model of a state as it ought to be, artificially constructed by enlightened ideologues, but the historical state itself, with its language and literature, its art, religion, and philosophy, conditioned by the felt presence of many other states, is the actualized "consciousness of freedom" on earth, in Hegel's sense of that term. We need to stress that, in the *Philosophy of Right,* the reality under study, from the beginning, is the system of inter-related nation-states taken, with all its complexities, as a whole. Hegel's exposition is indeed analytical, moving logically from the simple to the complex. But what is simple at the beginning, namely abstract right, is a product of analytical abstraction—pursued to facilitate study of a complex whole. Thus in a trenchant paragraph of his *Encyclopedia,* Hegel outlines the order of exposition pursued in his *Philosophy of Right:*

> We begin with something abstract, namely the notion of the will; we then go on to the actualization of the as yet abstract will in an external existent, to the sphere of formal right; from there we go on to the will

that is reflected into itself out of external existence, to the sphere of morality; and thirdly and lastly we come to the will that unites in itself these two abstract moments and is therefore the concrete ethical will. In the ethical sphere itself we again start from an immediate, from the natural, undeveloped shape possessed by the ethical mind in the *family;* then we come to the *splitting up* of the ethical substance in *civil society;* and finally, in the state, attain the unity and truth of those two one-sided forms of the ethical mind. But this course followed by our exposition does not in the least mean that we would make the ethical life *later in time* than right and morality, or would explain the family and civil society to be antecedent to the state in the *actual* world. On the contrary, we are well aware that the ethical life is the foundation of right and morality, as also the family and civil society with their well-ordered distinctions already presuppose the existence of the state.[14]

In other words, while analytical exposition takes us from the simple to the complex, we need to be aware throughout that the *person* of abstract right, the moral *subject* with rights of conscience, the family *member* with rights of love, and the isolable *burgher* with linked needs in civil society, are but roles distinguishable by analysis in the higher actuality of the *citizen* of a sovereign political community which has articulated an individualized personality of its own.

First and last, according to Hegel, *personality* is the basis of right; hence the imperative of right is: "Be a person and respect others as persons." But the historic truth is that we attain personality as individuals only *after* a "more perfect union" of men—an *e pluribus unum*—has come into being. That is why, as Hegel so convincingly stresses in his *Philosophy of Fine Art,* tragedy with its persons of the drama (*dramatis personae*) is conceivable only in states which, like those of ancient Greece, have manifested a self-conscious personality in relations of separate and equal station with other states.

In the fully matured political community, what we have, according to Hegel, is precisely the "basic moment of personality, abstract at the start in immediate right, which has matured itself through its various forms of subjectivity, and now . . . has become the personality of the state, its certainty of itself."[15] To leave no doubt about his meaning, Hegel says categorically: "A state is as little an actual individual without relations with other states as an individual is actually a person without rapport with other persons."[16] Personality is essentially awareness of one's existence as a unit in sharp distinction from others. It manifests itself on the level of the state as a relation to other states, each of which is autonomous *vis-a-vis* the others. This autonomy embodies mind's actual awareness of itself as a unit and hence it is the most fundamental freedom which a people possesses as well as its highest dignity. . . . Those who talk of the 'wishes' of a 'collection' of people to renounce its political center and autonomy in order to unite with others to form a new whole, have very little knowledge of what a 'collection' is or the feeling of selfhood which a nation possesses in its independence.[17]

As rationally comprehended, says Hegel, a state in its very idea "is entitled in the first place and without qualification to be sovereign from the point of view of other states, i.e. to be recognized by them as sovereign." But this title, he adds, is in itself "purely formal, and the demand for this recognition of the state, merely on the ground that it is a state, is abstract." A unilateral Declaration like that of 1776, we may add, is thus not enough. Whether a new state has independence worthy of *de jure* recognition depends, in Hegel's words, "on its content, i.e. on its constitution and general situation; and recognition, implying as it does an identity of both form and content, is conditional on the neighboring state's judgment and will." There is, of course a sense in which the assertion of independent political authority is an essentially domestic matter, in which foreign states ought not to meddle. Yet it is "no less essential," Hegel insists, "that this authority should receive its full and final legitimation through its recognition by other states, although this recognition requires to be safeguarded by the proviso that where a state is to be recognized by others, it shall likewise recognize them, i.e. respect their autonomy; and so it comes about that they cannot be indifferent to each other's domestic affairs."[18]

That last point is one that Alexander Solzhenitsyn has made in protesting continued "recognition" by Western states of regimes that have committed themselves ideologically to destroy the system of recognition. Implied in true recognition is shared acceptance of the first principle of international customary law, which is, in Hegel's words, that "treaties, as the ground of obligations between states, ought to be kept." The "ought to be" of that principle is what ensures juridical recognition of the continuing independence, in separate and equal stations, of the parties to an international treaty. What inevitably happens, therefore, in a system of independent states is that, as Hegel says, "international relations in *accordance* with treaty alternate with severence of those relations."[19] That is the condition *sine qua non* of true autonomy.

But why not a United Nations Organization with a world court and power enough to enforce treaty obligations so that they cease to be a mere 'ought to be'? Hegel raises the question in terms very like Henry Kissinger's in his inaugural speech as American Secretary of State—an inaugural speech which he chose to address to the United Nations General Assembly. Kissinger there cited Kant as his authority for the kind of enforceable peace he was prepared to help achieve. Hegel also cites Kant, but to an opposite purpose. "Kant," he notes, "had an idea for securing 'perpetual peace' by a League of Nations to adjust every dispute. It was to be a power recognized by each state, and was to arbitrate in all cases of dissension in order to make it impossible for disputants to resort to war in order to settle them." The idea, Hegel continues, "presupposes an accord between states resting on moral or religious or other grounds"; yet obviously, so long as the league remains a mere league, enforcement "would still have to depend ultimately on particularized sovereign wills and for that reason would remain infected with contingency."[20] To eliminate contingency, the league would have to cease to be voluntary and become, juridically, what imperial Rome finally became: a *uniquely* sovereign regime of coldly impersonal might, admitting of no equal.

Hegel's point is that a universal state capable of enforcing global peace is, in its very concept, a *defective* state. It can prevent war while it enjoys a monopoly of coercive power; but it cannot secure its citizens, or rather, subjects, in personal freedom because it is not itself, as a state, free in any meaningful sense. And in the end, even its global dominance without a peer—which is to say its uncheckable and therefore tyrannically irresponsible dominance—must reveal itself to have been illusory. Time will bring it under the judgment of history, where it at once ceases to be perceived as unique. Building a world government today or tomorrow cannot undo the fact that there has been a severalty of states in the past, and that this latest imperial regime without a peer is but another in a long series.

According to the Hegelian analysis, free men make *states* to regulate their freedom; free *states* in turn regulate their freedom not by making "still another" state, however irresponsibly large, but by making *history*, whose court of judgment is indeed a *world* court in the profoundest sense. Above history, transcending the ambitious statecraft of ideologues to interrupt its course with an illusory reign of "perpetual peace," are the absolute time-arresting moments of artistic beauty, religious grace, and philosophic truth in its highest reaches, where beauty, goodness, and truth are one. History rules the nations, but the art, religion, and philosophy in which national genius fully expresses itself in the course of history exercise an ultimate spiritual sovereignty on earth that bows only to heaven.

That, briefly, sums up Hegel's doctrine of the nation-state system of international relations. My concern throughout has obviously been to show how deeply rooted it is in history as well as in his system as a whole. It is a doctrine that accounts for but denies the rational validity of all political aspirations to impose a single law, whether Assyrian, Alexandrian, Roman, Mosaic, Islamic, Holy Roman, Napoleonic, liberal-capitalist, fascist, communist, or nuclear-terrorist, upon the entire world. But it also accounts for and affirms the rational validity of the political realism of the American founding fathers. It confirms their view that government is a necessary evil; that, as the coercive element in the political order, government performs its hard necessities best— which is to say, consistently with personal freedom—when its legitimized local monopoly of power is rationally limited; and that the limitations most supportive of individual freedom are those that are applicable internally, through a separation of powers checked and balanced to preserve them as members or branches of an organic whole, and externally, through deliberate preservation of a system of comparably free states each willfully yet respectfully determined to hold its own in voluntary association.

Such a system of international relation was once limited to Europe. The United States led the way in breaking that European monopoly. Now the system is on the verge of becoming global, admitting to full membership every people sufficiently conscious of freedom, in Hegel's sense, to claim for itself, and then maintain, a truly separate and equal station among the powers of the earth.

NOTES

1. Lincoln's First Inaugural Address, March 4, 1861, cited in *Documents of American History,* H. S. Commager, ed., New York, 1948, Vol. 1, p. 385.
2. *Hegel's Philosophy of Right,* T. M. Knox, trans., Oxford, 1956, P. 2, § 2. This work is hereafter cited as *Ph. R;* translations adapted slightly in accordance with German text (Gans 1933, 1952), making use also of the translation by S. W. Dyde (London, 1896).
3. *Ph. R,* pp. 20-21, § 4.
4. *Hegel's Philosophy of History (Ph. H),* J. Sibree, trans., New York, 1956, pp. 64-65. Translations adapted slightly in accordance with German text (Lasson, 1930).
5. *Ph. H,* p. 308.
6. *Ibid.,* p. 265.
7. *Ibid.,* p. 308.
8. *Ibid.,* p. 399.
9. *Ibid.,* pp. 430-32.
10. *Ibid.,* pp. 432-34.
11. *Ibid.,* pp. 440-41.
12. *Ibid.,* pp. 442-44.
13. *Ibid.,* pp. 452-53.
14. *Hegel's Philosophy of Mind* (Part III of *Enzyklopädie*), W. Wallace and A. V. Miller, trans., Oxford, 1971, p. 130, § 408.
15. *Ph. R,* p. 181, § 279.
16. *Ibid.,* p. 212, § 331.
17. *Ibid.,* p. 208, § 322.
18. *Ibid.,* pp. 212-13, § 331.
19. *Ibid.,* p. 213, § 333.
20. *Ibid.,* p. 214, § 333.

COMMENT ON

Harris's "Hegel's Theory of Sovereignty, International Relations, and War"

and

Paolucci's "Hegel and the Nation-State System of International Relations"

JOSEPH C. FLAY

Professor Harris and Professor Paolucci have offered us two interesting papers on Hegel's theory of the state and of international relations. But they are no less interesting than they are radically different from each other both in form and intent and in content. In my remarks I shall address myself in three stages to what they have argued. First I shall offer my objections to Professor Paolucci's paper, especially to the "Bicentennial thrust" and what this reveals about his interpretation of Hegel. Second, I shall suggest a way in which I think that Professor Harris's analysis can be extended to make a more philosophically satisfactory case for an extension to Hegel's analysis, given the extension in history which has stood between Hegel and ourselves. Finally, I must, for the purposes of philosophical honesty, offer a caveat to my remarks, a caveat on the issue of the overall validity of Hegel's theory in the context of his system of philosophical sciences.

I

Most of what Professor Paolucci has to say about Hegel is this paper would appear on the face of it to have validity. However, if we take note of his opening remarks about the relation between Hegel and the "Founding Fathers," and then note also his summary remarks at the end of the paper concerning the same matter, as well as the way in which he conceives of the "supra-national" state, it becomes apparent, at least to me, that we have here a very strange Hegel.

First of all, I would argue that such a link between Hegel and the American state cannot be forged, simply because that state was founded upon and still today reflects the social contract theory of the British, a theory refused by Hegel throughout his nature writings. The atomistic individualism on which that theory and that society are based is directly counter to Hegel's analysis of the state in the *Philosophy of Right,* the *Encyclopedia,* and the *Lectures on the Philosophy of History.* And we can be certain that Professor Paolucci has no special interpretation of the American state in mind, for at the end of his paper he becomes specific concerning the nature of the American state. He affirms in his paper what Hegel's doctrine

> accounts for and affirms the rational validity of the political realism of the American founding fathers. It confirms their view that government is a necessary evil; that, as the coercive element in the political order, it performs its hard necessities best—which is to say, consistently with personal freedom—when its legitimized local monopoly of power is rationally limited; and that the limitations most supportive of individual freedom are those that are applicable internally, through a separation of powers checked and balanced to preserve them as members or branches of an organic whole. . . .

This view clearly reflects the context of orthodox social contract and its essentially negative stand toward the state and the government; whereas the state, for Hegel, is not negative in that manner, but rather is the dialectical development of the Greek view of the polis.

Second, Professor Paolucci finds it "ironic" that American thinkers who make a case against the nation-state system look "to Immanuel Kant and his evolutionary design for perpetual peace." But surely there is nothing ironic about this; rather, it is a simple logical and dialectical necessity, since Kant never got completely beyond the abstract understanding of British political theory and of British empiricism in general. He therefore furnishes a natural "idealism" (in the non-Hegelian sense) on which to base an "ought" with no grounds in actuality.

From an Hegelian point of view the United States necessarily remains in *Existenz* at a very low level of the actualization of the State, for the atomistic individualism on which it was theoretically based still stubbornly stands reflected in the actuality of both civil society and the state. If we use the American Declaration of Independence for our "text," as Professor Paolucci intends, then we must ideologize Hegel's theory of the state and thereby violate the philosophical validity of Hegel's system. To use Hegel to "affirm" and "confirm" one view or another (as opposed to simply comprehending actuality) is to do what he explicitly proscribes in his political writings. Thus I must conclude that the validity that appears on the surface of Professor Paolucci's paper does not belong to it in reality.

II

In contrast, Professor Harris has given us a sound analysis of Hegel's views and has attempted to show that, philosophically (as opposed to ideologically), there are some changes to be brought to the Hegelian system in light of historical developments since Hegel's time. At the heart of Harris's analysis of Hegel is his characterization of the three forms in which the ideal unity of sovereignty operates—a far cry from Professor

Paolucci's contention that "the least government is the best." What one must do here—and what Harris has done well—is to comprehend correctly the category of "Ideality" as it is articulated in the *Science of Logic* and thus as it must be employed and understood in any of the other philosophical sciences. This is of course true of all Hegelian categories and the way they contribute to a comprehension of actuality. This particular category of "Ideality" will be important in a moment, when I shall suggest a way in which Hegel must necessarily and dialectically be developed.

A second important point made is that concerning "the general will" and how it is distinguished from the will of all and the will of the majority. I would think that Professor Harris's paper could benefit from a more detailed analysis of Hegel's rise above Rousseau on this matter.

But I should like to concentrate on the thrust of Professor Harris's paper, viz., to suggest a way in which, given Hegel's analysis of international relations and war, we can philosophically develop that theory in light of historical developments which have altered both the existential and the actual constitution of international relations. Professor Harris in large part proceeds from the outside, i.e., from the perspective offered by the horror and absurdity of contemporary wars. I should like to proceed from the inside, from an analysis of Hegel's own point of view and on the basis of a very important conditional on which his whole argument is based. The conditional occurs in paragraph 334 of the *Philosophy of Right*. In the paragraph preceding, Hegel cites the fundamental proposition of international law to be "that treaties, as the ground of obligations between states, ought to be kept. . . . The universal proviso of international law therefore does not go beyond an ought-to-be. . . . " He then continues in paragraph 334: "It follows that if states disagree and their particular wills cannot be harmonized, the matter can only be settled by war." In paragraph 340 in this same section on International Law Hegel summarizes his view of the relations between states.

> It is as particular entities that states enter into relations with one another. Hence their relations are on the largest scale a maelstrom of external contingency and the inner particularity of passions, private interests and selfish ends, abilities and virtues, vices, force and wrong. All these whirl together, and in their vortex the ethical whole itself, the autonomy of the state, is exposed to contingency.

I think that this is an accurate analysis of the nineteenth-century western world and, given Hegel's categories, his conclusions from the conditional are correct. Thus it is true for Hegel that the general wills of the several states constituting history were still such that they could be isolated from each other to a large extent—to the extent that war could be avoided and treaties kept most of the time. But I would now like to put Professor Harris's point about the change in historical actuality in the following way: general wills and thus nation states are no longer isolable in this fashion. And this is due not to some external change in relations between states, but to the fact that there is now hardly a facet of the realities constituting the actuality and ideality of our nation states which does not entail directly in its own meaning the immediate general wills of other states. This means that the actuality and ideality of international relations are no longer the matter of external contingency they once were and to which Hegel looked to discover the rationality of international relations. Let me expand on this.

States are in their Being the realities which constitute the ideality of history as concrete; in their Essence they constitute the reciprocity of the absolute relation in this sphere of science. Thus, both in their Being and in their Essence (and whether we consider sovereignty or the interrelation of states in history) the abstract analytic of the understanding consciousness of British theory—and thus of the founding fathers—is totally inadequate to the truth. In the case that the several idealities and actualities of nation-states enter into contingent relations, no general will of international relations can arise, and Hegel's view is sufficient. But in the case (which is our own contemporary case) that the several general wills are inextricably and necessarily bound up with each other, on economic as well as on social and political grounds, then there arises a configuration of relations which are not contingent, but which are necessary in Hegel's sense of Absolute Necessity. There is literally nothing in the general will of one nation-state today which is not a real moment of the general will of every other nation-state. International relations are therefore different and the Hegelian analysis, on Hegel's own terms, no longer holds.

Thus, the bare concept (in the Hegelian sense) of an international unity is now at hand which was not accessible to Hegel. The concept of "balance of power" is no longer an actuality, but an *aufgehobene* moment. It is no longer the case that *at times* conflicts *can* or *might* occur; it is now *always* the case that they *necessarily* occur. A bare concept of international unity now rests upon the historical emergence of the bare concept of the general will of international relations. We must acknowledge and act in accordance with this bare concept and thus transform it into the Idea which it must inevitably become.

A unity in international relations is not the emergence of a supra-state. This is still not possible given that Hegel's analysis of the state is correct. What emerges is something different from a state, but which is nevertheless in some way analogous to the state. It would remain to work out in the Concept what this unity would be. But that it is neither a state nor a Kantian league of nations is clear from the start.

In summary, then, I think that a philosophical analysis of the nature of the several general wills which constitute international relations today yields a dialectical (and essentially Hegelian) revision to the theory of International Relations between nation-states. The ideality of the sovereignty of one state in relation to that of another state or states is no longer the external affair it was in Hegel's time. Because of the development of economic, social, and political relations *within* the independent nation-states, there is an internal relation, in regard to content as well as to form, existing *between* the independent general wills of independent nation-states. This does not involve a dispute with Hegel's theory, only a philosophical dialogue with it, and in terms of his own categories and of his own comprehension of how categories should properly be applied to the various subject-matters of the philosophical sciences. I conclude therefore that a non-ideological, philosophical analysis of Hegel's theory in light of present historical actuality yields a category of the Philosophy of Right which was not explicitly present within Hegel's own analysis, but which follows from it. The "newborn" child whose entrance into world history Hegel heralded, the new epoch, has grown a bit and has revealed aspects of itself not apparent at its birth.

III

But I must now add to all of this Hegelian analysis in which I have engaged a shadow of a doubt. I have, in responding to these two papers, carefully employed Hegel's own language and meaning. Several times I have added a phrase to my comments, to the effect that something followed *if* Hegel's system were adequate or correct. I must now explain that I did this because I have some doubts that the system, beyond the *Science of Logic,* is valid. Both of these papers intended to address themselves to problems within parameters acceptable to Hegel's sciences of the *Philosophy of Spirit.* To respond to them from a perspective outside of these parameters would have been non-dialectical and question-begging. And so my remarks were based on the proviso that in his move from the science of logic to the other philosophical sciences Hegel did nothing non-dialectical. I think, on the contrary, that a lacuna exists between these parts of the system of philosophical sciences and that, therefore, until we ascertain precisely the nature of this break in the system of sciences, we shall not be able to judge forcefully the validity of the analyses given in the philosophical sciences of nature and spirit.

COMMENT ON

Harris's "Hegel's Theory of Sovereignty, International Relations, and War"

and

Paolucci's "Hegel and the Nation-State System of International Relations"

PAUL THOMAS

In responding to the papers of Professors Harris and Paolucci, I find myself in the curious position of, on the one hand, having no substantive disagreements with anything they say—which I am prepared to endorse heartily—and, on the other hand, of wishing to extend the terms of the discussion. What I should like to do is to indicate what I take to be a connection—a little observed one, but a connection nonetheless—between what Hegel says about war (which both Professor Harris and Professor Paolucci discuss) and what he says about civil society (which is treated more fully by Professor Harris).

Professor Harris indicates that sovereignty in Hegel's *Philosophy of Right,* while it is something represented or personified in the figure of the monarch, operates in actual fact in three ways. *First,* it operates in and through the principles of order or common interest underlying *die bürgerliche Gesellschaft.* The commonality of interest is both cause and consequence of the system of (broadly) economic activity in civil society.

The *second* sense in which sovereignty is said to operate seems not to be sharply distinguished from the first; it consists in "control of private professional and business activities." I hope I am not untrue to Professor Harris' own distinction between these two expressions of sovereignty in choosing to portray it as a distinction between state action (the *second* respect) and a Montesquienian *esprit générale* (the *first* respect) which is both cause and consequence.

The *third* way in which sovereignty is expressed and made manifest in Professor Harris' view is more hypothetical or contingent. In times of emergency, private interests, Hegel tells us, are more or less readily sacrificed to the common weal. The question here is what is the nature of the emergency and whether it is generated externally (by war) or internally (by civil discord). In fact, it seems with Hegel—who lived through the French Revolution—to be generated, or is capable of being generated, by *both.* War, he insists, *inter alia* shows up or points up the relativity of the goods and goals pursued in civil society; that is, as Professor Harris' criteria, number three points up the ultimate relativity (if one can speak of ultimate relativity) of number one, if not number two. This I take to be a point of some considerable importance to which I shall return presently, but it is not the only such point. If we take civil discord, Hegel makes it clear that there is, so to speak, a dynamic within civil society and its "system of needs" which tends and leads, *ceteris paribus,* to social dislocation of a certain type. I shall return to this, too, in a moment; suffice it to say, in a preliminary sense, that in Hegel's account of civil society, luxury and indigence tend to proceed in parallel and proportionately one to the other; and the problem of poverty in the modern state, in particular, as Hegel admits, is acute and may be actually incapable of solution.

Before proceeding to these points, I feel I should indicate at this juncture that my comments are concerned, not with the three areas of sovereignty Professor Harris has outlined, but with the relationship among them, which may be a closer one than has seemed apparent to many of Hegel's commentators.

Hegel's own argument on the ethical aspect (or ethical *Moment,* in the German sense of the word) of war, an argument which *is* an attack on the Kantian *Friedensbund,* and is *not* remotely militaristic, is, I suggest, more pointed with respect to Hegel's depiction of civil society than Professor Harris perhaps allows. And it is also more pointed chronologically. Here Professor Paolucci puts the picture into focus, and I should like to register my agreement with what he says—with the minor reservation that there seems to me to be a rather important distinction between the bearing of the American Revolution and that of the French Revolution. The American Revolution, in spite of its resonance in pre-revolutionary France, was anything but a revolution *for export.* But the same cannot be said for the French Revolution which, from the time of Brissot's curdling and crusading declaration of principles, most certainly *was* a revolution for export, as Kant (whose response Hegel attacked) was readily aware. Hegel himself had first-hand experience of this exported revolution, as the well-known story of the relationship of the proofs of *The Phenomenology of Mind* to the battle of Jena bears witness. But overlap in time is not the whole story. The French Revolution represented something altogether unprecedented to Hegel not simply *because* it was the first real revolution for export, but also by virtue of the *reasons why* it became one.

As Hegel himself put it, in Professor Paolucci's citation, the French "immediately passed over from the theoretical to the practical." The word "immediately," as usual with Hegel, does not simply mean "instantly." The sentence which tells us that "what Rousseau defined, Robespierre institutionalized and Napoleon attempted to impose on all the peoples of Europe" is one I would call too telescoped. What Hegel means by "immediately" is also "lacking in mediation," or lacking in the felt need *for* mediation; and this gives his critique of Kant (the possibly unlikely "theoretical counterpart" of the French Revolution) added bite. War, to the French Revolutionists, may justifiably be fought for the sake of "the rights of man," their securing and their extension. This revolutionary argument is the more obverse—at least in terms of abstraction—of Kant's argument for perpetual peace which, it is argued, may be (as it were) waged for the same ends.

Hegel, to his eternal credit, pointed out in his defense of war that war, by its very nature, must necessarily offend against every single "right of man"; to the extent that it fails to guard against the onset of wars, Kant's scheme for "perpetual peace" can be condemned in the same breath. But be this as it may: it seems to me that Hegel's argument on war has a great deal of substance to it as well as a welcome conceptual clarity; and here I seem to be in complete agreement with Professors Harris and Paolucci. However, Hegel's argument amounts to a telling denial that war can be justified by the utilitarian motives of the defense of life and property; it is absurd to demand that men sacrifice, in the act of war, the very things toward the "preservation" of which it is waged in the first place (*Philosophy of Right*, § 324: Knox, pp. 209-10). This would base war, not upon the states that actually wage it, but upon civil society; and this Hegel resolutely refused to do. Hegel's justification—force is a moment of right—is quite different from any argument that would reduce war in this way to the level of civil society. War, he tells us, is "ethical" (*Sittlich*) in as much as it *exposes* the accidental, the arbitrary, the finite in everyday life; and the point here, I take it, is not just that Hegel is sanguine about war in much the same way that Marx is sanguine about *class* war, although both could, I think, be referred back to the Ancients' belief that war (particularly war without greed) calls forth civic virtue, the highest political ethos. The point is, really, that *the realm of the accidental, the finite, the arbitrary is precisely civil society itself* as Hegel outlines it.

This, it seems to me, leads into a point of some considerable importance. War to Hegel is important not simply because, in the words of George Bernard Shaw's *Man and Superman*, "when the military man approaches, the world locks up its spoons," for war's effect of highlighting the relativities of civil society is *not* an incidental by-product of its incidence. Hegel is talking about something much more fundamental. War is not just *an* integrative institution, it is *the* significant integrative institution of the modern state. It does what the French Revolution wanted to do but failed to carry out until *it* turned to war; it helps us focus on one another. The French revolutionaries had thought—wrongly, as Hegel was well aware—that participation could provide this mutual focus; Hegel insists that war alone can do so. War has an ethical value in the sense that the internal order guaranteed by the state has something to define itself *against;* this order is, in other words, connected to and dependent upon the existence of outer chaos. It's a serious mistake, in my opinion, to depict Hegel as saying that the outer chaos signified by war is a sphere of irrationality defeating the achievements of Reason in civil society; for, whether we like it or not, the opposite is the case, at least according to Hegel. The possibility of war—which is a probability, all things considered—serves to dry up potentially stagnant pools of irrationality in civil society; war, which "preserves the ethical health of peoples," in Hegel's words, is compared to the "blowing of winds preserving the sea from the foulness which would be the result of a prolonged calm" (§ 324, p. 210). This, of course, is a hit at Kant; it is perpetual peace that leads away from morality to corruption. Increasingly settled expectations in a liberal market society, where not all injustices are visible, and where class differences and pauperism are rampant, will lead to an abuse of justice on the part of the rich; this undermines everything orderly, on which *all* the rational expectations of civil society depend. And these orderly expectations *need undermining,* by war.

Let me, in conclusion, put these points into context. Theorists such as Hobbes, Locke, and Kant all, in their various ways, contribute to a certain liberal vision of "the sublimation of politics" (to use Sheldon Wolin's happy phrase). The argument is this: commerce breeds peace. Because of this the dilemmas of politics are solved. The state, standing in between the promise of justice and social order, on the one hand, and the menace of war, on the other, is integrated into a more comprehensive set of relationships based on the peaceable market. But, says Hegel, the market isn't peaceable in the required sense; it may be systematic, but this is something else again. The hypocrisy of the liberal model, Hegel is telling us, caricatures the moral possibilities of social realities. Commerce does not sublimate politics; it exemplifies conflict. Neither does politics sublimate commerce. But war does. Commerce is shown up, and torn from its illusions of peace by war—war which is, with Hegel, as class war was to be with Marx, a moral resource. It establishes the identity of a people, and it serves in this way the purpose of an integrative rationality, the need for which Hegel had outlined in the *Phenomenology.* The function of war, I am suggesting, is analogous to the function of the paradigmatic "struggle for recognition" in the *Phenomenology,* and, by extension, to the function of class war in Marx. Hegel, as I put it at the American Political Science Association convention—somewhat vividly but, I believe, not inaccurately, is *advocating violence.* His reasons for doing so connect directly with his depiction of civil society, which breeds extravagance and want, luxury and penury, in proportion to each other. Poverty is not an accidental by-product of the regular operation of civil society, Hegel was writing at a time when the "unincorporated poor," as they were called, were beginning to constitute a numerical majority in many German states, including Prussia. In Hegel's view, the rabble of paupers, the *Pöbel,* was the other side of the coin of luxury. The decadence of the rich increases in tandem with the degradation of the poor; both are a species of social degeneration, and both are intrinsic to the smooth and regular operation of civil society. The question is how under such circumstances can anything integrative exist at all? The answer is war: "under its agency the ethical health of peoples is preserved in their indifference to the stabilization of finite institutions." War undermines complacency. "Property and life," says Hegel, "should be definitely established as accidental. . . . The rights and interests of individuals are established as a passing phase. . . . War . . . deals in earnest with the vanity of temporal goods and concerns."

Hegel's Concept of Marriage and Family: The Origin of Subjective Freedom

by

RUDOLF J. SIEBERT

It is the aim of this study to explore, analyze, and critically evaluate Georg W. F. Hegel's philosophy of marriage and family.[1] Hegel's philosophical concept of the family reaches from his *Early Theological Writings,* the *Jenaer System Fragments,* and the *Phenomenology of Spirit,* over the *Philosophical Propedeutic,* the *System of Philosophy,* the *Philosophy of Right,* and the *Philosophy of History,* to the *Aesthetics* and the *Philosophy of Religion.*[2] The particular goal of this paper is to demonstrate to what extent for Hegel the family is the origin, the realization, and the protector of man's subjective freedom or his free subjectivity.[3] This question seems to be of utmost importance at the present stage of the world historical transition period from the old European civilization to a new post-modern culture, the beginning of which Hegel already predicted in the preface of his *Phenomenology of the Spirit,* and which continues today, and which is characterized by a powerful trend toward the totally administered society and toward the end of the dignity and freedom of the individual.[4] It is the intent of this essay to answer this question concerning the beginning and realization of subjective freedom in marriage and family in the context of Hegel's view of man's liberation history.[5] We will proceed dialectically from historical macrology to social micrology, from world history to its smallest and empirically most concrete units—marriage and family and the individual human subject.[6]

Particularity

According to the social philosopher Hegel, the right of the human subject to find himself or herself satisfied in his or her particularity—or which is the same, the right of subjective freedom of free subjectivity—constitutes the turning and center point in the differentiation between Greek and Roman antiquity and modern time.[7] This right of the particularity of the subject in its infinitude has been expressed in Christianity. Through Christianity, this right has been made into the universal, real principle of a new form of the world—medieval and modern Europe. To the concrete formation of this principle of subjective freedom belong romantic love, the purpose of the eternal happiness of the individual, as well as personal morality, including individual resolution and guilt, intention and well-being, goodness and conscience. The principle of free subjectivity is further concretized in the individualism of early civil society and as moment in the constitution of civil states as well as generally in modern world history, in political history, but particularly also in the modern history of art, religion, science, and philosophy.[8] Likewise, the principle of free individuality is present in the modern European form of marriage and family.[9]

Dialectics of Love

According to Hegel's *Philosophy of Right* of the year 1821, the family is the immediate substantiality of man's spirit.[10] It is the self-feeling unity of human spirit. As such, the family has love for its essential determination. In the family, it is the intent of the individuals to have the self-consciousness of their individuality in this self-feeling unity, in this love, as a reality, which is in and for itself. In the family, the individuals no longer want to exist as persons for themselves as they do in the area of abstract right characterized by property, contract, and punishment for injustice, or as mere isolated subjects with their private resolutions, intentions, conscience, or as bourgeois for themselves, as they do in the sphere of civil society determined by need system, administration of justice, police and corporation, but as real social members, living with each other.[11]

In Hegel's socio-ethical perspective, love is the consciousness of my unity with another.[12] In love I am no longer isolated for myself. In love I gain my self-consciousness and come to myself and am with myself and am therefore free only through the abandonment of my being-for-myself and through my knowing myself as the unity of myself with the other and of the other with myself.[13] For Hegel, love is first of all feeling. As such, love is social morality in the form of the natural. Love as feeling and therefore as something natural, in Hegel's view, no longer exists in the realm of objective spirit beyond the level of the family, that is, in civil society or the state.[14] In the dimension of civil society, the selfishness of the bourgeois prevails, which excludes love.[15] In civil society, every individual is his own purpose. For each individual, the others are either nothing or merely means for the purpose of his own particularity. In the dimension of the state, the citizens are aware of their unity in the form of law.[16] Here the political content must be rational, not in terms of instrumental, but rather of substantial rationality.[17] The citizens must know this rational content of the law and of the state to which they belong.

In Hegel's perspective, the first moment in the totality of love is that the individual no longer wants to be an independent person, subject, or bourgeois for himself.[18] In case the individual would be such an isolated person, subject, or bourgeois, he would feel insufficient and incomplete. The second moment in the totality of love is that the individual gains himself in another individual; that he finds his validity in the other individual; that the other individual finds her validity in him. Because of those two moments, the totality of love is for Hegel the most enormous contradiction. According to Hegel, the understanding of the positive social sciences cannot solve this contradiction of love.[19] It cannot comprehend the totality of love. It can merely understand the external conditions under which the process of love can commence and proceed. Only positive dialectical reason can comprehend love in its contradictory totality.[20]

Love is such an immense contradiction, since in its totality the punctuality of the self-consciousness of the individual—there is nothing harder than this in the world—is negated and at the same time also affirmed.[21] Love is the production and the solution of this contradiction of the negation and affirmation of the self-consciousness of the individual. This is the dialectics of love. Love, as the solution of this contradiction, is the dialectical ethical unity of the individuals. In this dialectical unity, the individuals not only lose their abstract self-consciousness, but also gain their concrete, subjective freedom. The dialectics of love is the source and medium of the development of free personality.

Right

In Hegel's socio-ethical view, the right—which is due to the individual on the basis of the family unity and which is first of all his life in this totality itself—takes the form of right as the abstract moment of the definite individuality only insofar as the family disintegrates and goes over into the sphere of civil society and state.[22] In this process of familial disorganization, the individuals who ought to exist as members in the family become independent persons, subjects, bourgeois, and citizens in their mind as well as in their reality. What the individuals made out in the family as determinate moment in its totality—the familial property, alimony, costs for education, etc.—they receive now in the separation from the family according to its external aspects.

According to Hegel, the right of the family consists really in the fact, that its substantiality should have external existence.[23] It is, therefore, a right against the externality of nature, civil society, and state. It is a right against the individuals leaving the unity of the family. Contrary to the right of the family, love is again a feeling, something subjective, against which the familial unity cannot give validity to itself. If, therefore, unity is demanded in the family, then this can happen only in relation to such things, which by their very nature are external, and as such belong to the sphere of familial property, and are as such not conditioned by feeling, by love. Right is powerless versus the love of the individuals who constitute the family.

Taking into consideration the moments of familial love and right, we are now able to determine the notion of the family as it presents itself in Hegel's social philosophy.[24] According to Hegel, the family develops itself in three aspects. First, the family realizes itself in the form of its immediate notion as marriage. Second, the family evolves in the external existence, in the familial property and possession and in the care for it. Third, the family completes itself in the education of the children and in its transition and disintegration into society, state, and history. For Hegel, the family is not only an integral part of the social totality. His social ethics is more than state ethics. For Hegel, the family is a social totality in itself and in its own right. The moments of marriage, familial property, and education of children constitute this totality of the family. I concentrate on the emancipation of the individual in the spheres of marriage, family property, and child education.

Subject–Object

Already in his early theological writings of 1797, 23 years before the philosophy of right, the twenty-seven-year-old Hegel is concerned with the loving emancipation of the individual in marriage and family.[25] According to the young Hegel, true union or love proper exists only between living subjects who are alike in power, and thus, in one another's eyes, living beings from every point of view. In no respect is either individual dead for the other. This genuine love excludes all oppositions. Love is not the understanding, whose relations always leave the manifold of related terms as a manifold and whose unity is always a unity of opposites which are left as opposites.[26] Love is not negative dialectical reason either, because such reason sharply opposes its determining power to what is determined.[27] Love neither restricts nor is it restricted.[28] It is not finite at all. It is infinite. It is a feeling. But it is not a single feeling among other single feelings. A single feeling is only a part and not the whole of life. The life present in a single feeling dissolves its barriers and drives on till it disperses itself in the manifold of feelings with a view to finding itself in the totality of this manifold. This whole life is not contained in love in the same way as it is in this sum of many particular and isolated feelings. In love, life is present as a duplicate of itself and as a single and unified self. Here life has run through the circle of development from an immature to a completely mature unity. When the unity was immature, there still stood over against it the world and the possibility of a cleavage between itself and the world. As development proceeded, reflection produced more and more oppositions, unified by satisfied impulses, until it set the whole of man's life in opposition to objectivity. Finally, love completely destroys objectivity and thereby annuls and transcends reflection. It deprives man's opposite—the world—of all foreign character. It discovers life itself without any further defect. In love, the separate does still remain, but as something united and no longer as something separate. Life in the subject senses life in the object. Subject and object are united in the mutual sensing of each other's life.

The Lovers

In his early theological writings, Hegel determines love as the subject's sensing of something living in the object.[29] According to Hegel, lovers can be distinct only insofar as they are mortal and do not look upon this possibility of separation as if there were really a separation or as if reality were a sort of conjunction between possibility and existence. According to Aristotle, natural objects are composite of matter, that is, mere inactive and inactual potentiality, and of form, intelligible actuality.[30] In the lovers, there is no matter. They are a living totality. To say that the lovers have an independence and a living principle peculiar to each of themselves means only that they may die and may be separated by death. To say in positivistic biology that salt and other minerals are part of the make-up of a plant, and that these carry in themselves their own laws governing their operation, is the judgment of external reflection. It means no more than that the plant may rot. But love strives to annul even this distinction between the lover as lover and the lover as a physical organism. Love tends to annul this possibility of separation between the lover as such and the lover as organism as a mere abstract possibility. Love wants to unite with itself even the mortal element within the lover—the organism—and to make it immortal. For Hegel, the idealist, it is impossible to assume that the consciousness of the lovers may be as mortal as their bodies.

Shame

If the separate element persists in either of the lovers as something peculiarly his own before their union is complete, it creates a difficulty for them.[31] The lovers have a problem if either of them does not surrender himself completely to his beloved. He is, as it were, dividing himself into separate compartments. He is reserving one of those departments for himself and thereby deprives the other lover of it. There is a sort of antagonism between surrender or the only possible cancellation of opposition in complete union on one hand and a still subsisting independence on the other hand. Union feels the latter as a hindrance. Love is indignant if part of the individual is reserved and held back as a private property. This raging of love against exclusive individuality is shame. Shame is not a reaction of the mortal body. It is not an expression of the freedom of the individual to maintain his life, to subsist. The hostility in a loveless assault does injury to the loving heart itself. The shame of this now injured heart becomes the rage which defends its right, its property. If shame, instead of being an effect of love—an effect which only takes an indignant form after encountering something hostile—were something itself by nature hostile which wanted to defend an assailable property of its own, then we would have to say that shame is most of all characteristic of despots, or of girls who will not yield their charms except for money, or of vain women who want to fascinate. None of these really love. Their defense of their mortal body is the opposite of indignation about it. They ascribe an intrinsic value to their mortal body and are therefore shameless.

Romantic Love

According to the young Hegel, a pure heart is not ashamed of love.[32] But it is ashamed of its love being incomplete. It upbraids itself, if there is some hostile power which hinders love's culmination. Shame enters only through the recollection of the body, through the presence of an exclusive personality or the sensing of an exclusive individuality. It is not a fear *for* what is mortal, for what is merely one's own. It is rather a fear *of* what is mortal. It is a fear which vanishes as the separable element in the lover is diminished by his love. Love is stronger than fear. It has no fear of its fear. But led by its fear, it cancels separation, apprehensive as it is of finding opposition which may resist it or be a fixed barrier against it. Love is a mutual giving and taking. Through shyness, love's gifts may be disdained. Through shyness, an opponent may not yield to love's receiving. But love still tries whether hope has not deceived it, whether it still finds itself everywhere. The lover who takes is not thereby made richer than the other. He is enriched indeed, but only so much as the other is. So too, the giver does not make himself poorer. By giving to the other, he has at the same time and to the same extent enhanced his own treasure. Hegel bases this, his early phenomenology of love, on the tragedy of Romeo and Juliet by William Shakespeare. Romeo expresses beautifully the enrichment of the giving lover:

My bounty is as boundless as the sea.
My love as deep; the more I give to thee,
The more I have.[33]

Hegel here sees romantic love symbolized in Romeo and Juliet and describes it as a form of the Christian principle of free personality.[34]

The Child

Love acquires this wealth of life, presented by Romeo and Juliet, in the exchange of every thought, every variety of inner experience.[35] This is so, since love seeks out differences and devises unifications *ad infinitum*. It turns to the whole manifold of nature in order to drink love out of every life. What in the first instance is most the individual's own is united into the totality of love in the lovers' touch and contact. In this totality of love all consciousness of a separate self disappears. All distinction between the lovers is annulled. The mortal element, the body, has lost the character of separability. The lovers beget a child. A living child, a seed of immortality, of the eternally self-developing and self-generating human genus, has come into existence. What has been united in the child is not divided again. In love and through love, God has acted and created. The theological element is present in Hegel's philosophy of the family, as in any other part of his social philosophy.[36]

Child Development

In Hegel's socio-ethical perspective, as far as it is developed in his early theological writings, this unity of the lovers, their child, is only a point, an undifferentiated unity, a seed.[37] The lovers cannot so contribute to the child as their undifferentiated unity as to give it a manifold life in itself at the start. The union of the lovers is free from all inner division. In it there is no working on an opposite. Everything which gives the newly begotten child a manifold life and a specific existence, it must draw into itself, set over against itself and unify with itself. The seed breaks free from its original unity. It turns ever more and more to opposition. It begins to develop. Each stage of its development is a separation. The child's aim in each stage of its development is to regain for itself the full riches of life, which have been enjoyed by the parents. Thus the dialectical process of the notion of the family is: unity—separated opposites—reunion. The child is in a certain sense the parents themselves. After their union the lovers separate again. But in the child, their union has become unseparated and inseparable.

Marital Property

This union of the lovers in love is complete.[38] But it can remain complete only as long as the separate lovers are opposed solely in the sense that the one loves and the other is loved, that each separate lover is one organ in a living totality. But the lovers are necessarily continually in contact with much that is dead. External objects belong to each of the lovers. This means that a lover stands in relation to things opposed to him in his own eyes as objects and as opposites. This is why lovers are capable of a multiplex opposition in the course of their multiplex acquisition and possession of property and rights. The dead object, in the power of one of the lovers, is opposed to both of them. A union of the lovers, in respect to the dead object, seems to Hegel to be possible only if it comes under the dominion of both. The one lover who sees the other in possession of a property must sense in the other the separate individuality which has willed this possession. He cannot himself annul the exclusive dominion of the other, for this once again would be an opposition to the other's power, since no relation to an object is possible except mastery over it. He would be opposing a mastery to the other's dominion and would be cancelling one of the other's relationships, namely, his exclusion of others from his property.

In Hegel's estimate, since possession and property make up such an important part of man's life, cares, and thoughts, even lovers cannot refrain from reflections on this aspect of their relations. Even if the use of the property is common to both, the right to its possession would remain undecided, and the thought of this right would never be forgotten because everything which man possesses has the legal form of property. But if the possessor gives the other the same right of possession as he has himself, community of goods is still only the right to the thing of the one or the other of the two lovers. For Hegel, community of goods or communism is not even possible or desirable between lovers. Like Epicurus, Hegel rejects community of goods among friends or between lovers, since it would demonstrate a distrust.[39] But those who distrust each other cannot be friends or lovers.

From Desire to Love

Hegel continues his philosophy of the family, which began in the *Early Theological Writings* in his *Jenaer System Fragments* of 1803-1804.[40] Those fragments constitute to a large extent a preparation for Hegel's *Phenomenology of the Spirit.* They are themselves already phenomenology—science of the development of different formations of consciousness. Besides a phenomenology of language, work and struggle for mutual recognition, the *Jenaer Fragments* contain also an early phenomenology of marriage- and family-consciousness, an anticipation and preparation of the later phenomenology of family consciousness of 1807.[41]

According to Hegel's phenomenology of marriage, the relation of the lovers begins with desire.[42] Sexual desire, for the thirty-three-year-old Hegel, is destruction on grounds of sexual need. But this destructiveness, rage, or hostility rooted in sexual need is restrained in sexual desire. Such desire is something entirely external, natural, physical. But the freedom of man's consciousness supercedes the sexual need and it curbs thereby the destructiveness of sexual desire through sexual pleasure. The freedom of man's spirit accomplishes this task all by itself. It thereby makes both sexes into consciousness for each other. It turns the two sexes into individuals who are and continue to be for each other not only as mortal bodies, but particularly as consciousness. Man's freedom produces a situation in which each sex partner is himself or herself in the other's being for himself or herself. Through human freedom it happens that each sex partner is conscious of himself or herself for himself or for herself in the consciousness of the other, that is, in his or her individuality or in his or her being for himself or herself. Through freedom of consciousness, the sexual relationship becomes one in which each sex partner is himself or herself one with the other in the being of the consciousness of each of them. Thereby, the external, natural sexual relationship turns into an inner, ideal relationship. In this metamorphosis, sexual desire emancipates itself from its relation to external pleasure. Sexual desire becomes an immediate oneness of the sex partners in their absolute being for themselves, their individuality. So sexual desire turns into love. Now in the sphere of love, sexual pleasure consists in each lover's perception of himself or herself in the being of the other's consciousness. The relationship of the lovers itself becomes in the same way the being of both of them. It remains the permanent being of both lovers. The relationship of the lovers becomes marriage.

In marital love, the woman becomes for the man a being for herself.[43] The woman ceases to be a mere object of man's desire. She becomes a subject for man. Man's desire for the woman becomes ideal. It turns into man's perception of and inclination toward the woman. As desire so liberates itself from its relation to pleasure and makes itself into permanent love, it does not die in pleasure. Desire turns into a lasting bond. Through reason, desire becomes marriage.

In marriage, each partner is mutually in the consciousness of the other with his or her total individuality.[44] Here the partners give to each other a whole common existence. The conjugal partners are united in this common existence not in connection with any individual thing or a particular purpose. They rather are one with each other in their marital existence according to their totality with which they belong to nature. In this conjugal bond, each partner has the consciousness of the totality of the other and of himself or herself. Precisely because of this mutual consciousness of totality, the marital bond is sacred. On this ground, marriage is completely distant from the notion of contract. Only isolated persons conclude contracts concerning dead things.[45] Contrary to his great predecessor, Immanuel Kant, Hegel breaks already in his *Jenaer Fragments* with the old European tradition to determine marriage as a contract.[46] For Hegel, the marriage is the only social dimension in which individuals become united in their totality. In society and state, individuals encounter each other fragmentarily according to some aspect of their being.

From his Jenaer phenomenology of marriage on, Hegel excludes the organisms of the lovers from his consideration.[47] This does not mean that Hegel's philosophy of the family becomes less materialistic and more idealistic the further it proceeds. In Hegel's objective and absolute idealism, materialism is never only negated, but also preserved and elevated.[48] When the phenomenologist of marriage, Hegel, puts the bodies of the lovers under *epoché* from the *Jenaer Fragments* on, then this is merely a methodological device. Hegel brackets out the organisms of the lovers in order to concentrate completely on their mutual consciousness. At the same time, he relegates their bodies to the organic dimension of nature and to the anthropological spheres of man's subjective spirit.[49] Never does Hegel become forgetful of the rock bottom biological base structure of family life or of social life in general, as his materialistic disciples and opponents on the Hegelian Left are sometimes prone to do when they discuss the withering away of the family.[50] For Hegel, the lovers remain always body-subjects and as such part of nature.[51] Hegel's social philosophy is built not only on his *Logic* or logos-theology or on his *Phenomenology of Spirit*, but also on a very extensive *Philosophy of Nature,* which takes almost as much room in his *Enzyklopaedia* as his whole *Philosophy of Spirit,* including subjective, objective, and absolute spirit.[52]

Education

According to Hegel's Jenaer phenomenology of marital consciousness, in the living oneness of the conjugal partners the consciousness of each of them has exchanged itself for that of the other.[53] The consciousness of each lover is his own and also that of his or her partner. At the same time, the consciousness of the lovers is necessarily also the center in which both of them differentiate themselves from each other, but in which they are also nevertheless one with each other as well. This center is the marriage partners' existing dialectical unity. In this center, the lovers recognize themselves in their unity as superceded poles of their own opposition. In this center of their unity, the conjugal partners are therefore also again opposed to each other. This center of the marital partners' unity exists not only for them, but also for itself in its own right, versus the conjugal partners in their separate, abstract individuality. What precisely is this center of the conjugal partners?

In Hegel's view, this center in which the lovers recognize themselves as being one with each other, and as being superceded poles of their own abstract opposition, is necessarily in itself a consciousness.[54] This must be so, since the marital partners are substantially one with each other only as consciousness. Their external union in sexual intercourse is contingent and sporadic. The real center of unity of the marital partners is the consciousness of their child. It is their child, in which the lovers recognize themselves as being one with each other in one consciousness, that of their child. In the consciousness of their child, the lovers know themselves as the annuled poles of their opposition. The conjugal partners perceive in the consciousness of their child their being progressively superceded. The marital partners recognize themselves in their child as *genus*. They know themselves in their child as something else than that what they are themselves, namely, as an accomplished unity. But this evolved unity is itself a consciousness in its own right. It is a consciousness in which the annulment of the parents perceives itself. It is a consciousness in which the consciousness of the parents is developing. That means that the parents must educate their child. They must form the child's consciousness.

In Hegel's perspective, as the parents educate the child, they posit their own evolved consciousness into the consciousness of the child.[55] The parents produce their own death as they animate their child toward its own consciousness. At the same time as the parents internalize their own consciousness into that of the child, they realize the reflection of their own consciousness into itself. They produce for themselves the emptiness of absolute individuality. The parental consciousness, as evolved consciousness, becomes inorganic nature. The child elevates itself to the totality of the inorganic nature of the consciousness of its parents. In the family, consciousness becomes another consciousness for itself. The consciousness of the parents becomes for itself the consciousness of the child. The consciousness of the child becomes for itself the consciousness of the parents. The education of the child consists precisely in that, that the consciousness which has been posited into its own consciousness by the parents as another than its own, becomes its own. The child's inorganic nature, which it consumes into itself, is an evolved consciousness. The process of the individuality of the child is a formation process. The child, which here consumes the developing form of consciousness into itself, is the evolved individuality.

According to Hegel's Jenaer phenomenology, in familial education the consciousness of the child becomes one which posits another consciousness into itself.[56] In education, the unconscious unity of the child annuls itself. The unity of the child's consciousness differentiates itself in itself. It becomes an educated consciousness. The consciousness of the parents is the material for the prize of which the consciousness of the child forms itself. The parents are for the child an unknown dark presentiment of itself. The parents annul the child's compact, squat, stumpy being in itself. What the parents give to the child, they themselves lose. The parents die in the child, since what they give to it is their own consciousness. Here the consciousness is the evolution of another consciousness in itself, the evolution of the parental consciousness in that of the child. The parents perceive in the development of the consciousness of the child their own annulment.

In Hegel's view, in the family the world does not come to the consciousness of the child, as long as it is developing, in the absolute form of externality, but only as having passed through the form of the parental consciousness.[57] The inorganic nature of this consciousness is the knowledge of the parents. The external world, when it reaches the consciousness of the child, has already been prepared by the parents. The child is mediated with the world through the parents. The world comes to the child in the form not of reality, but ideality. As the world comes to the evolving consciousness of the child not as real but as ideal world, it is the task of the consciousness of the child to find the meaning, the reality of this ideal world, presented by the parents. The child must discover how this ideal world exists. The child must realize the ideal world presented to it by the parents. For the child, there is present the contradiction between the real world and the ideal world mediated to it by the parents. For the child, there is sooner or later present the contradiction between the real world, which it experiences on its own, and the ideal world, mediated to the child by its parents. This contradiction annuls itself for the evolving consciousness of the child, as it posits the real world, which so far has been unconscious to it, as ideal world, and as it realizes the ideal world of the parents which has been conscious to it throughout its more mature life in the family. The activity of the consciousness of the child is this entirely opposite activity. The consciousness of the child unites both those opposite activities. Only that way the consciousness of the child is evolved for itself. The consciousness of the child supercedes the externality of the external world as it annuls the internality of the parental ideal world. Both worlds are present to the consciousness of the child as something external.

According to Hegel's Jenaer phenomenology, in the family the totality of consciousness is the same as a consciousness evolving for itself.[58] The individual perceives itself in the other. The other is the same totality of consciousness. The other has his or her consciousness in the begotten child. The child perceives its totality in the parents. The parents are the same totality of consciousness as the child. The parents have the totality of their consciousness in the child begotten by them.

Ethical Moment

On February 7, 1807, an illegitimate son, Ludwig, was born to Hegel by the wife of his landlord in Jena, Christiana Charlotte Burkhardt, née Fischer.[59] Shortly afterwards, the landlord died. Hegel has been said to have promised marriage to the widow. But he then supposedly forgot about his promise after he had left Jena.

In the same year, 1807, the thirty-seven-year-old Hegel determined in his *Phenomenology of Spirit* the family as a natural ethical community.[60] Here, the first time in the evolution of his philosophy of marriage and family, Hegel makes explicit its specifically ethical sphere beyond its natural dimension. To be sure, the ethical sphere of marriage and family was implicitly present, besides its natural region, already in the early Hegelian philosophy of the family, as it is contained in Hegel's *Early Theological Writings* and in his *Jenaer Fragments*.[61] But the phenomenological description of the socio-ethical consciousness of the old Greeks, particularly as it is crystalized in the Sophoclean tragedies of Antigone and King Oedipus, gives Hegel in the framework of his *Phenomenology of Spirit* the opportunity to bring forth into full light the ethical aspects of marriage and family.[62] Hegel may be called not only the last Christian philosopher, but also the last Greek philosopher.[63] But to be sure, Hegel's own ethical consciousness is far beyond the Greek consciousness on the ladder on which the human spirit climbs to absolute knowledge according to his phenomenology.[64] But the Christian principle of subjectivity, which constitutes Hegel's Christian notion of the family, is already anticipated in the principle of individuality, which characterizes the Greek family on the height of its development as it is expressed in classical Greek poetry.[65] In his phenomenology of the Greek family, Hegel concentrates particularly on the privileged position of the individual in the latter.[66]

According to Hegel's phenomenology of spirit, the family is as ethical community the indwelling notion of sociality.[67] It operates in an unconscious way. It stands opposed to its own actuality, when it is explicitly conscious. That happens in the nation or in the state. The family is fully actualized in the nation. The familial principle of sociality becomes fully conscious in the state. The family is the basis of the nation. As fundament of the state, the family stands in opposition to it. As the acorn stands in contrast to the oak, in which it is fully realized, so the family is opposed to the state. The family is the immediate ethical existence. The state is the mediated ethical existence. The family stands over against the mediated ethical order of the nation, which shapes and preserves itself by work for universal ends. The family works for the particular needs of its individual members. The Penates of the family stand therefore in contrast to the universal spirit of the nation. In opposition to the state, the family becomes that dimension in which the individual can evolve in his or her totality.

The ethical moment of the family has the character of immediacy or naturalness.[68] It is nevertheless within itself an ethical entity. But it is ethical not insofar as it is the natural relation of its component parts, its members, or insofar as their connection is one which holds immediately among individual concrete beings. The ethical element is always intrinsically universal, not particular or individual. The familial relation established by nature, by desire, is essentially never only a matter of nature, but also and as much a spiritual fact. The relation among the different individual members of the family is ethical only by being spiritual, not by being natural. More still than in the *Jenaer Fragments,* Hegel stresses in his phenomenology proper the spiritual and ethical side of marriage and family and brackets out their external natural aspect. All becomes inwardness, a matter of consciousness. Against this idealism of Hegel, his materialistic opponents on the Marxist Left and on the positivistic Right will throughout the nineteenth and twentieth centuries emphasize externality and naturalness and give them the absolute primacy over the spiritual and ethical element in marriage and family as in other dimensions of social life. Wherein does the peculiar ethical character of the family consist according to Hegel's new science?

In the first place, for Hegel, because the ethical moment is the intrinsically universal element in the family, the ethical relation among its members is not that of sentiment or of love.[69] Feeling and sexual love belong to the natural realm inside of marriage and family. The universal ethical element seems bound to be placed in the relation of the individual familial member to the totality of the family as the real substance, so that the purpose of his or her action and the content of his or her actuality are taken from this familial substance. They are derived solely from family life. But the conscious purpose which dominates the action of the totality of the family, so far as that purpose concerns the familial whole, is itself the individual family member. For Hegel, the family is the only social unit, which has the individual as such for its purpose. Neither the state nor the society are, as such, concerned with the individual. The family is therefore of utmost importance for the development of the individuality of the individual. In the family, free subjectivity arises.

Individual

In the social dimension, the procuring and maintaining of power and wealth turn, in part, merely on needs and wants and are a matter that has to do with desire.[70] In part, they become in their higher object something which is merely of mediate significance. This object does not fall within the family itself. It concerns what is truly universal, the community, the nation, the state. We cannot yet speak of "society" on the Greek level of socio-ethical consciousness. The reality of society belongs to modern times. In the modern era, the procurement and maintaining of power and wealth belongs not only into the dimension of the state, but also and very much so into the sphere of civil society.[71] Already in the Greek world, the nation or the state, with its concern for power and wealth, acts rather in a negative way on the family.[72] The nation consists in setting the individual outside of the family. In modern time, the civil society pulls the individual out of the familial unity.[73] Already in Greece, the state subdues the individual's merely natural existence and his or her mere particularity he or she may enjoy in the family.[74] So the nation draws the individual on towards self-sacrificing political virtue, toward living in and for the universal, the state.[75] In the state exists extreme identity-compulsion.[76] It is at work also in the modern society and state.[77] In the family, the individual finds a degree of collective non-identity or free subjectivity.[78] At least on the Greek level of spiritual culture and ethical consciousness, in the family there is place for negative dialectics.[79] Here is even room for that which Hegel calls the "foul existence," that is, non-conceptual individuality and particularity disconnected from the universality of society, state, history, and religion.[80] In the family, individuality is not a mere negligible quantity as it is in state and society.

In Hegel's reflection upon the Greek ethical consciousness, the positive purpose peculiar to the family is the individual as such. In order that this relationship of the family to the individual may be ethical, neither the individual who does an act nor he or she to whom the act refers must show any trace of contingency as obtains in rendering some particular help or service—like cooking a meal.[81] The content of the ethical act must be substantial in character. It must be total and universal. Hence, it can only stand in relation to the entire individual or the individual in his or her totality, to the individual not only as particular but rather as universal. This again must not be taken as if it were merely in the idea, that an act of service furthered the individual's entire happiness, whereas the service, taken as an immediate or concrete act, only does something particular in regard to him or to her. According to Hegel, we must also not think that the ethical act, like a process of education, really takes the individual, the child, as its object and, dealing with it, as a whole, in a series of efforts, produces it as a kind of work. For in the process of education—apart from its purpose, which operates in a negative way on the family since it really serves the state or later on also the society—the real educational act has merely a limited content, like teaching the child to wash or to read or to write, Finally, just as little should we take it, according to Hegel, that the service rendered is a help in time of need, by which in truth the entire individual is saved, as in the case of administering help to a very sick family member. For such help is itself an entirely casual act, the occasion of which is an ordinary actuality, which can as well be as not be. It is contingent.

In Hegel's phenomenological view of the Greek world, the ethical act which embraces the entire existence of the blood relation does not concern the citizen, for he does not belong to the family, but to the state.[82] It also does not deal with one who is going to be a citizen and so will cease to have the significance of a mere particular individual. In modern times the ethical act, which embraces the total existence of the family member, does not concern the *bourgeois,* since he belongs into the sphere of civil society.[83]

This ethical act rather has as its object and content this specific individual which belongs to the family.[84] It takes this individual as a universal or total being, divested of his sensuous or particular reality. The act no longer concerns the living, but the dead. The dead family member has passed through the long sequence of his broken and diversified existence. He has gathered up his being into its one completed embodiment. He has lifted himself out of the unrest of a life of chance and change into the peace of simple universality. Since the individual is really real and substantial only as a citizen of the city-state, the full actualization of the family, so he is as non-citizen and family member merely the unreal, marrowless shadow in comparison to the real citizen.

Antigone's brothers, Enteocles and Polynices, who were real and substantial as citizens of Thebes, return as unreal marrowless shadows into the circle of their family waiting to be buried by their sisters.[85]

According to Hegel, this condition of universality which the individual family member as such reaches, is mere being, death.[86] It is the immediate issue of the process of nature. Death is not the action of a conscious mind. The duty of a member of a family is on that account to attach this aspect of conscious mind too, in order that this last phase of being—this universal being of the dead family member—may also not belong to nature alone, and remain something irrational, but may be actually done, and the right of consciousness may be asserted in it. The family member has the duty to bury the blood relation. The significance of the act of burial of a family member is that, because in truth the peace and universality of a self-conscious being does not belong to nature, the apparent claim which nature has made to act in this way of death may be given up and the truth reinstated.

Family Versus State

According to Hegel, the act of burying the dead blood relation is the highest expression of reverent devotion.[87] Such piety finds in Hegel's view the most sublime artistic representation in the Sophoclean Antigone. Here reverent devotion is stated as the law of the woman. It is the law of the feeling subjective substantiality, or substantial subjectivity, of the inwardness, which has not yet achieved its complete realization. Piety is the law of the old Greek gods, of the netherworld. It is the eternal law of which nobody knows from where it appeared. Sophocles represents this law of reverent devotion as standing in contrast to the law of the state. Antigone dutifully reinstates the truth, against the claim of nature, when she sees to it that both of her brothers, not only Enteocles, but also Polynices be buried in conformity to the divine law of the netherworld, but in violation of the human law of the state represented by Creon, the king of Thebes. For Hegel, this conflict between the family, which is concerned with the individual in his particularity and universality, and the state contains the highest socio-ethical and therefore the most tragic opposition in the social world. This opposition is individualized in Antigone and Creon, more generally in womanliness and manliness.

Brother and Sister

According to Hegel's phenomenology of Greek spirit, the divine law which holds sway in the family, has on its side, distinctions and stages within itself, as does, on the other side, the human law which dominates the state.[88] The relations among those distinctions make up the living process of realization of the family on one hand, as well as of the state on the other hand. We limit ourselves to the relations among the distinctions in the family.

In Hegel's perspective of Greek life, the family contains three relationships: the relationship of husband and wife, parents and children, brothers and sisters.[89] Among those three relationships, the relation between husband and wife is, to begin with, the primary and immediate form in which one consciousness recognizes itself in the other and in which each consciousness knows this reciprocal recognition. The relationship between husband and wife, being natural self-knowledge— knowledge of self on the basis of nature and not on the foundation of ethical life—merely represents and typifies in a figure the life of objective spirit. It is not yet objective spirit as being actually realized. Figurative representation, however, has its reality in another than it is. The relationship of husband and wife therefore finds itself actualized not in itself as such, but in the child. The child is the other, in whose coming into being the conjugal relationship consists and with which it passes away. This change from one generation onwards to another generation is permanent in and as the life of a nation, society, state.

In Hegel's phenomenological perspective of Greek family life, the reverent devotion of man and woman toward one another is thus mixed up with a natural relation and with feeling.[90] Their relationship does not return into itself. Only spirit has such self-reflection. The relationship of man and woman as such is natural and as such, does not reflect back into itself. It loses itself in the "bad" infinity of the generations.

Likewise, the second relationship, the reverent devotion of parents and children to one another is, as such, not self-complete.[91] The devotion of parents toward their children is affected with emotion just by their being consciously realized in what is external to themselves, namely, the children and by their seeing them becoming something on their own account without thereby returning to their parents. As the oak is foreign to the acorn, so the independent existence on the part of the children remains as a natural entity a foreign reality to the parents, a reality all the children's own. The devotion of children, again, towards their parents is conversely affected by their coming into being from or having their essential nature in, what is external to themselves, namely the parents, and what passes away. The children attain independent existence and a self-consciousness of their own solely through separation from the source whence they came. In this separation of the children, the spring, the life of their parents gets exhausted.

So, according to Hegel's phenomenology of Greek ethical life, both these relationships—the relation between husband and wife, and the relation between parents and children—are incomplete insofar as they are merely natural.[92] They are constituted by and hold within the natural transience and the dissimilarity of the two sides, which are assigned to them. Things are different with the third relationship in the family, the relation between brother and sister. For Hegel, between brother and sister an unmixed intransitive form of relationship exists inside the family. Brother and sister are of the same blood. But the blood in them has entered into a condition of stable equilibrium. Brother and sister therefore stand in no such natural relation to each other as husband and wife. They do not desire one another sexually. Also, brother and sister have not given to one another or received from one another, like husband and wife, their independence of individual being. Brother and sister are free individualities with respect to each other. The feminine element, therefore, in the form of the sister, gives a premonition of and foreshadows most completely the nature of ethical life. The sister does not become conscious of the ethical life in the family and does not actualize it, because the divine law of the family is her inherent implicit inward nature, which does not lie open to the daylight of consciousness. It rather remains the sister's inner feeling and the divine element exempt from actuality. The feminine life is attached to the household divinities, the Penates. The sister sees in the Penates both her universal substance and her particular individuality. But the sister so views the Penates, that this relationship of her individuality to them is at the same time not the natural one of pleasure as in the case of the wife. Obviously, Hegel's phenomenology of the feminine element or the sister is based on the image of the sisters Ismene and Antigone, the daughters of Oedipus in the Sophoclean Theban plays.[93] Hegel anticipates Freud's concern with the unconscious moment in the Oedipus myth, but remains pre-Freudian insofar as the sexual unconsciousness of brother and sister is concerned.[94]

According to Hegel's phenomenology of the Greek family, the woman, as a daughter, must see her parents pass away with natural emotion and yet also with ethical resignation, for it is only at the cost of this condition that she can come to that individual existence of which she is capable.[95] She thus cannot see her independent existence positively attained in her relation to her parents. The relationship of mother and wife, however, are individualized partly in the form of something natural, which brings pleasure. Partly, they are individualized in the form of something negative, which finds simply its own evanescence in those relationships of mother and wife. Partly again, the individualization of the relationship of wife and mother is just on that account, something contingent which can be replaced by another particular individuality. In a household of the ethical kind, a woman's relationships are not based on a reference to *this* particular husband, *this* particular child. In the ethical dimension of the household, a woman's relationships are based on a reference to a husband, to children in *general*—not to feeling, but to the universal. The distinction between the woman's ethical life and that of her husband, while it certainly determines her particular existence and brings her pleasure, consists nevertheless just in this, that it has always directly universal significance for her, and is quite alien to the impulsive condition of mere particular desire. On the other hand, in the husband these two aspects of ethical life and particular pleasure get separated. Since the husband possesses, as a citizen in the state, the self-conscious power belonging to the universal ethical life, the life of the social whole, he acquires thereby the rights of desire, and keeps himself at the same time in detachment from it. So far then for Hegel, as particularity is implicated in this relationship in the case of the wife, her ethical life is not purely ethical. But insofar as the life of the wife is ethical, the particularity is a matter of indifference. In the ethical household as it appears in Greek history, the wife is without the moment of knowing herself as *this* particular self in and through another.

In Hegel's phenomenological view of the Greek family, the brother is, in the eyes of the sister, a being whose nature is unperturbed by desire and is ethically like her own.[96] The recognition of the sister in her brother is pure and unmixed with any sexual relation. The indifference of particular existence and the ethical contingency thence arising are, therefore, not present in the relationship between sister and brother. Instead, the moment of *individual selfhood,* recognizing and being recognized, can here assert its right, because it is bound up with the balance and equilibrium resulting from the brother and sister being of the same blood, and from their being related in a way that involves no mutual desire. The loss of a brother is thus irreparable to the sister, and her duty toward him is the highest. Therefore, Antigone was under the sacred obligation to bury her brother Polynices, in spite of the fact that he had become guilty under human law by attacking the city state of Thebes and in it, King Creon and his brother Enteocles, and had died in this process.[97] For Hegel, the individualization of the individuals in the family reaches its highest peak not in the relationship between husband and wife, parents and children, but in the relationship between brother and sister.[98] In this relationship, the partners find their individual selfhood. Here, free subjectivity appears as fully as this can happen in the realm of the family, at least in the Greek world.

According to Hegel, this relationship between brother and sister at the same time is the limit, at which the circumscribed life of the family is broken up, and passes beyond itself.[99] The brother is the member of the family in whom its spirit becomes individualized, and enabled thereby to turn towards another social sphere, towards what is other than and external to itself and to pass over into consciousness of universality. The brother leaves this immediate, rudimentary, and therefore, strictly speaking, negative ethical life of the family, in order to acquire and produce the concrete ethical order which is conscious of itself—the state. Of course, Antigone's brothers, Enteocles and Polynices, find in the service of the state only their death on the battlefield. Here on the level of the state, the family and the individual come into their real crisis. In the Greek world, at least, the state does not seem to realize the promise the family gave. For Hegel, nevertheless, inside of the substantial unity of the family, the individualization of the individuals reaches its highest peak in the relationship between brother and sister. Here, free subjectivity appears as fully and completely united with the principle of universality as this can possibly happen in the sphere of the family, at least on the Greek level of man's liberation history.

Hegel's Marriage and Family

One year after the completion of the *Phenomenology of Spirit,* in 1808, Hegel was appointed by the King of Bavaria as professor of the preparatory sciences in and as principal of the Agidien Gymnasium in Nürnberg.[100] Three years later, the forty-one year-old Hegel married the twenty-year-old Marie von Tucher, in Nürnberg.

In Hegel's life, nothing had indicated so far that he would seriously consider putting into practice the philosophy of the family, which he had developed in his *Early Theological Writings,* in the *Jenaer Fragments,* or in the *Phenomenology of Spirit.*[101] For Hegel, his profession as a philosopher was at the same time his whole existence. Like Moses, Hegel had a heavy tongue. He used to say that God had condemned him to be a philosopher. His intellectual restlessness made Hegel doubt if he were really created for a purely earthly happiness, not to speak of making another human being happy in marriage. Hegel shows his intellectual restlessness particularly in his phenomenology of the spirit, where the negativity of doubt and even desperation drives him from one formation of human consciousness to the other, from one stage of reflection to the other, from consciousness over self-consciousness to free concrete mind, including the objective spirit, the ethical order of family and state in the Greek world, and beyond that, to religion and absolute knowledge or knowledge of the Absolute.[102] Certainly, the continual philosophical encounter with the problems of man and his world does not exactly dispose a philosopher for a comfortable family existence.[103] Philosophy obligates the philosopher to absolute truthfulness. But the truth can be found only in critical examination and verification. A small shift of emphasis can already lead to wrong results in theory as well as to disastrous practical consequences.[104] This critical attitude throws the philosopher only too easily off the course of the normal, naive, unreflected human existence. His negative attitude can make the philosopher under certain circumstances unbearable to people living close to him. Up to the end of the Middle Ages, philosophers were almost without exception priests and monks, and as such lived in celibacy. But the modern philosophers Descartes, Malebranche, Spinoza, Leibnitz, Wolff, Locke, Hume, and Kant also remained unmarried.[105] By the age of 40, Hegel no longer had much hope that happiness was part of his destination and that he could gain the love of a woman and find contentment in marriage and family, which he had interpreted so eloquently in his philosophy so far.

In a letter to his young bride, Marie, who worried about the philosopher's melancholical tendencies, Hegel reminded her that her own deeper sense has taught her that in hearts which are not shallow, all feelings of happiness are connected with feelings of sorrow.[106] A decade later, at the end of his philosophy of religion, Hegel would sharply criticize the bourgeois enlighteners, who have perverted love into love and pleasure without pain.[107] Hegel also reminds his bride that she promised to heal him in his heart from the residuals of disbelief in human contentment.[108] Hegel hopes that Marie, as his wife, will reconcile his true inwardness with the mode in which he only too often behaves against and in the external social world. Ten years later, Hegel stated in his philosophy of religion that in the late European civilization, as once before in the late Roman empire, the unity between man's interiority and exteriority is no longer present.[109] In such an end-time-situation, philosophy must be a separate sanctuary and its servants must form an isolated priesthood, which is not allowed to go along with the world and must preserve the possession of the truth. The truth becomes the more fragile the more the present historical transition period progresses.[110] Hegel reminds his bride that this viewpoint, namely, the reconciliation of the philosopher's true inwardness with his critical attitude toward the empirical reality, gives her destination a higher meaning and value.[111] Hegel also reminds his bride of his trust that she will have the strength to reconcile the truth in his subjectivity with his critique of the outside world. Hegel trusts that this strength lies in his and Marie's mutual love.

For Hegel, in spite of his absolute devotion to truth and his corresponding extreme seriousness, celibacy was not the right style of life.[112] In Hegel's socio-ethical view, celibacy was not, like for some bourgeois enlighteners, simply unnatural. Before Freud, Hegel knew of the necessity of instinctual renunciation for the growth and survival of any spiritual culture, particularly of marriage and the family.[113] According to the Lutheran Hegel, celibacy is unethical.[114] It contradicts the social morality and sacredness of marriage and the family. When Hegel got married, as Fichte before him and Schelling before and after him, he ceased merely to theorize about the family, as innumerable philosophers and theologians, had done before him, and practiced it as well.[115]

According to the witness of his family and his friends, Hegel's marriage with Marie von Tucher lasted 20 years in untroubled happiness and mutual love. Hegel and his wife had one daughter, who died soon after birth, and two sons of their own, Karl and Immanuel. After having been informed about Hegel's earlier relationship to Christiana Burckhardt, Marie had sufficient trust in her own love to take his four-year-old natural son, Ludwig, into her marriage and to raise him and educate him in her family together with her two sons. Hegel died in the arms of his family on 14 November 1831.[116] In the judgment of his wife, Marie, Hegel died as a saint and like being transfigured.[117]

Honest Love

Hegel's philosophy of the family reaches the peak of its elaboration, expansion, and determination in form and content and of intelligibility a decade after the conclusion of his own marriage, in his *Philosophy of Right* of 1821.[118] Here the fifty-one-year-old Hegel sums up his whole perception of the essence of the family. He collects here all the theoretical and practical insights he has gained into marriage and family life in the quarter of a century since his *Early Theological Writings*.[119] In his *Philosophy of Law* Hegel no longer presents the family as it existed in the Greek or any other pre-Christian-European world. Here Hegel develops the notion of the family as it resulted from Christian-European experience. At the same time, Hegel points to a new type of family, possibly to be realized in a post-European world.[120] Now to return to Hegel's philosophy of the family as it finds its final form in his *Philosophy of Right*.

In his philosophy of law, Hegel defines marriage—the immediate notion, structure, potential of the family—as the immediate socio-ethical relationship.[121] As such, marriage contains first of all the moment of natural vivacity. It carries in itself as substantial relationship liveliness in its totality, namely as the reality of the human genus and its process. But secondly, the unity of the natural sexes, which is first of all only internal and as such and exactly thereby in its existence merely external, is in the self-consciousness of the sex partners transformed into a spiritual, a self-conscious love. Already the younger Hegel of the *Jenaer Fragments* spoke of this transformation of external sexual desire into love through the freedom of consciousness.[122] Hegel's complete philosophy of the family preserves in itself with astonishing consequence its earlier developmental stages.

Hegel's determination of marriage as socio-ethical relationship stands in opposition to theories of the family produced by philosophers and theologians in antiquity, the Middle Ages, and in the first period of modern times.[123] Hegel criticizes earlier theories, particularly natural law theories, from antiquity and the Middle Ages for looking at marriage only in terms of its physical aspect; according to that which it is by nature. As we find forms of marriage and family already in the animal kingdoms—among woodpeckers, ostriches, seals, lions, orangutans—so there is certainly also a natural dimension in the human family. Hegel never ceased to stress this materialistic point. But Hegel opposes the traditional thinkers, particularly the old natural lawyers, because they saw nothing else in marriage than a natural sexual relationship. Thereby they closed for themselves any way to the other determinations of marriage.

Hegel finds the moral philosophers no less rude and barbarous than the traditional philosophers and theologians. They, like Kant, understand marriage merely as a bourgeois contract, in which the mutual arbitrariness of the individuals comes to a consensus concerning their bodies and property.[124] Up to today, bourgeois thinkers differentiate in marriage between a contract of love and a contract of property. In Hegel's view, the bourgeois moralists degrade marriage into a form of the sex partners' mutual contractual usage of their bodies. The Hegelian Left, particularly Marx, later on continues Hegel's critique by defining the bourgeois marriage contract as legalized prostitution.[125] The Hegelian, Theodor W. Adorno, affirms in late civil society what Hegel had observed in its earlier developmental stage: the bourgeois mind ends always in barbarism.[126]

Hegel opposes in his philosophy of law still a third type of theory about the family, which has become popular in his own time.[127] This newest theory posits marriage exclusively into love. Marriage is nothing else than love. According to Hegel, this modern theory is untrue and must therefore be rejected since love, which is a feeling, allows for contingency in every respect. But social morality, according to its very notion, must not have the form of contingency. The socio-ethical idea contains not only the element of accidental particularity, but also especially the moment of necessary universality. Therefore, in his philosophy of right, Hegel determines marriage as not only the life of the loving subject sensing life in the beloved object, as he had done in the early theological writings, or as sexual desire, need, and pleasure transformed into love, as he had done in the *Jenaer Fragments,* but rather as honest, socio-ethical love. According to Hegel, the elements of arbitrariness, capriciousness, transitoriness, and of a bad subjectivism disappear from marriage as honest and ethical love.

Decision and Inclination

Finally, Hegel's reflections upon the starting point of marriage in his philosophy of right throw light once more not only on the principle of subjective freedom in the dimension of marriage and family, but also on its reunion with the principle of substantiality.[128] For Hegel, social morality is nothing else than the negative or differentiated unity of the subjective and the universal will.[129] The family is this unity in the form of feeling. Therefore, the free constitutional state must have the highest respect for the reverent devotion of the family.[130] Through the family, the constitutional state has for its citizens such individuals who already have a socio-ethical character for themselves. Individuals are not yet socio-ethical as persons, who can own property, or as subjects, who are able to have their private resolution and guilt, intention and well-being, goodness and conscience, or as bourgeois, who are entitled to satisfy their particular material needs.[131] Through the family, the constitutional state has for its citizens such individuals who bring with them already the solid foundation of being able to feel themselves as being one with its socio-ethical concrete totality.[132] The family anticipates and prepares the socio-ethical reconciliation between the subjective freedom of the individual and the objective and universal freedom of the social whole which, on the level of objective spirit, finds its full realization in the truly free constitutional state.

In Hegel's socio-ethical view as it is expressed in the philosophy of law, the subjective starting point of marriage and family can either be the particular inclination of the two persons, determined for marriage, or the provision and arrangement of the parents, kinship group, tribe, etc.[133] In Hegel's perspective, the objective starting point of marriage is the free consent of the persons who are going to be married, for the purpose of constituting together one person. That means that the two persons agree to give up their natural and individual personality in the unity of marriage. In that sense the marital union is a self-limitation for the two persons entering it. But at the same time this conjugal union is also a process of liberation for the two persons joining each other in marriage, insofar as they gain in their mutual union their substantial self-consciousness, free subjectivity, or subjective freedom.

For Hegel, the objective starting point of marriage is the marital partners' decision to enter into the dialectics of love, which is the very core of marriage.[134] In this dialectics of love, the marriage partners exchange their abstract accidental for their concrete substantial subjectivity.[135] Marital unity does not only not exclude subjective freedom. In Hegel's view, the dialectical conjugal unity and the emancipation of man and woman into their really free freedom are identical.[136] Man cannot find true subjective freedom outside the solidarity with others. Without solidarity, man cannot come to himself and be with himself, and thereby be free. Marriage is the first form of genuine human solidarity, in which man and woman can come home to themselves and can be with themselves in each other's consciousness and can so find their free substantial self-consciousness.

According to Hegel, it is man's objective determination, that is, not only his right, but also his socio-ethical duty, to enter into the estate of individuality, into marriage.[137] How the external subjective starting point of marriage is exactly constituted is for Hegel, as such, accidental. It is a historical matter. It depends mainly on the level of the formation of reflection, which has been achieved in a certain epoch of history. There exist in history two extremely different types of external subjective starting-points for marriage. According to the first type, the arrangement of the well-meaning parents initiates their children's new marriage and family. In the two persons who are in the process of being determined for each other for the union of love by their parents, the inclination for each other grows as it becomes known to them that they are to become husband and wife. This type of maritial starting-point belongs to the old patriarchal world of Africa, Asia, Greece, Rome, and the European Middle Ages.

The other type of external starting-point for marriage consists, according to Hegel, in that the inclination for each other appears first in the two persons who are going to get married.[138] The inclination—including sexual desire, need, pleasure, love as life of one sex partner sensing life in the other—rises first in these two infinitely particularized individuals, who later will get married.[139] This type of subjective marital starting point belongs to the modern world of Europe.[140]

At the time of the development of his philosophy of law, Hegel considers the first type of external starting-point of marriage to be the more ethical way, since here the decision to get married makes the beginning and has the sexual inclination for its consequence, so that then in the case of actual marriage, both elements are united.[141] It is closely connected with the universal principle of the old worlds—the principle of substantiality.[142] In the second type of subjective marital starting-point, the infinitely particularized peculiarity of the two persons who will get married makes valid its pretension. It hangs closely together with the subjective principle of the modern world, the principle of subjective freedom or free subjectivity.[143]

In modern dramas or in other artistic productions of civil society, in which the love of the sexes constitutes the fundamental interest, Hegel meets—long before Ibsen and Strindberg—with the element of a penetrating psychic frostiness.[144] According to Hegel, modern artists carry this element of psychic frigidity into the heat of the represented passion of the sex partners by showing it to be entirely contingent. Furthermore, the bourgeois artists in their artistic products bring frostiness into the passion of the sex partners, by demonstrating that the whole interest rests only on *these* sex partners. According to Hegel, that may be of infinite importance for these partners. But it is not important in itself, in relation to the notion of marriage or the idea of the family or to the idea of social morality in general.

According to Hegel's perspective, in nations in which the female sex stands in low esteem—in the old worlds of Africa, Asia, Greece and Rome, and partially also still of medieval Europe—the parents dispose over the marriage of their children according to their own arbitrariness without asking the individuals determined for marriage, concerning their personal inclinations, their sexual needs, desire, pleasure, love.[145] The individuals let the parental arbitrariness happen to themselves passively, since the particularity of their feeling does not yet make a pretension. This is so, since they do not know yet that they are free by their very humanity.[146] The girl is only concerned with *a* man, not with *this* man.[147] The man is only interested in *a* woman, not in *this* woman. Under other circumstances, concerns for property, social connections, or political purposes are the determining factor in the parents' arrangements of their children's marriage, rather than mere arbitrariness. Here great severity and hardship can happen, since marriage is made into a means for other purposes.

In Hegel's view, on the other hand, in the modern world of Europe, in contrast to the old worlds, people consider the second subjective starting-point, inclination or falling in love, as exclusively important.[148] Men and women living in European civil society imagine that everybody must wait until his hour of falling in love has come. They are of the opinion that they can give their love only to this definite particular individual.

Toward the Future

The social philosopher Hegel is critical in his philosophy of right of both types of external, subjective starting-points of marriage and family.[149] He rejects the parental arrangement of marriage, customary in the old worlds of Africa, Asia, Greece, Rome, and the Western Middle Ages, because all too often it represses the element of personal inclination in the potential marital partners: their sexual need, desire, pleasure, their love as life sensing life in the other, the reflectiveness and differentiation of their consciousness, the particularity of their feelings, their subjective freedom.[150] But Hegel opposes also the entirely individual arrangement of marriage and family on the basis of sexual inclination and falling in love alone, which has become customary in the modern world of Europe, since only too often it is completely contingent, lacks all ethical universality and inner necessity, is deficient of emotional warmth, reinforces the hard punctuality of self-consciousness, and blocks exactly thereby the start and the continuation of the dialectics of marital and familial love.[151] It is not enough to fall in love. One must stand in it. In Hegel's view, each of the two antagonistic types of external subjective marital starting-points is for itself abstract and as such, untrue. For Hegel, the truth lies in the reconciliation of the two opposite ways of the old and the modern world to initiate marriage and family. This truth negates, but also preserves and even elevates the old and the modern type of family and marriage. At the same time, this truth points beyond the old and the modern to a possible post-modern post-positivistic American or Slavic world.[152]

According to Hegel's social ethics, the truth of a more rational and freer marriage and family type of the future post-bourgeois world consists in the dialectical unity of marital decision and sexual inclination.[153] Hegel's family ethics inherits from the world of antiquity the element of marital decision. It takes over from the world of modern Europe the moment of sexual inclination. Hegel learns from the old and the modern world, but he is not captive of either. He emancipates himself through his dialectical reflection from the captivity of antiquity and modernity. Precisely therefore, he is able to produce a dialectical socio-ethical construct or model of the marriage and the family of the future. According to this construct, marital decision or free consent of the potential marriage partners to enter the dialectics of conjugal love on one hand, and their sexual inclination, need, desire, pleasure, love, on the other hand, are dialectically related to each other. The marital decision is present in the sexual inclination. Sexual inclination remains present in the marital consent. In the future spiritual culture to be born in the post-European American or Slavic world, marital decision no longer represses sexual inclination. That was the irrationality of antiquity. Also sexual inclination no longer explodes marital decision. That is the irrationality of bourgeois modernity. In the arrangement of the marriage and the family of the future, the girl is not only concerned with *a* man, like in the old world, or merely with *this* man, like in the modern world, but with *a* man who becomes *this* man or with *this* man who becomes *a* man. Here the man is not only interested in *a* woman, as in antiquity, or *this* woman like in modernity, but with *a* woman who turns for him into *this* woman or with *this* woman who becomes for him *a* woman. The particular is the universal. The universal is the particular. While the old world gravitated toward the universal and the modern world emphasizes the particular, according to Hegel's logic of history, the post-modern world brings into balance the particular and the universal in family, society, and constitutional state.[154]

In the world of the future, if Hegel's construct of marriage and family is true and is not demolished by *facta bruta,* the totality of marriage and family, as well as of the constitutional state, has the infinite energy not only to contain, but even to enhance in itself the free subjectivity of the individuals.[155] At the same time, the subjective freedom of the individuals has in itself the infinite strength not only to contain, but even to enhance the substantiality of marriage and family as well as of the constitutional state. In the future post-modern American or Slavic world in family and state comes about what has never happened before either in the old world of Africa, Asia, Greece, Rome, Medieval Europe, or in the modern world of Europe: the balance of free subjectivity and free substantiality. Exactly by tracing the historical development of marriage and family from antiquity to the modern world of Europe, Hegel was able in the power of his negative and positive dialectical method to project a new model of a more rational and freer type of the family than has existed in the past, into the future, possibly to be realized through the new social praxis of a post-European, post-positivistic American or Slavic culture.[156]

NOTES

1. This paper is a shorter version of a manuscript of greater length on the same topic and having the same title.

    G. W. F. Hegel, *Grundlinien der Philosophie des Rechts* (Stuttgart—Bad Cannstatt: Friedrich Frommann Verlag, 1964), 237-262. Hereinafter cited as: *WW* 7.

2. H. Hohl, Hegel's *Theologische Jugendschriften* (Tubingen, 1907), 378-382; G. W. F. Hegel, *Jenaer Systementwürfe* X, Hamburg: Felix Meiner Verlag 1975, i, 301-306; Hegel, *Phänomenologie des Geistes* (Stuttgart—Bad Cannstatt: Friedrich Frommann Verlag, 1964), 340-354, 354-367, hereinafter cited as: *WW* 2; Hegel, *Philosophische Propedeutik* (Stuttgart: Fr. Frommann Verlag, 1961), 220; Hegel, *Enzyklopädie der Philosophischen Wissenschaften im Grundriss* (Stuttgart: Fr. Frommann Verlag, 1956), 293-294, hereinafter cited as: *WW* 6; Hegel, *System der Philosophie* (Stuttgart—Bad Cannstatt:Friedrich Frommann Verlag, 1965), III, 399-400, hereinafter cited as: *WW* 10; *WW* 7, 237-262; Hegel, *Vorlesungen über die Philosophie der Geschichte* (Stuttgart: Fr. Frommann Verlag, 1961), 74-75, hereinafter cited as: *WW* 11; Hegel, *Asthetik* (Frankfurt a.M.: Europaische Verlagsanstalt, 1951), II, 564; I, 188-189, 447-448, 489-490; Hegel, *Die Religionen der Geistigen Individualität* (Hamburg: Verlag von F. Meiner, 1966), Hb.2, 61, 147, 220; Hb. 1, 81-83, 101, 215.

3. *WW* 7, 237-262; 265-267; 182-184, 99-101.

4. *WW* 2, 18-19; E. Voeglin, *From Enlightenment to Revolution* (Durham, North Carolina: Duke University Press, 1975), 74; P. Tillich, *Morality and Beyond* (New York: Harper and Row, 1963), chap. V; M. Horkheimer, *Die Sehnsucht nach dem Ganz Anderen* (Hamburg:

Furche Verlag, 1970), 83-89; J. Habermas, *Legitimation Crisis* (Boston: Beacon Press, 1975), 117-130; Th. W. Adorno, *Negative Dialectics* (New York: The Seabury Press, 1973), 3-57; B. F. Skinner, *Beyond Dignity and Freedom* (New York: Vintage Books, 1972), chaps. 2 and 3.

5. *WW* 11, 43-47, 74-75.

6. K. Röhring, "Theodor W. Adorno" in W. Schmidt, ed., *Die Religion des Religions Kritik* (Munich: Claudius Verlag, 1972), 91-93, 117-119.

7. *WW* 7, 164-224, esp. 182-183; Hegel, *Die Religionen*, Hb. 2, 133-134, 137, 141, 164, 177, 185; *WW* 10, 380-381.

8. *WW* 7, 182-183, 262-270; 367-432; *WW* 11, 43-69; Hegel, *Ästhetik*, I, 155-162, 180-196; 503, 504, 511-512; II, 346, 415, 423-437, 515, 560, 564; Hegel, *Religionen*, 133-134; Hegel, *Vorlesungen über die Philosophie der Religion* (Stuttgart—Bad Cannstatt: Friedrich Frommann Verlag, 1965), I, 24-36, hereinafter cited as: *WW* 15; Hegel, *Vorlesungen über die Geschichte der Philosophie* (Stuttgart—Bad Cannstatt: Friedrich Frommann Verlag, 1965), III, 551-683, hereinafter cited as: *WW* 19; J. Habermas, *Erkenntnis und Interesse* (Frankfurt a.M.: Suhrkamp Verlag, 1971), chap. III.

9. Hegel, *Jenaer Systementwürfe*, 301-306; *WW* 2, 340-354; *WW* 7, 237-270; *WW* 3, 220; Hegel, *Enzyklopädie*, 323; *WW* 6, 293-294; *WW* 10, 339-400.

10. *WW* 7, 237-238.

11. Ibid., 88-163; 262-328; 164-225.

12. Ibid., 237-238.

13. Ibid.; *WW* 11, 44-45; M. Horkheimer, *Zur Kritik*, 15-62.

14. *WW* 7, 238; 262-328; 328-456.

15. Ibid., 263.

16. Ibid., 238; 328-440.

17. Ibid., 328-440; M. Horkheimer, *Zur Kritik*, 15-62.

18. *WW* 7, 238, 272.

19. Ibid., 238; Hegel, *Enzyklopädie*, 49, 103, 129-130.

20. *WW* 7, 238; Hegel, *Enzyklopädie*, 44, 73, 102-103, 184, 316.

21. *WW* 7, 238.

22. Ibid., 238-239; 255-260; 261-262; 262-328; 328-456.

23. Ibid., 238-239.

24. Ibid., 239.

25. H. Nohl, *Hegel's Theologische Jugendschriften* (Tubingen, 1907), 379.

26. Ibid., 379-380; Hegel, *Enzyklopädie*, 49, 103, 124-130.

27. Nohl, *Hegel*, 380; Hegel, *Enzyklopädie*, 44, 73, 102-103, 184, 316; Adorno, *Negative Dialectics*, 134-207.

28. Nohl, *Hegel*, 379-380.

29. Ibid.

30. Ibid., 380; Hegel, *Vorlesungen über die Geschichte der Philosophie*, (Stuttgart—Bad Cannstatt, 1965), II, 318-337, hereinafter cited as: *WW* 18.

31. Nohl, *Hegel*, 380.

32. Ibid., 379-380.

33. Ibid.; W. Shakespeare, *Complete Works* (Albany, New York: James B. Lyon, 1878), 1031-1068.

34. Nohl, *Hegel*, 380; *WW* 7, 183.
35. Nohl, *Hegel*, 380-381.
36. Ibid.; *WW* 7, 237-262.
37. Nohl, *Hegel*, 381.
38. Ibid., 381-382.
39. Ibid.; *WW* 7, 100; Diogenes Laertius L.X.n.VI.
40. Hegel, *Jenaer Systementwürfe*, 301, 306.
41. Ibid., 282-296, 297-300, 300-306, 307-315; *WW* 2, 340-367; Habermas, *Theory and Practice* (Boston: Beacon Press, 1971), 142-169.
42. Hegel, *Jenaer Systementwürfe*, 301.
43. Ibid., 301-302.
44. Ibid.
45. Ibid.; *WW* 7, 130-142.
46. Hegel, *Jenaer Systementwürfe*, 302; *WW* 7, 239-240.
47. Hegel, *Jenaer Systementwürfe*, 301-306; *WW* 2, 339-367.
48. *WW* 11, 43-45; Hegel, *Enzyklopädie*, 85, 17-18, 117, 132-134, 201, 213-215, 319; 39, 77, 81, 441; 70, 114, 297; 114; 4, 6, 47, 51, 80-83, 181-183, 193-195, 284, 462.
49. Hegel, *Enzyklopädie*, 291-309; 318-344; *WW* 10, 93-109.
50. Nohl, *Hegel*, 378-382; Hegel, *Jenaer Systementwürfe*, 301; Hegel, *Enzyklopädie*, 323; W. Gunther, "Sexualerziehung, beispielsweise," *FH* 25 (July 1970) H. 7, 501-508; H. Kentler, "Sexualerziehung—wozu?" *FH* 25 (July 1970) H. 7, 508-511; W. Dirks, "Familie, beispielsweise," *FH* (August 1970) H. 8, 561-570; G. Raeithel, "Der anatomische Schicksalsglaube und die amerikanische Frau," *FH* 31 (January 1976) H. 1, 25-34.
51. Hegel, *Jenaer Systementwürfe*, 302; *Enzyklopädie*, 323.
52. Hegel, *System der Philosophie* (Stuttgart—Bad Cannstatt: Friedrich Frommann Verlag, 1964), Erster Teil. Die Logik, hereinafter cited as: *WW* 8; *WW* 2, 335-516; Hegel, *System der Philosophie* (Stuttgart—Bad Cannstatt: Friedrich Frommann Verlag, 1965), Zweiter Teil. Die Naturphilosophie, hereinafter cited as: *WW* 9; *WW* 6, 147-224; 227-310.
53. Hegel, *Jenaer Systementwürfe*, 302.
54. Ibid., 303.
55. Ibid., 303-306.
56. Ibid., 304-306.
57. Ibid.
58. Ibid., 306.
59. F. Wiedmann, *Hegel*, 7, 45.
60. *WW* 2, 342.
61. Nohl, *Hegel*, 304-308; Hegel, *Jenaer Systementwürfe*, 301-306.
62. *WW* 2, 339-367; Sophocles, *The Theban Plays* (Baltimore, Maryland: Penguin Books, 1964), 126-162, 25-124; Josef Nolte, "Widerstand und Wirklichkeit," *FH* 31, 7 (July 1976) 51-61.
63. A. Pazanin, "Das Problem der Geschichte bei Husserl, Hegel, und Marx," in *Phänomenologie Heute* (Den Haag: Martinus Nijhoff, 1967), 182.
64. *WW* 2, 339-367, 569-601, 602-620.
65. *WW* 7, 182-183, 266, 237-260; H. Küng, *Menschwerdung Gottes* (Freiburg: Herder, 1970), 364-381; M. Theunissen, *Hegel's Lehre vom absoluten Geist als theologisch-politischer*

Traktat (Berlin: Walter de Gruyter, 1970), 77-100; Sophocles, *The Theban Plays,* 25-162.
66. *WW* 2, 339-367; Horkheimer, *Studien,* 64-76.
67. *WW* 2, 342-367.
68. Ibid., 342.
69. Ibid., 342.
70. Ibid., 342-343.
71. *WW* 7, 270-286, 310-328, 328-446.
72. *WW* 2, 342-343.
73. *WW* 7, 253-262.
74. *WW* 2, 343.
75. Ibid.
76. Ibid., 354-367; *WW* 7, 328-446.
77. *WW* 7, 262-328.
78. *WW* 2, 340-354.
79. Ibid.; Adorno, *Negative Dialectics,* part II.
80. Adorno, *Negative Dialectics,* 8; *WW* 15, 23.
81. *WW* 2, 343-346.
82. Ibid.; *WW* 7, 328-446.
83. *WW* 7, 262-328.
84. *WW* 2, 343-346.
85. Ibid.; Sophocles, *Antigone,* 126-162.
86. *WW* 2, 344-346.
87. *WW* 2, 343-346; *WW* 7, 246-247; Sophocles, *Antigone,* 126-162; Nolte, "Widerstand,"
    51-61.
88. *WW* 2, 346-354.
89. Ibid., 347-348.
90. Ibid., 348.
91. Ibid.
92. Ibid., 348-349.
93. Ibid.; Hegel, *Ästhetik,* I, 448; Sophocles, *The Theben Plays,* 126-162.
94. *WW* 2, 348-354; Hegel, *Ästhetik,* I, 187-188, 206, 211-212, 352, 545; 218, 448, 454,
    541, 545; II. 236, 522, 564-565, 568, 522, 565; I, 224, 269, 453; II, 522, 565,
    569-570; S. Freud, *On Creativity and the Unconsciousness* (New York: Harper and Row,
    1958), 49, 109; Sophocles, *The Theben Plays*, 25-124; 126-162.
95. *WW* 2, 349.
96. Ibid., 349-350.
97. Ibid.; Hegel, *Ästhetik,* I, 448; II, 564.
98. *WW* 2, 348-354.
99. Ibid., 350.
100. Wiedmann, *Hegel,* 38-47.
101. Ibid., 42; Nohl, *Hegel,* 378-382; Hegel, *Jenaer Systementwürfe,* 301-306; *WW* 2, 339-
    367.
102. *WW* 2, 81-138, 139-181, 182-334, 335-516, 517-601, 602-620.
103. Ibid.; Wiedmann, *Hegel,* 42.
104. Wiedmann, *Hegel,* 42; Hegel, *Enzyklopädie,* 387-388.

105. Wiedmann, *Hegel,* 42; *WW* 19, 331-417, 449-485, 417-439, 493-500, 551-611.

106. Wiedmann, *Hegel,* 43; R. J. Siebert, "Max Horkheimer: Theology and Positivism I," *The Ecumenist,* 14, No. 2 (January-February, 1976), 19-24, esp. 21; Siebert, "Max Horkheimer: Theology and Positivism II," *The Ecumenist,* 14, No. 3, (March-April, 1976), 42-45.

107. *WW* 16, 355.

108. Wiedmann, *Hegel,* 43.

109. *WW* 16, 355.

110. Adorno, *Negative Dialectics,* 33-35.

111. Wiedmann, *Hegel,* 43.

112. Ibid.; *WW* 7, 242; Hegel, *Enzyklopädie,* 434-435.

113. *WW* 7, 242-243; 251-253; S. Freud, *Civilization and its Discontent* (New York: W. W. Norton, 1962), 12-20, 20-32.

114. Hegel, *Enzyklopädie,* 434-435.

115. Wiedmann, *Hegel,* 42-46.

116. Kung, *Menschwerdung,* 499-500.

117. Ibid.; K. Rosenkranz, *G. W. F. Hegel's Leben* (Darmstadt, 1963), 423.

118. *WW* 7, 231-262.

119. Ibid.; Nohl, *Hegel,* 378-382.

120. *WW* 7, 237-262; *WW* 11, 126-130, 149.

121. *WW* 7, 239.

122. Ibid.; Hegel, *Jenaer Systementwürfe,* 301.

123. *WW* 7, 239.

124. Ibid., 239-240.

125. K. Marx, *Die Frühschriften* (Stuttgart: Alfred Kroner Verlag, 1953), 25-27, 111-112, 355, 543, 528, 545.

126. Adorno, *Negative Dialectics,* 71.

127. *WW* 7, 240.

128. Ibid., 240-241.

129. *WW* 11, 74-75, 84.

130. Ibid., 75; *WW* 7, 328-440.

131. *WW* 11, 75; *WW* 7, 272-276, 88-163, 164-225.

132. *WW* 11, 75; *WW* 7, 237-262, 328-456.

133. *WW* 7, 240-241.

134. Ibid., 238.

135. Ibid.; *WW* 15, 67-68.

136. *WW* 7, 237-241; *WW* 11, 43-47.

137. *WW* 7, 240; *WW* 6, 293.

138. *WW* 7, 240.

139. Ibid., 240-241; Hegel, *Jenaer Systementwürfe,* 301-302; Nohl, *Hegel,* 379.

140. *WW* 7, 240-241, 182-184.

141. Ibid., 240-241.

142. Ibid., 240-241, 265-267.

143. Ibid., 240-241, 182-184.

144. Ibid., 241.

145. Ibid.; Hegel, *Jenaer Systementwürfe,* 301-303; Nohl, *Hegel,* 378-382.
146. *WW* 7, 241; *WW* 11, 45; Hegel, *Enzyklopädie,* 388.
147. *WW* 7, 241.
148. Ibid.
149. Ibid., 239-241.
150. Ibid., 239-241, 182-184; Nohl, *Hegel,* 378-382; Hegel, *Jenaer Systementwürfe,* 301-306.
151. *WW* 7, 182-184, 237-241, 242-243, 265-267.
152. Ibid., 237-241, 265-267; *WW* 11, 126-130, 149; Hegel, *Ästhetik,* II, 423.
153. *WW* 7, 237-241; Hegel, *Ästhetik,* II, 423.
154. *WW* 7, 237-249; *WW* 5, 35-171; *WW* 11, 568-569.
155. *WW* 7, 237-249, 265-267.
156. *WW* 2, 339-367; *WW* 7, 237-262; *WW* 11, 126-130, 149; Hegel, *Ästhetik,* II, 423.

Hegel in St. Louis

by

JOHN E. SMITH

The St. Louis movement in philosophy, sparked by the founding of the St. Louis Philosophical Society in 1866, represents one of the most fascinating and at the same time most bizarre intellectual developments ever to take place on the American scene. It would be difficult to find anywhere another example of applied philosophy to equal the efforts of the St. Louis Hegelians, as they came to be called, in their attempt both to shape and interpret the life of their time from the vantage point of Hegel's philosophy. Although initially some dozen students of Hegel's thought were involved, there were three men at the center of the movement—Henry C. Brokmeyer, a lawyer who was later to become Lt. Governor of Missouri; William Torrey Harris, a school teacher born in Connecticut and sometime United States Commissioner of Education; and Denton J. Snider, a student of the Classics who taught at the Christian Brothers College in St. Louis. Of the three, Brokmeyer, who made a translation of Hegel's *Larger Logic* which remains unpublished to this day, was the most faithful representative of Hegel's ideas, struggling to understand and translate the text as accurately as possible. Harris was somewhat more original philosophically, more critical of Hegel, and hence less of a mirror image of the master. Snider, to whom we are indebted for much of what we know about the Movement, was voluble and lyrical in his appreciation of the importance to be attached to Hegel's thought, but apart from knowledge of some key ideas in the *Philosophy of History* and the *Philosophy of Right,* he does not show any intimate acquaintance with the full scope of Hegel's categoreal scheme.

Although the professors making up the academic establishment at Washington University (founded in 1853) were inclined to laugh at what they regarded as the unprofessional approach of these three men, it is nevertheless true that, through their devotion, the tradition of German Idealism was introduced to American thinkers, and with lasting results. Not only did Brokmeyer translate Hegel's *Larger Logic,* but Harris, almost single-handedly, founded the *Journal of Speculative Philosophy* in 1867 and sustained it for twenty-two volumes! In pages filled with translations from the works of Kant, Fichte, Schelling, Goethe, and Hegel on the topics of art, education, social order, and speculative metaphysics, Harris was attempting nothing less than the transplantation of German culture to America, both for the large population of Germans who emigrated to America at mid-century and for the thinking public at large. While members of the Society were studying Hegel's *Logic* with Brokmeyer (Snider always called him "university Brokmeyer"), a sub-section of the members was meeting at the home of Harris for the purpose of translating the *Phenomenology*. They were all enthusiasts—Hegel-intoxicated men—and they did more than think *about* Hegel; they tried to understand all that was happening in Civil War St. Louis by means of Hegel's ideas. How serious they were in this undertaking is illustrated by Snider. Referring repeatedly to Hegel's *Logic* as the "Book of Fate," Snider described the capture of the arsenal at Camp Jackson—the first Union victory of the war—as a "world historical event" in the odyssey of the Absolute Spirit, an event which was supposed to catapult the city of St. Louis into the middle of the struggle to achieve a union of the One and the Many. As one can see, Snider was more a prophet than a sober philosopher.

It is not my aim to tell the story, as it were, of the St. Louis Movement. Much work on that historical task has been done, although to be sure much remains. My purpose is primarily philosophical and therefore I shall try to extract several ideas which these men found in Hegel and to indicate how they were employed in the task of comprehending the time in which they lived and in pointing out the future course of American life. This undertaking is not easy because of the disjointed character of the sources and the mixture of exposition and commentary on Hegel's texts with flashes of insight, prophetic claims, and vague intimations of the relevance of Hegel's doctrines which fall far short of Hegel's demand that the matter be worked out.

I single out for consideration three themes; first, the prophetic interpretation of the role to be played by the city of St. Louis as representative of the Union and the American West and as the instrument of the *Weltgeist* in determining the future shape of America; secondly, the belief that Hegel's concept of the community and the state at the level of objective *Geist* provide resources for combating the excessive individualism at the heart of American political thinking since colonial times, plus the tendency to think of government as a merely external mechanism or abstract unity of power; thirdly, the vision of America as the super-Hegelian State wherein the unity of many states and a Union has been realized through the activity of the *Weltgeist* to serve as a model, first for a United States of Europe and ultimately for the world.

(1) *The Role of St. Louis* Although the leaders of the Movement referred repeatedly to the *Logic*, we must not overlook the fact that Sibree's translation of the *Philosophy of History* was the only published work of Hegel's available in English at the time and its influence is readily detected. On the other hand, it is necessary to bear in mind that Snider, especially, invariably understood the *Logic* as an expression of the true pattern of world *history* or, as he says, "the movement of the pure essences of the world, stripped from their outer illusory vesture."[1] It is against this background that we must understand their perception of the manner in which Hegel's thought was to interpret the role of St. Louis. His philosophy of world history was to provide, first, the basis for understanding the historical career of St. Louis on the world stage and, second, to help bring about, through an application of the concept of community, a new synthesis or cultural unity among the diverse elements which lived side by side in the city. Snider distinguished four groups—Roman Catholics, New Englanders, Southerners, and Germans—and sought to describe their essential and at certain points conflicting characteristics and interests. A unified St. Louis, he thought, capable of performing its historical role, required a harmonizing principle and a proper sense, on the part of each group, that they were participating in events of world historical proportions.

The Roman Catholics, according to Snider's account, formed the largest and most diversified group, embracing people of French, Irish, Slavic, and German descent. Through the world character of their religion and the unity of their "Catholic soul," they contributed a sense of the *universal,* of order and structure. The religious faith which unified them remained intact, and whatever differences arose between these groups were invariably the result of divergent political interests.

The smallest but most homogeneous group were the New Englanders. By contrast with the religious unity displayed by the Catholics, this group was sharply divided theologically by the Trinitarian/Unitarian cleavage. Their special contribution, however, was a powerful concern for education manifested in the establishment of public schools and of Washington University. These schools, thought Snider, would provide the main channel for the spread of those ideas and ideals which defined the St. Louis Movement, and it was indeed significant that Harris served as school principal for a time.

The third group, the Southerners, helped to establish St. Louis as a "Southern" city whose life was pervaded by the social graciousness, in Snider's words, characteristic of the pre-war South. Members of this group were distinguished by their talent for politics and political leadership, as evidenced by the fact that the leading figures in every political party at the time were Southerners. Unfortunately, the war led to bitter divisions among them which served to curtail sharply, if not actually nullify, their influence as a group in the development of the new metropolis.

Snider's fourth group, the Germans, he described as the "strongest element," possessing a unity of spirit rooted in intelligence and aggressiveness, and reinforced by the disciplines of education and military training. Snider underlined the powerful contribution to the Union cause made by the German contingent in the capture of the arsenal at Camp Jackson. This event was, to Snider, a pivotal one in the Civil War—the first victory for the Union and the arrest of secession in a southern state. Though the event was in St. Louis, the Teutonic spirit of the Fatherland, says Snider, was at work, and, he writes, "we were unconscious participators in a globe-encircling world-movement."[2] It was the conviction of these Hegelians that Hegel's philosophy had revealed to them the existence and interpreted the significance of the subterranean *Geist* at work in the New World.

Earlier on it was said that, to perform its historical mission, the city of St. Louis would have to be transformed through an integration of its constituent elements. To this end, Snider cited "the fifth element"— the St. Louis Movement—which, through culture, education, and religion of an "unofficial" sort, was to bring about the grand synthesis, overcoming the separateness of the "four transmitted cultural elements." It is of the utmost importance that Snider, though he could describe Hegel's thought as "handed down from Europe" and as a product of European conditions, did not regard Hegel's philosophy as "transmitted" in the same sense as the four cultural elements. In his view, Hegel was expressing the Universal, the essence and spirit of world history as a power transcending the four elements. "We took," he wrote, "a foreign traditional philosophy to countervail the tradition which had already been imported."[3]

These men were groping to find the meaning of the Civil War; the time called for some first principles, among which was the need for a conception of a transcending unity beyond the polarity of the One (the Union) and the Many (the separate states). They sought the answer in Hegel's *Logic*! They believed that if they could find the original, indigenous soul of the city of St. Louis they would uncover a reality transcending all the separate groups and that this would serve as a model for the integration of the nation at large. In their view, St. Louis had become the medium whereby the problem of Union vs. the supremacy of the single states was brought into the clearest focus. The solution in the form of a unity of the Union and the single states provides a model for the world. For Snider, this unity is the highest unity of Hegel's world spirit in the sphere of political organization.

These sublime thoughts about the destiny of St. Louis, however, were to be rudely contradicted by subsequent events. The inhabitants of the actual city failed to perceive their world historical role and deceived themselves with illusions and allegiance to false gods. In his disillusionment and disappointment, Snider declared the appearance in St. Louis of what he called the "Great Illusion," and he appealed to Hegel as the means of unmasking it. That illusion consisted in the belief that the greatness of the city lies in wealth, increasing population, and success in competition with the fortunes of other cities. Hegel's philosophy, however, according to Snider, demands that we see the naked truth underlying all reality, and hence that the greatness of a city does not manifest itself in the goals of the river gods, but rather in the contribution which it is to make to the realization of the world design. St. Louis, Snider continued, further revealed its unworthiness in the *hubris* the city displayed in its contest with Chicago for supremacy in commerce and the size of its population. While Snider was thus engaged in exposing the "Great Illusion" in St. Louis, Brokmeyer could not forego striking an Hegelian blow in the other direction. *Hubris,* he insisted, was not confined to St. Louis. The city of Chicago had likewise exhibited an overwhelming pride in its struggle for recognition, and retribution came in the form of the great fire of 1870. Brokmeyer saw this conflagration as a judgment of history and declared that Chicago was negated by its own negativity as expressed in its own *hubris.* It should now be clear that the St. Louis Hegelians were far from content merely to talk about Hegel's philosophy; they saw it as the convenient vantage point from which to interpret all the events through which they lived.

(2) *Hegel's Doctrine of Community vs. Individualism* The main point to be emphasized here is quite clear: it concerns the importance of introducing Hegel's basic philosophical outlook into the American consciousness as a corrective and antidote to the dominance enjoyed by the British tradition, especially, in our political thinking. Harris was fully aware of the influence exercised by the particularism and individualism of British empiricism and he was calling for Hegel's perspective on the community and the rational state to counteract a trend which was inaugurated by the Founders of the Republic when they conceived of government as no more than an instrument for securing individual rights. In an editorial note which launched the first issue of the *Journal of Speculative Philosophy* in 1867, Harris made at least one of his philosophical aims quite clear:

> Likewise, it will be acknowledged that the national consciousness has moved forward on a new platform during the past few years. The idea underlying our form of government had hitherto developed only one of its essential phases—that of brittle individualism—in which national unity seemed an external mechanism, soon to be entirely dispensed with, and the enterprise of the private man or of the corporation substituted for it. Now we have arrived at the consciousness of the other essential phase, and each individual recognizes his substantial side to be the state as such.

Time and again Harris objected that acts of the will, though self-determining in their essential character, become mere "self-will" and hence the opposite of the rational will, when they stand unrelated to the mediating function of the state which brings "home" to the individual the universal import of what he has done. On a lesser level—that of civil society—the institutions of the spirit bring the individual to an awareness of his essential uncompleteness when viewed in isolation. "It is the whole *community*," he wrote, "only, that furnishes the complete outfit for each individual, and hence it acts as one organism, and each individual, though this act of transcending himself and making himself *for* all, receives in turn the service *of* all; and thus all are for him and he is *for himself* through the reciprocal relation thus established."[4] For Harris as well as the others, Hegel's thought seemed to provide exactly what was needed to mediate the conflicting demands of an especially difficult social and political situation. On the one side stood the powerful tradition of individualism—individuals are primordial and their being together in society is a subsequent affair—and of individual unalienable rights which it is the supreme task of government to protect. On the other side there were the legitimate demands made by society and by a federal government for a loyalty and an acknowledgment of responsibility adequate for sustaining a national community and overcoming the conflicts of interest inevitable in a quite heterogeneous collection of peoples. Harris saw in Hegel's concept of self-determining and self-differentiating life the proper model of the Universal which is embodied in the state as rational will. The individual doer is to learn to will rational deeds which have a rational or universal content, which is to say that, unlike evil deeds which negate civil society or family, they do not harm the doer when they are brought back to his own person in the form of their consequences.

For Harris, the living *ethos* of a people, finding its fullest and most concrete realization in the state, stands as a way of overcoming the external and mechanical view of government which determined the political thinking of the eighteenth century. When Harris complained that philosophical thinking in America had been far too much under the sway of English empiricism (if German thinkers, he said, are "unamerican," so are the English), and proposed Plato, Aristotle, Schelling, and Hegel as the needed antidote, he was seeking to overcome the conception of government as no more than an instrument designed to ensure the rights of individuals considered one at a time. An instrument is something to be used; it is wielded by some men in the process of controlling or regulating the activity of others, whereas, on Hegel's view, as Harris saw so well, the state is a rational order in which all members participate and wherein all live a common life. An instrument or mechanism allows for neither life nor participation. It is most noteworthy that for Harris and his contemporaries, the so-called "organic" state proclaimed by Hegel was *not* envisaged, as it later came to be, as an absolute or totalitarian whole swallowing all individuals or demanding a total sacrifice on the part of all citizens. Several reasons help to explain this fact. First, Harris and his colleagues could approach Hegel's thought directly and free of any polemical context of the sort that existed (and still exists) in the discussions of Hegel's *Philosophy of Right* following the advent of Nazism and the Second World War. Hence they could more readily lay hold of the liberal orientation of Hegel's views and understand his emphasis on objective *Geist* as a modern recovery of the concept of an *ethos* prevalent among the ancient philosophers. Second, the American Hegelians saw Hegel's philosophy of the state against the background of American individualism and they were firm in their belief that, while that element could be transformed in the direction of the Universal, it would never be eliminated and would therefore continue to serve as a counterweight against the development of a monolithic collectivism on the basis of the organic theory.

(3) *America the Super-Hegelian State* On this topic the basic ideas were developed by Snider in his book, *The State,* published in 1902. In this work he shows first-hand acquaintance with Hegel's *Philosophy of Right,* citing specific sections to support his argument. Snider's first claim is that Hegel's state, though informed "by certain English ideas," is still an absolutism. That doctrine, Snider contended, could have been avoided if Hegel had paid attention to the American Constitution, something, says Snider, which had been working for thirty years by the time Hegel published his book. Hegel, however, is not to be blamed because most Europeans knew little or nothing about our Constitution until Tocqueville brought it to their attention. Hegel, on the other hand, is culpable because, while announcing the principle that the "real is the rational," he managed to overlook some of this reality in the New World. "One may wonder," says Snider, "why he did not search a little for the latest reality in the unfolding of his world-spirit."[5] Fortunately, Snider was referring here to the American Republic and its Constitution, and he sedulously avoided any hint that Hegel would have found this "latest reality" had he directed his attention to St. Louis.

Snider's central criticism of Hegel concerns the thesis that single states confront each other as *independent, sovereign wills,* each of which pursues its own welfare so that armed conflict is the only final restraining power. "Hegel declares," says Snider, "that the principles of morality belong to the relation of individual to individual, but not to the relation of State to State."[6] The only possible emperor with power over the collection of single states is the world spirit—the Emperor of

Emperors—and Snider saw in that conception a principle of caprice whereby individual states are established or destroyed according to the particular will of the world *Geist*. But, says Snider, if evolution is a reality, this is not the end of the matter; we must look to what the world spirit has disclosed when we pass "from its European to its American manifestation."[7] Taking a page from Hegel's own book, Snider declared that embodied in the American experience of creating a union of states on a constitutional basis is a new and non-capricious principle, the most recent form of the world spirit, which is that of a state-producing state—*America*. This principle of achieving the unity of a one and a many expresses the *one which must be made universal* in a United States of the World. Until this happens, all states—including America—must continue to exist in a temporal and spatial environment of conflicting states. Snider thought that Hegel and European philosophy generally were seduced by absolutism and the imperious spirit which projects absolute and automatic principles so that the individual "has nothing to do but look on and see it work and obey its behest."[8] But, again, this is not the whole story because, according to Snider, the world spirit in its American manifestation has not only taught the new truth about the state-producing state but has made it clear, as well, that man must always *recreate* the principle operative in political affairs. "In America the state too is imperial and commands the people, who obey its law; but the people are also imperical and command the state, creating it anew if they so will."[9] The odyssey of the Hegelian world spirit is clear—the United States has already arrived on the scene, bearing in its political structure the principle destined to become the *Begriff* of all future political reality; the United States of Europe even now has a kind of being in the thought and aspirations of many, and both point on to the concrete realization of the union of all states throughout the world. This was Snider's Hegelian vision.

From our present vantage point of over a century after the St. Louis Movement was launched, the question is what we are to say about its significance for the development of philosophical thinking in America. At least two considerations present themselves. In the first place, there can be little doubt about the influence of these men in establishing the tradition of German Idealism in America. As they rightly perceived, American philosophical thinking, especially in matters social and political, had been dominated by the British tradition, especially Mill and

Spencer (Harris called attention to the fact that Spencer's works sold more than eight times the number of copies in America than they did in London). The introduction of Hegel's thought provided not only a new metaphysical and speculative depth, but it established as well the basis for an idealist critique of naturalistic and materialistic philosophies. Hegel's influence was double-barrelled; on the one hand, there was the positive development of Absolute Idealism at the hands of Royce, the first American thinker to construct a comprehensive metaphysic in the tradition of the classical system builders. On the other hand, idealist critics of Hegel's Absolutism, like Howison and others, developed pluralistic and personalistic idealisms which have had a continuing influence on American thought. It seems quite clear that on the basis of the developments cited, Hegel and German Idealism greatly enriched our philosophical fare. But that is not all; a more complete account would include the enormous influence exercised by the Hegelian way of thinking on the philosophical work of John Dewey and the metaphysics of Charles Peirce.

The second comment is more sobering, but it may even be salutary in an academically oriented meeting about Hegel. Surveying the activity and thought of the St. Louis Hegelians furnishes insight into what it means *really to believe in Hegel's thought* in relation to a *present*, historical situation. Even allowing for the enthusiasm and the naivete, we can see in these men what Hegelianism meant in action and not only as a standpoint to be studied in its application to distant times and places. When one reads Snider especially, but Brokmeyer as well, there comes the sense that the world spirit is at work in the very street where one is walking and that all things surrounding are living examples of becoming and dynamic synthesis. Snider was aware of the extent to which Hegel had captivated them and he admitted that his philosophy had become for them a kind of religion. To see such earnestness and commitment to a philosophical position is certainly refreshing in a situation where philosophy has become something of an *industry*, the products of which are largely for internal consumption.

NOTES

1. D. J. Snider, *The St. Louis Movement* (St. Louis, 1920), p. 12.
2. Ibid., p. 23.
3. Ibid., p. 26.
4. *The American Hegelians,* Ed. W. H. Goetzman (New York, 1973), p. 111.
5. D. J. Snider, *The State, The American Hegelians,* Ed. W. H. Goetzman, (New York, 1973), p. 186.
6. Ibid., p. 187.
7. Ibid., p. 188.
8. Ibid., p. 189.
9. Ibid., p. 190.

Some Observations on Social and Political Philosophy Among the St. Louis Hegelians

by

JOHN O. RIEDL

The topic for discussion at this session, the social and political thought of the St. Louis Hegelians, is interesting partly because it is not the chief concern of the St. Louis Movement, and therefore not usually treated with more than passing mention by its historians, and because, in effect, it takes Hegel's doctrine that everything that happens in society is the product of reason and history, and examines it in the context of American political ideals and social aspirations.

As evidence of the minor role of the topic in discussions among the St. Louis Hegelians, I submit that I was able to find only seven relevant articles in the twenty-two volumes of *The Journal of Speculative Philosophy*.[1] In the seventh volume H. H. Morgan wrote on "Foundation of Authority in the State" (January, 1873, 42-46); in the sixteenth volume there are Mary Wright Sewall on "The Idea of the Home" (1882, 274-85), treating of family life and forms of domestic tyranny, and J. Burns-Gibson, "On Some Idols or Factitious Unities" (1882, 386-95); in the seventeenth volume is J. G. Woerner, "On the Nature of Property and its Devolution" (1883, 141-53); in the eighteenth volume, Walter B. Wines wrote "On Hegel's Idea of the Nature and Sanction of Law" (1884, 9-20); and in the twenty-second volume there are Simon N. Patten, "Can Economics Furnish an Objective Standard for Morality?" (1893, 322-32), and Leonora B. Halsted, on "Friendship" (1893, 400-11). In addition, W. H. Kimball contributed, under the pen-name Theron Gray, several more or less pertinent articles, namely, "The Grand Man" [VIII (1874), 73-84], "Science in Government" [X (1876) 290-307] "The Nation and the Commune" [XII (1878), 44-67], and "Fate and Freedom" [XVI (1882), 337-42]. James Hutchison Stirling contributed four "Lectures on the Philosophy of Law" [VI (1872), 313-32; VII (April 1873), 20-39; VII (July 1873), 24-43; VIII (1874), 123-43]. None of the authors is a major figure in the St. Louis movement.[2]

Several translations from Hegel should be mentioned, namely, "The Science of Rights, Morals, and Religion," translated from Hegel's

Philosophische Propaedeutik by William Torrey Harris [IV (1870), 38-62, 155-92], and "Hegel's Philosophy of the State," translated from Hegel's *Philosophy of Spirit* by Edwin D. Mead [XVI (1882), 71-84, 194-208].[3]

Among the Book Notices, two reviews by William Torrey Harris are noteworthy: of Hermann Ulrici, *Grundzüge der Praktischen Philosophie. Naturrecht, Ethik und Aesthetik,* in which Harris speaks of the true classification of the American Republic in the Philosophy of Right [VII (October 1873), 90-92], and of Britton A. Hill, *Liberty and Law under Federative Government,* in which Harris discusses the function of nurture in the State and the nature of paper money [VIII (1874), 186-191].[4]

The entire list of articles, translations, and reviews shows minimal interest in social and political thought compared to the interest in logic, metaphysics and, within practical philosophy, the theory of education. What does exist is by less well-known writers, except for William Torrey Harris, whose name is prominent among both the translators and the reviewers.

Another good place to test the importance of social and political philosophy among the St. Louis Hegelians is in the courses of lectures offered at the Concord Summer School of Philosophy. Early in 1879, a faculty of philosophy was organized informally at Concord, Massachusetts, and in the spring, A. Bronson Alcott was made Dean of the faculty, and F. B. Sanborn, Secretary. Although both officers were of Concord, William Torrey Harris was deeply involved in the planning.[5] The report of the 1879 summer indicates that there were ten lectures by David A. Wesson, of Medford, on *Political Philosophy*, and two lectures by F. B. Sanborn, on *Philanthropy and Social Science.* There were in all nine courses of ten sessions each, with some additional lectures. The charges were $3.00 per course, board in the village could be had for from $6 to $12 a week. The report was carried by *The Journal of Speculative Philosophy* [XIV (1880), 135-38].

The prospectus for the summer of 1880 indicates that similar courses of lectures were planned. Among the additional lectures were one by Julia Ward Howe on *Modern Society*, and two by F. B. Sanborn on *The Philosophy of Charity* [XIV (1880), 251-53]. In the 1881 program, there was a lecture by E. Mulford, on *The Philosophy of the State* [XV (1881), 75-77].[6] The program for 1883 included nothing on either social or political philosophy [XVII (1883) 213-15]. The same was true of the program for 1884, which dealt with Ralph Waldo Emerson (1803-1882), and of the program for 1885, which dealt mostly with Goethe

[XIX (1885), 220-21].[7] The program for 1886 was an elaborate study of Aristotle. The *Journal of Speculative Philosophy* printed "Suggestions to those beginning the study of Aristotle" [XX (1886), 430-38] and an elaborate "Bibliography" on Aristotle [XX (1886), 439-43]. Among the lectures planned were the following:

> 10. Aristotle's Theory of the State (particularly in relation to the individual), compared with Modern Views on the same subject.
> 11. Aristotle's Views on Education and on the State's Relation to it, compared with Modern Views on the same subject.
> 12. Aristotle's Views on Profit and Interest, compared with Modern Views [XX (1886), 426-29].

The ninth, (and last) summer of the Concord School, 1887, continued the interest in Aristotle. Among the lecturers were: A. P. Peabody, on "The Ethics of Aristotle"; Luigi Ferri, of Rome, on "Aristotle's *Politics* and Montesquieu's *Esprit des Lois*"; F. B. Sanborn, on "Social Science in Plato and Aristotle"; and Ellen M. Mitchell, on "Friendship in Aristotle's Ethics."

In the interest of completeness, it should be mentioned that two of the prominent members of the St. Louis Hegelians had practical experience in government. Henry Conrad Brokmeyer (1826-1906) was Lieutenant-Governor of Missouri from 1875 to 1879, Acting Governor in 1876-1877.[8] William Torrey Harris (1835-1909) was United States Commissioner of Education, 1889-1906. In addition to his publications in the *Journal,* he wrote "Edward Bellamy's Vision."[9]

The one of the triumvirate of founders most concerned with social and political philosophy was Denton Jaques Snider (1841-1925), who held no government position. Among his many books, mostly on literary and psychological subjects, are: *Social Institutions in their Origin, Growth and Interconnection, Psychologically Treated* (1901) and *The State* (1902).[10]

Harvey Gates Townsend contributed an article, "The Political Philosophy of Hegel in a Frontier Society," to a volume commemorative of the centenary of Harris's birth.[11] Thomas Henry Clare wrote a doctoral thesis on *The Sociological Theories of William Torrey Harris,*[12] and Frances Adele Harmon (Bolles), on *The Social Philosophy of the St. Louis Hegelians.*[13]

These are remarks contributed by Professor Riedl as Chairman of a session on the relation of Hegel's political and social thought to the St. Louis Hegelians in which Professor Smith's paper on "Hegel in St. Louis" was presented.—ED.

NOTES

1. Published quarterly from January 1867 through 1887; then sporadically for four more numbers, ending with that of December 1893. William Torrey Harris was the editor.

2. Some articles, more on ethics than on social and political philosophy, may also be useful. They are: James Edmunds, "Kant's Ethics" [V (1871), 27-37, 108-18, 289-307; VIII (1874), 339-51; X (1876), 416-31]; Josiah Royce, "Schiller's Ethical Studies" [XII (1878), 373-92]; R. G. Hazard, "Man's Freedom in his Moral Nature" [XVII (1883), 421-30]; Francis Ellingwood Abbot, "The Moral Creativeness of Man" [XVIII (1884), 138-52]; A. D'Orell, "The Problem of Evil" [XVIII (1884), 188-94]; S. W. Dyde, "Martineau's Idiopsychological Ethics" [XXII (1888), 138-69]; James Hutchison Stirling (1820-1909), *Four Lectures on the Philosophy of Law* (New York: D. Appleton & Co., ca. 1880), is a republication in book form of the lectures in the *Journal*. Stirling is also the author of *The Secret of Hegel: Being the Hegelian System in Origin, Principle, Form and Matter* (London: Longman, Green, Longman, Roberts and Green, 1865). His lectures at Concord were probably commissioned because of an appreciation of his lectures before the Juridical Society of Edinburgh, 1871, which had appeared in the *Journal of Jurisprudence and Scottish Law Magazine,* January-April 1872, and in book form under the title, *Lectures on the Philosophy of Law. Together with Whewell and Hegel, and Hegel and Mr. W. R. Smith, A Vindication in Physico-Mathematical Regard* (London: Longmans, Green & Co., 1873, 139 pp.).

3. Other translations, of peripheral interest, are: "Hegel as Publicist. By J. K. F. Rosenkranz," translated by G. S. Hall [VI (1872), 258-63; "Hegel, Prussia, and the Philosophy of Right. By J. K. F. Rosenkranz," Translated by G. S. Hall [VI (1872), 263-79]; "Anthropology. By Immanuel Kant," translated by Adolph E. Kroeger [IX (1875), 16-27, 239-45, 406-16; X (1876), 319-23; XI (1877), 310-17, 353-63; XIII (1879), 281-89; XIV (1880), 154-69, 299-304; XV (1881), 62-66; XVI (1882), 47-52, 395-413 (end of first book)]; cf. also "Adolph E. Kroeger—Obituary," by William Torrey Harris [XVI (1882), 433-39]; "On the Study of History and Jurisprudence," being F. W. J. Schelling's tenth lecture "On the Method of University Study" *(des akademischen Studium)*, translated by Ella S. Morgan [XIII (1879), 310-19]; "Facts of Consciousness. By J. G. Fichte," translated by Adolph E. Kroeger [XVII (1883), 130-41, 263-83; XVIII (1884), 47-71, 152-61]; "The Problem of Anthropology. By Ludwig Noire," translated by M. B. Bonner [XVIII (1884), 337-55].

4. There are also some, from short to very short, notices of the following books: Britton A. Hill, *Absolute Money. A New System of National Finance under a Cooperative Government* [IX (1875), 442]; Robert D. Allen, *An Effort to Analyze the Moral Idea* [IX (1875), 444]; William B. Weeden, *The Morality of Prohibitory Liquor Laws. An Essay* [IX (1875), 444]; R. S. Guerney, *Municipal Law and its Relations to the Constitution of Man* [XII (1878), 108]; J. G. Woerner (a judge of the Probate Court of St. Louis), "The Jurisdiction of Probate Cases," *Southern Law Review,* June-July 1877 [XII (1878), 109]; R. J. Wright, *Principia or Basis of Social Science; Being a Survey of the Subject from the Moral and Theological, Yet Liberal*

and Progressive, Stand-Point (on Socialism) [XII (1878, 218]; James Parsons, *A Series of Essays on Legal Topics* [XII (1878), 218]; James Edmunds, *Kant's Ethics: The Clavis to an Index. Including Extracts from several Oriental Sacred Scriptures and from certain Greek and Roman Philosophical Writings* [XIII (1879), 428-29]; cf. also a circular advertising same [XXI (1887), 112]; Jeremy Bentham, *An Introduction to the Principles of Morals and Legislation* (Oxford: Clarendon Press, 1876) [XV(1881), 103]; George Whale, *A Fragment on Political Education,* noticed by J. Burns-Gibson [XVII (1883), 440].

5. Harris was so interested in the project that he left St. Louis and his position as Superintendent of City Schools in 1880, "and devoted himself to lecturing on pedagogy, and the pursuit of literature." Cf. Henry Ridgley Evans, "William Torrey Harris: An Appreciation," in Edward L. Schaub, editor, *William Torrey Harris 1835-1935* (Chicago: The Open Court Publishing Company, 1936), pp. 1-14, especially pp. 5-6. Cf. also the article by Cleon Forbes, published in five parts in the *Missouri Historical Review,* under the title, "The St. Louis School of Thought" [XXV, no. 1 (October 1930), 83-101; XXV, no. 2 (January 1931), 289-305; XXV, no. 3 (April 1931), 461-73; XXV, no. 4 (July 1931), 609-23; XXVI, no. 1 (October 1931), 68-77], especially part II, "William Torrey Harris— Exponent." Morris R. Cohen makes a brief statement about Harris's social philosophy, in *American Thought, a Critical Sketch* (Glencoe, Ill.: The Free Press, 1954), p. 266.

6. The lectures for 1882 were not mentioned in the *Journal of Speculative Philosophy,* except to announce, in a "Report of the Lectures on the Concord School" [XVII (1883), 317-18] their impending publication under the title, *Concord Lectures on Philosophy.* The volume appeared in 1883 with the sub-title, "Comprising outlines of all the lectures at the Concord Summer School of Philosophy in 1882, with an Historical sketch. Collected and arranged by Raymond L. Bridgman. Revised by the lecturers. Approved by the faculty" (Cambridge, Mass.: Moses King, Publisher, 1883, 168 pp.).

7. Collected into a book by Franklin Benjamin Sanborn, editor, *The Life and Genius of Goethe; Lectures at the Concord School of Philosophy* (Boston: Ticknor and Company, 1886, 454 pp.). The 1884 series also appeared in book form: F. B. Sanborn, editor, *The Genius and Character of Emerson, Lectures at the Concord School of Philosophy* (Boston: J. R. Osgood and Company, 1885, 447 pp.).

8. His only published book, *A Mechanic's Diary,* which appeared posthumously in 1910, was made up of entries from his diary for the period May 1, 1856 to November 8, 1856. It has some observations about social and political problems.

9. *Forum,* VIII (1889), 199-208. The article was republished by William H. Goetzmann, editor, *The American Hegelians, An Intellectual Episode in the History of Western America* (New York: Alfred A. Knopf, 1973) pp. 193-201.

10. Both published privately in St. Louis. His *The St. Louis Movement in Philosophy, Literature, Education, Psychology, with Chapters of Autobiography* (St. Louis: Sigma Publishing Co., 1926, 608 pp.), is the definitive work on the subject. It has no chapters on social and political philosophy.

11. Edward Leroy Schaub, editor, *William Torrey Harris 1835-1935* (Chicago: The Open Court Publishing Company, 1936), pp. 68-80. See also Harvey Gates Townsend, "Philosophy in St. Louis," in his *Philosophical Ideas in the United States* (New York: American Book Company, 1934), pp. 116-30.

12. Thesis (Ph.D.), St. Louis: Washington University, 1934, 262 pp. Published in book form,

Belleville, Illinois: C. Hepp Printing Co. 1935, 262 pp. For this reference, I am indebted to Edward I. Pitts, College of Education, Division of Education Policy Studies, The Pennsylvania State University.

13. Thesis (Ph.D.), New York: Columbia University, 1943, 112 pp.

COMMENT ON

The Relationship of Habermas's Views to Hegel

RICHARD J. BERNSTEIN

There are several ways in which the topic "Habermas and Hegel" may be approached. Before outlining how I will deal with the topic, I want to indicate what I will not do. Hegel has had a profound influence on the intellectual career of Habermas. On several occasions, Habermas has explicitly encountered and written about various aspects of Hegel's philosophy. One might then focus on Habermas' explicit treatment of Hegel in order to evaluate Habermas' contribution as a critic and scholar of Hegel. While I will not do this, I do want to claim that Habermas' treatment of Hegel has the distinctive quality of the most penetrating commentaries. For whether one agrees or disagrees with Habermas' interpretations and criticisms, they open up new perspectives on Hegel and compel the reader to return to the texts in order to rethink basic issues in Hegel. One might also interpret the topic of this symposium as raising the question, "Is Habermas an Hegelian?" But the difficulty with this question is that it presupposes an answer to the complex question, "What does it mean to be an Hegelian in our time?" I will be suggesting how some key Hegelian themes run through Habermas' work, but I believe that the question can be best answered by approaching it indirectly.

In my brief comment, I intend to focus on four interrelated Hegelian themes in Habermas' writings. My purpose is systematic, for I want to raise some basic questions about what appear to be deep conflicting tendencies in his most recent philosophizing. The four themes are: (1) Habermas' general strategy of argumentation; (2) the Hegelian type of argument exhibited in *Knowledge and Human Interests;* (3) the centrality of the concept of self-reflection; and (4) the relation between Habermas' comprehensive theory of rationality and *Vernunft.*

(1) Even a superficial acquaintance with Habermas' writings leaves one with a strong impression of his erudition and wide range of knowledge. In *Theory and Practice,* he traces the fate of these concepts from their classical Greek origins through medieval philosophy, the Renaissance, to early modern thought, culminating with a discussion of Hegel and Marx. In *Knowledge and Human Interests,* we follow the theme of the nature and conditions of human knowledge through Kant, Fichte, Hegel, Marx, Nietzsche, Comte, Dilthey, Peirce, and Freud. Not only is Habermas' historical knowledge penetrating, but his systematic interests range over sociology in its various schools, linguistics, philosophy of language, philosophy of science, hermeneutics, phenomenology, psychoanalysis, and psychological theories of cognitive and moral development. One is tempted to say that his knowledge is almost encyclopedic. Some

critics have accused him of a facile ecclecticism. But I believe that we gain an insight into his range of concerns and what Habermas is doing by returning to Hegel.

My primary text is that marvelous passage in the Introduction to the *Phenomenology* where Hegel describes how science (*Wissenschaft*) and natural consciousness (*Das Natürliche Bewusstsein*) initially appear to each other to be topsy-turvy or inverted. Hegel writes:

> For science cannot simply reject a form of knowledge which is not true, and treat this as a common view of things, and then assure us that itself is an entirely different kind of knowledge, and holds the other to be of no account at all; nor can it appeal to the fact that in this other there are pressages of a better. By giving that assurance it would declare its force and value to lie in its bare existence; but the untrue knowledge appeals likewise to the fact that it *is,* and assures that to it *science* is nothing. One barren assurance, however, is of just as much value as another.[1]

While Habermas rejects the Hegelian claim to the actualization of science (*Wissenschaft*), nevertheless there is an extremely important moral to be drawn from this passage. One of the primary characteristics of contemporary cultural life is the virtual insularity of competing and conflicting orientations—where, in effect, we are confronted with one barren assurance as over against another, each claiming truth for itself and that its competitors are "of no account at all." Against this dominant tendency, Habermas is a dialectical thinker in the best Hegelian sense. He always attempts to immerse himself in the "moment" or the "shape of consciousness" that he critically examines, to comprehend it from the inside in order to grasp both its truth and its falsity. He does this with the systematic intent of passing beyond the "given" position in order to achieve a genuine synthetic comprehension that preserves the truth of the "moment." Furthermore, as I read Hegel, the task of the philosopher is *always* to start with what is "given," with what is taken to be the "common view of things"—not to turn his back on this with the assurance that "there are pressages of a better" type of knowledge. The philosopher must *work through* what is taken to be the common view of things or the conventional wisdom in order to show its internal conflicts, to bring out its truth, to show how by following out the dialectic of the subject matter we are compelled to move to a more adequate Concept (*Begriff*). I believe that this is the method that is most characteristic of Habermas' own strategy of argumentation, and provides the necessary perspective for grasping what he seeks to show us in his treatment of a wide variety of positions. It also provides the clue for comprehending the way in which he overcomes the entrenched dogma of so much of analytic philosophy—that there is an unbridgeable categorical distinction between historical and systematic knowledge.

(2) I can make the above observations more concrete by turning to *Knowledge and Human Interests.* Only someone who had Hegel in his "bones" could have written that

study. Although its scope is far less ambitious .than Hegel's *Phenomenology,* both the spirit and the letter of the book have deep affinities with the *Phenomenology.* Consider what Habermas says about Hegel's *Phenomenology:*

> For reflection destroys, along with a false view of things, the dogmatic attitudes of a habitual form of life: this holds even for the first stage, the world of sense-certainty. In false consciousness, knowing and willing are still joined. The residues of the destruction of false consciousness serve as rungs on the ladder of the experience of reflection. As shown by the proto-typical area of experience in life history, the experiences from which one learns are negative. The reversal of consciousness means the dissolution of identifications, the breaking of fixations, and the destruction of projections. The failure of the state of consciousness that has been overcome turns at the same time into a new reflected attitude in which the situation comes to consciousness in an undistorted manner, just as it is.[2]

Knowledge and Human Interests follows the course of such an overcoming of false consciousness. It is a historically oriented journey that seeks "to reconstruct the prehistory of modern positivism with the systematic intention of analyzing the connections between knowledge and human interests."[3] Habermas' *telos* is "to recover the forgotten experience of reflection"[4] which lies at the very heart of Hegel's thinking. Beginning with Hegel's critique of Kant, in which the enterprise of epistemology is replaced by the phenomenological self-reflection of mind, Habermas uses an Hegelian approach to bring out the truth and the falsity of each of the moments in this development. Just as in Hegel, where we witness how in each "shape of consciousness" there is a deep tension, an essential conflict, a moment of despair, and indeed a dialectical movement from *Gewissheit* to *Wahrheit,* so this is also exhibited in Habermas' narrative. In each stage there is a disparity between what is *nur gemeint* and the actual consequences of the position when its full dialectical consequences are developed. Thus, for example, Habermas shows the disparity between the scientistic self-understanding that both Marx and Freud have of their disciplines and their actual contributions to a form of critique which is based upon self-reflection.

Against the opposing and seductive tendencies of an unreflective objectivism and a self-defeating subjectivism that has dominated so much of intellectual and cultural life since Hegel, Habermas develops a comprehensive theory of knowledge and rationality which is at once a social theory and is based upon the three primary cognitive interests: the technical, the practical, and the emancipatory. Habermas' path is also one of determinate negation where, despite the attempts to suppress or repress the "experience of self-reflection," the point of the study is to show how such a project fails, and how self-reflection breaks forth in Marx's critique of ideology and Freud's understanding of the therapeutic situation.

(3) The preceding discussion brings into the foreground what I take to be the most

central concept—the Archimedian point—of Habermas' philosophic outlook: the concept of self-reflection. It is the basis of his identification of reason and the "will to reason." It is the dynamics of self-reflection that has the *power* to overcome false consciousness, to destroy a false view of things and the dogmatic attitudes of habitual forms of life. It is through the power of negativity of self-reflection that the emancipatory interest of reason is furthered. It is the basis of Habermas' understanding of *critique* or critical theory. The origins of this concept can be traced back to classical philosophy, especially in the Platonic portrayal of Socrates. Self-reflection became the central concept of German Idealism and is exhibited in the highway of despair that is followed in the *Phenomenology*. [5]

Habermas has followed out this concept beyond Hegel, and shows how it has been transformed by Marx and Freud. It is the basis for understanding a type of knowledge that is different from and not reducible to the "objectivistic" knowledge exhibited in the empirical-analytic sciences, which is governed by a cognitive technical interest. This model of self-reflection presupposes that there are agents (or classes of agents) who are at once shaped by hidden causalities of the past, but have the capacity of self-reflection by which they can achieve self-understanding and thereby further the processes of their own self-formation through reflection. Genuine self-reflection involves both theoretical and practical insight. When critique is appropriated by the agents to whom it is addressed, then it becomes a *necessary* condition for furthering the processes of rational self-formation.

There are two vital points that must be stressed in Habermas' development of the concept of self-reflection. Both of these are emphasized in his interpretation of Freud. The first is that a necessary (although not a sufficient) condition of a "successful" therapeutic situation—one in which there is a movement on the part of the subject toward an emancipation or liberation from the distorting hidden causalities of the past—is that the subject himself must appropriate the interpretation of his situation. The subject must come to a self-understanding—a moral insight—into his condition. I stress this point—as does Habermas—because without such an appropriation there is always a danger that the relation between the patient and the analyst can be reduced to one of manipulation or strategic action rather than communicative interaction. Second, as Freud himself so acutely realized, the type of knowledge that is required by a patient in order to effect a therapeutic movement is not merely intellectual assent to a set of propositions. It is a type of knowledge that has theoretical, practical, and affective consequences; it is a type of knowledge that is potentially transformative. Such knowledge requires the breaking down of subtle resistances and complex defense mechanisms, and the motivation of the subject is directly related to his suffering. In speaking of this type of moral insight, Habermas says:

> First it includes two movements equally: the cognitive and the affec-
> tive and motivational. It is critique in the sense that the analytic power
> to dissolve dogmatic attitudes inheres in analytic insight. Critique

terminates in a transformation of the affective-motivational basis, just as it begins with the need for practical transformation. Critique would not have the power to break up false consciousness if it were not impelled by a *passion for critique.*[6]

Habermas claims to base his conclusions on the therapeutic situation as it is comprehended by Freud. But I think it is more accurate to say that Habermas is offering an *interpretation* of the therapeutic situation which underscores the dynamics of self-reflection. Further, this interpretation is one that is shaped by Habermas' understanding of Hegel. For when we think of the phenomenology of Spirit, not exclusively from the perspective of the philosophic "we" who is comprehending the process, but from the perspective of the agents who are undergoing this dialectic, then we can see how Hegel brilliantly understands the pain, conflict, and internal tension that is experienced by the subjects who break through the dogmatic attitudes of false consciousness.

(4) The preceding discussion of self-reflection leads directly to what has become Habermas' most central preoccupation—the development of a comprehensive theory of communicative competence and a theory of social evolution. Both of these can be considered aspects of an attempt to give a reconstruction of the universal conditions of human rationality. There are some striking parallels with Hegel's grasp of the dynamics of *Vernunft*. Let me try to pin this down. I have already mentioned that Habermas strongly objects to the Hegelian claim to totality, finality, system, and self-contained completeness of *Geist* and *Vernunft*. If one maintains that to be a Hegelian requires the acceptance of these ambitious and ambiguous claims in Hegel, then Habermas is certainly not a Hegelian. But I believe that Hegel had a incisive grasp of the deficiencies of abstract understanding. Hegel already showed us how skepticism, nihilism, and relativism are only dialectical mirror images of abstract *Verstand*. If we think of *Vernunft* as a process or project to move beyond the falsity of these frozen abstractions—a movement which aspires to concrete universality—then I submit this is the fundamental characteristic of Habermas' own attempts to understand the universal claims to validity which underlie communicative interaction.

Let me approach this point from a slightly different perspective. I believe that Hegel was unduly optimistic about the power of *Vernunft* to transcend the oppositions between abstract understanding and skepticism. Indeed, we can read a good deal of intellectual and cultural life since Hegel as a fluctuation between these extremes. In the philosophy of science, the philosophy of language, the understanding of social reality, ethics, and politics we can detect similar patterns of fluctuation—from the extreme that we can state, with finality, abstract universal criteria of rationality, or meaning, or verification to the opposing extreme, where there is skepticism about any universal standards and where we are somehow locked up in incommensurable conceptual schemes or language games. At present we seem to be living in a period of rampant relativism. And this epistemological skepticism has significant practical consequences—for it all too easily leads to a moral and political despair where ultimately one point of view, orientation, or basic norm is taken to be "one barren assurance" which has just as much value as another.

Habermas at once perceives the pervasiveness of the temptation to fluctuate from abstract understanding to skepticism, and the pernicious theoretical and practical consequences of this movement. It is a false nostalgia to believe that one can find a way out of this dilemma by a return to Hegel—that it is sufficient to cite the appropriate texts about the power and all-embracing significance of *Vernunft*. Rather, one must try again, in new ways, to do what Hegel attempted to do and failed to achieve—to show how, in light of contemporary oppositions, tensions, and dialectical conflicts, it is possible to develop an understanding of human rationality in his theoretical and practical dimensions which does justice to the universality of the validity claims of Reason, and at the same time recognizes the role of historical variability and development. In this sense Habermas' project or program has deep affinities with Hegel's project.

On the basis of the four Hegelian themes in Habermas that I have sketched, I can now raise my basic questions. For it seems to me that there are deep tensions in Habermas, pulling him in different directions. I am not convinced that they are compatible. Let me label these as Kantian, Hegelian, and Marxist tendencies. Habermas' understanding of a universal pragmatics is in a direct line with Kant's attempt to develop a transcendental philosophy. Habermas rejects the notion of a transcendental ego or subjectivity, and he is far more pragmatistic or fallibilistic than Kant. Nevertheless, insofar as he thinks we can isolate the universal formal conditions for all speech acts, and state once and for all what these are, then this project is essentially Kantian. There is a direct line between the Kantian question, "What are the conditions for the possibility of human knowledge or experience?" and Habermas' question, "What are the conditions for communicative action?" Just as Kant thought that this type of question could be answered in a way that would "transcend" historical differences, Habermas appears to be committed to the same endeavor.

But alongside this Kantian bias, there is, of course, the Hegelian strain in Habermas. This comes out prominently in his interest in social development—especially the development of learning processes. It is also reflected in his conviction that such a theory can be only retrospective, not prospective. It is only after the fact that we can see the order and "logic" of social evolution.

Although Habermas thinks of himself as working in a Marxist tradition, it seems to me that the Marxist elements are more and more muted, and soften, in his most recent work. In developing his notion of critique and self-reflection, the issue must be posed: who are the subjects or agents to whom such critical theory is addressed? What is the historically motivated agency (if any) for overcoming forms of distorted communication? Where does Habermas see the signs of the "passion for critique?" Hegel and Marx were both severely critical of Kant for failing to understand and illuminate the problem of historical agency. They saw that, unless one grapples with this issue, there is the danger that Kantianism becomes "merely" abstract and formal in both its theoretical and practical dimensions. But if one no longer believes that *Geist* is realizing itself in history, or that there are dynamics of human production and activity that lead to revolutionary *praxis,* then the question arises: What (if anything) in Habermas' scheme functionally replaces Hegel's understanding of the dynamics of *Geist* or Marx's understanding of the dynamics and power of *praxis*? Unless one confronts this issue (or rather complex of issues) in a clear and unambiguous form, then there is a serious danger that the very conception of critique is threatened with foundering. We may no longer be able to appeal to the proletariat as that class which is exploited and will come to the realization of its historical role in furthering human emancipation. But I submit that the very idea of critique or critical theory does not make sense—or carry conviction—unless one speaks to the question of who *are* or who *will be* the agents who appropriate critical understanding and thereby further the processes of rational self-formation.

I can summarize my questions to Habermas in a single question. If I am right about my identification of the Kantian, Hegelian, and Marxist poles in Habermas' thought, then I would like to know—in the words of the old union song—"Which side are you on?"

NOTES

1. G. W. F. Hegel, *The Phenomenology of Mind,* trans. J. B. Baillie (London: George Allen & Unwin, 1949), pp. 134-35.
2. Jürgen Habermas, *Knowledge and Human Interests* (Boston: Beacon Press, 1971), pp. 17-18.
3. Ibid., vii.
4. Ibid., vii.
5. In "A Postscript to *Knowledge and Human Interests* [*Philosophy of the Social Sciences,* 3 (1973), 182] Habermas writes: "The studies I published in *Knowledge and Human Interests* suffer from the lack of a precise distinction not only between objectivity and truth, but also between reconstruction and 'self-reflexion' in a critical sense. It occurred to me only after completing the book that the traditional use of the term 'reflexion,' which goes back to German Idealism, covers (and confuses) two things: on the one hand, it denotes the reflexion upon the conditions of potential abilities of a knowing, speaking and acting subject as such; on the other hand, it denotes the reflexion upon unconsciously produced constraints to which a determinate subject (or a determinate group of subjects, or a determinate species subject) succumbs in the process of self-formation."
6. *Knowledge and Human Interests,* p. 234.

COMMENT ON

The Relationship of Habermas's Views to Hegel

KENLEY DOVE

I

The topic of our symposium, "Habermas and Hegel" is provocative and perhaps even paradoxical. No contemporary thinker could be more fittingly juxtaposed with Hegel because no one has done more to raise the level of discourse concerning Hegel's social and political philosophy. Hegel's thought, and especially the theory of objective spirit, has provided the impulse for much of Habermas' work as a philosopher over the past two decades. While others have contributed useful historical studies of Hegel's texts, Habermas has argued with Hegel as one would argue with a contemporary. One result of this is that the Hegel who repeatedly surfaces in Habermas' work has indeed become, to a significant degree, our contemporary.

The conjunction of Habermas and Hegel is nevertheless provocative. There are, I believe, at least two reasons for this. The first is that the criticism to which Habermas has subjected Hegel's social and political thought is potentially devastating. Recognizing that Hegel's is a theory of the basic or categorial structures of human interaction, Habermas has attempted to show that these structures are theoretically generated according to a paradigm that is radically non-interactive. Or, to use an expression that Habermas has made familiar, the paradigm for the generation of social and political categories is said to be a "monological" subjectivity or the absolute ego as reflexive self-consciousness. The second reason why one might find the joining of Habermas and Hegel provocative lies in the theoretical project which Habermas has set for himself and tried to make plausible. This project aims at showing how the elementary structures of human interaction are "determined within the framework of a theory of social evolution."[1] If successful, this theoretical program might lay claim to being "more Hegelian than Hegel," that is, more truthful, even than Hegel himself, to what Habermas has called "Hegel's original insight:"[2]: that the ego as self-consciousness can only be comprehended in terms of spirit as interaction, not vice versa.

According to Habermas, Hegel uses the notion of spirit as interaction in his dialectical criticism of other philosophical theories. Each is shown to claim a theoretical legitimation that can only be redeemed in terms of a structure of interaction. Yet the systematic opposition between the required structure of interaction and the actual structure of the theory in question reveals this theory to be monological in character and thus unable to support *its own* claim to intersubjective validity. This polemical device will be familiar to all readers who have considered the sequence of shapes described in Hegel's PhG as manifestations of the "opposition of consciousness": the opposition, namely, between the standpoint of consciousness, what is "for it," and its principle of validation, what is said to be "in itself." In each case the principle of validation, when it is itself drawn into question, shows itself to have the status of being merely "for it" while the claim that it is a principle of validation would require that the principle be embedded in the structure of communicative action and not in the structure of consciousness or self-consciousness.

As several commentators have observed (e.g. Bubner, Henrich), the most widely known books and essays by Habermas have exploited precisely this dialectical strategy of argumentation derived from Hegel's *Phenomenology*.[3] In each of these an aporia is reached which manifests the need for a theory that will link and comprehend the two opposed theoretical tendencies. As directly opposed, however, each seems both to require and to negate the other. The monological method of reflective scientific theories is guided by principles that such a method cannot legitimate: either these principles are adopted from a tradition of communication not yet subjected to critical reflection or else they are simply the result of an arbitrary decision. The interpretative method of hermeneutical theories, as opposed to the nomological scientific theories, does attempt to immunize the shared traditions of communicative interaction against reflexive dissolution, but for this very reason it cannot show the interpreted structures to be universally valid independent of the particular and contingent traditions in which they are embedded.

Habermas knows, of course, that Hegel claimed to have brought this phenomenological dialectic of the "for it" and the "in itself" to its immanent consummation under the title "Absolute Knowledge." Habermas' reformulation of this same phenomenological dialectic under the titles "scientism vs. hermeneutics," or "monologism vs. interaction" has indeed revitalized the distinctive pattern of argumentation in Hegel's *Phenomenology*. But his claim that the *Phenomenology* radicalizes this aporetic opposition rather than overcoming it[4] seems to be based more on a semantic analysis of the term "Absolute Knowledge" than upon a consideration of the argument presented by Hegel under that heading.

Needless to say, this is a question of Hegel interpretation that we could hardly be expected to resolve here. Nevertheless, if I have correctly identified the Hegelian inspiration and impulse in Habermas' philosophical work, then we can also look to Hegel for clues in our attempt to understand the second, or "systematic," phase of Habermas' philosophical project—a phase which, it should be noted, is now in its earliest stages of development. The two most characteristic features of Habermas' most recent, or systematic, work are (1) the theory of social evolution and (2) what Albrecht Wellmer has aptly called "the linguistic turn" in his thinking.

Granting, for the sake of argument, that Hegel's philosophy of objective spirit (like his entire philosophy of spirit) fails because the structures of interaction that it presents (e.g., family, civil society, the state) are actually generated or determined by the absolute movement of spirit reflecting on itself, and thus by a monological structure writ large, how can the basic structures of interaction be generated in a way that does not ultimately trace back to a monological framework? This is the task Habermas assigns to a theory of social evolution. Of course, social evolution cannot merely be understood as an empirical history, for then the desired elementary structures could not be grasped abstractly "but only picked out inductively."[5] The problem is therefore to formulate a generative logic of social evolution that is interactional, rather than monological, at its most basic level.

II

Perhaps the most striking parallel between Habermas and Hegel is that both attempt to formulate a theory of categoreal genesis and that in both cases the theory is prepared for or introduced by an independent "critical theory." Thus Hegel introduces *his* theory of categoreal genesis, the *Science of Logic*, with the *Phenomenology of Spirit*. The point of departure for Habermas' theory of social evolution is an argument that philosophy has undergone a breakdown crisis. The mode of discourse which was originally born out of a critique of the truth claims of mythic and religious interpretations of the world, namely philosophy, has, in the course of its development, reduced itself to an opposed pair of methods, each of which can be shown to be irrational. These are the methods of (a) empirical-analytic and (b) interpretative or hermeneutic thinking. Each is said to be structured by an "anthropologically deep-seated interest": either (a) an interest in technical control or (b) an interest in intersubjective communication. But taken by themselves, as guides to philosophical thinking, each leads to aporias. As Habermas attempts to show in his *Knowledge and Human Interests*, the crisis of philosophical theories guided by these two basic interests has become manifest in the development of philosophy since Hegel. But if we come to see that the interests in technical control (work) and in intersubjective communication (interaction) *are* "deep seated" and invariant, then they need not be regarded as distorting prisms of objective knowledge. It rather becomes possible to link them as the joint conditions under which a plurality of individuals structures and reproduces itself collective life, comes to have a knowable experience as such.

The theory of social evolution, by which these basic structures are theoretically generated and determined, therefore takes the interests and activities of work and interaction as pre-given and linked a priori. The point is to show how the basic forms of this linkage alter. Unlike Hegel's *Logic*, Habermas' theory of categoreal genesis does not begin with "the indeterminate immediate"; work and interaction are already determinate notions and, inasmuch as the subject matter is taken to be social or irreducibly plural, work, as socially organized, is informed by and is accordingly dependent upon a structure of interaction just as a structure of interaction is dependent upon the activity of work for its material embodiment. Because of this two-fold dependency Habermas also calls this theory of social evolution a rational "reconstruction of historical materialism."

The theory is *materialist* because the structures it generates are, in each case, real in virtue of their participation in the reproduction of social life. But the development of work, or the forces of production, is not what gives the theory its historical significance. For, as Habermas argues, the development of work, the technical control over nature, proceeds in a merely cumulative way, with no systematically differentiable stages. The theory is *historical* because it exhibits a temporal logic (as opposed to Hegel's a-temporal logic) of social development with definite stages in a definite sequence. These are the transformations of the structure of communicative action or interaction on the basis of which a socio-economic system is organized. Finally, the theory is said to be a rational *reconstruction* because it uncovers anonymous rule systems in terms of which any subject participates in a structure of interaction and because these rule systems can be ordered. The ordering principle is said to be the relation of reciprocity that informs *all* interactions, not merely those linked to work.

Habermas then proceeds to argue that the interactional structures that organize the material reproduction of society have proceeded in three basic stages: (1) Primitive, (2) Traditional and (3) Modern. In the first of these *kinship* systems are said to provide the organizational principle; in the second, the principle is the *political* domination of classes and in the third it is the self-regulative market principle of *civil society*.

A student of Hegel's philosophy of objective spirit cannot fail to note that these are the same basic structures which are considered under the heading *Sittlichkeit* or Ethical Life. But whereas Hegel argues that the socialization process, by which everyone in the *modern* world is individuated, must involve *each* of these modes of ethical life, Habermas maintains that each *in turn* determines the totality of social intercourse. In other words, Hegel presents the interactive structures of the family, civil society and the state synchronically and not generatively, whereas for Habermas the structures must be presented diachronically because it is the theory of social evolution that bears the burden of generating the basic categories. As in other parts of Hegel's *Realphilosophie*, the guiding principles for the discovery of real structures in the sphere of objective spirit are already developed in the *Logic*.[6] But since Habermas' theory of social evolution is, at one and the same time, his theory of categoreal genesis and his theory of the structures of interaction, he forecloses the possibility of regarding individuation as a process involving three modes of interaction that are equally basic.

A practical motive for adopting this theoretical strategy is not difficult to detect. From the first of his major writings, Habermas has attempted to spell out a social theory "with a practical intent." In his most recent writings this has taken the form of a theory of "post-modern" society. Such a theory would make no sense to Hegel; he regarded his account of the basic structures of ethical interaction as logically complete. But Habermas, together with many Marxists, regards the structure that Hegel desig-

nates "civil society" to be, in effect, identical with liberal capitalism. In basic agreement with the young Marx, Habermas questions the universal character of the structure Hegel ascribes to civil society. (The putative reciprocity of the market structure of
interaction, the exchange of equivalents, is said to be a mere ideology.)

For Hegel civil society does have a universal character because it is the one structure
of interaction which is not merely necessary for individuation (like the family and the
state) but is also the very same real structure for every individual. In other words, a self
becomes an individual through participation in *this particular* family (e.g. the Smith
family) and in *this particular* nation state (e.g. the French), but civil society is unitary
and global. No instance of it is susceptible of bearing a proper name. Insofar as such a
structure can be systematically comprehended within a theory of the structures of
interaction, the theory itself will have an internal reference to universality and will
not, like hermeneutical theories of interaction as particular traditions of shared meaning, have a merely oblique reference to universal validity. Hegel's integration of such a
structure into his three-fold theory of ethical interaction was the result of his three-fold
logical theory of the universal, the particular and the individual *and* the result of an
antecedent social evolution that established civil society as an implicitly *global* institution. That is a major reason why Hegel's theory of interaction and ethical individuation is a theory of the *modern world*.[7]

In Habermas' theory of social evolution, however, the modern world is not characterized by the integration of civil society into a more embracing structure of ethical
interaction; modernity is instead characterized by the domination by civil society as
the structure providing the determining principle of organization for all modes of
interaction. For Habermas every social formation is a distinctive way of linking work
and interaction. When the determining principle or organization was kinship or
familial relations, the resultant structuring of the work process was defined by the
limits of a particular household or *oikos*. When the determining principle of organization became political, class differentiations arose and the work process was guided by a
public structure of interaction that was functionally different from the still essentially
private mode of economic reproduction. With the rise of modern civil society and the
structure of market interaction as the guiding principle of organization, the public
realm (*Öffentlichkeit*) is no longer differentiated from the realm of economic life.[8]

Habermas' theory of these stages in the linkage of work and interaction, his theory
of social evolution, has another essential component that must be mentioned here.
This is the linguistic dimension; it is critical for understanding what he calls the "inner
logic" of the stages of social evolution and for making plausible his claim that a
"post-modern" stage of social evolution is possible.

Each of the three structures of interaction that we have reviewed in the development
from the family structure through the political structure to the market structure are
regarded as institutional structures of interaction precisely because they do exhibit a
systematic link between work and interaction. The pure form of interaction is, one

might say, "schematized" by virtue of its embodiment in, its informing, a mode of economic reproduction, a mode of work. Considered in this way, it becomes plausible to inquire about the pure form of interaction, that is, interaction independent of its embodiment in a system of social work.

Habermas' theory of a pure form of interaction, whose conceptual articulation is still in its earliest stages, is based upon the types of reciprocity that obtain in a speech situation when all interests other than the interest in arriving at consensus about truth are "bracketed out." This is the ideal of undistorted communication that, in Habermas' theory, we necessarily affirm insofar as we engage in a process of communication at all.[9]

Each of the structures of embodied interaction, that is, modes of interaction linked with a mode of social work, may be read as a partial institutionalization of the pure form of interaction. But because the institutionalization is partial, the mode of communication obtaining at any given stage will be "systematically distorted." Nevertheless, as an institutionalization of pure interaction, each stage can be differentiated by the degree to which its particular linkage of work and interaction involves distortion.

This obviously leaves open the possibility of considering a future stage of social evolution that will embody or institutionalize the form of interaction without systematic distortion. Hence the "practical intent" of Habermas' theory of social evolution. What remains unclear to me is whether such a "post-modern" stage of social evolution could still be understood in terms of a linkage of interaction and social work. For it is the direct linkage of these two at the stage Habermas designates as modern or capitalist that seems to account for the peculiar distortion of communication at this stage.

The notion of distorted communication naturally seems to require a correlative notion of undistorted communication. And Habermas has acknowledged that the articulation of his notion of communicative action remains one of the most important pieces of unfinished business in his theoretical program. As I have tried to show, this program owes much of its inspiration to Habermas' interpretation of Hegel's failed program. Though he shares this interpretation with many readers of Hegel, Habermas stands out among our contemporaries as one who is resolved to redeem as much as he can of Hegel's original insight. Whatever the ultimate success of his program, all of us who work with Hegel can profit from his reidentification of this insight as the concept of interaction. When his notion of communicative action is presented as a theory, I am confident that we will be aided in our comprehension of Hegel as much as by any existing commentary.

In the meantime, much as I have been stimulated by Habermas' program, it remains to me an open question whether the category-generating argument of Hegel's *Logic* is, as Habermas contends, a basically monological process of absolute self-consciousness reflecting upon itself. I would rather contend that Hegel's genesis of the categories of interaction, his *Logic*, is distinguished by its absolute freedom from any reference to any real entities, including absolute consciousness as well as evolutionary society. As I noted at the beginning, this is the question of the meaning of "Absolute Knowledge" as the result of the *Phenomenology* and the beginning of the *Logic*. But in raising this question to prominence once again, Habermas has, I believe, made a singular contribution to our thinking with Hegel as our contemporary.

NOTES

1. J. Habermas, *Legitimation Crisis,* tr. T. McCarthy (Boston, 1975), p. 49.

2. J. Habermas, *Technik und Wissenschaft als Ideologie* (Frankfurt, 1968), p. 15.

3. The writings of Habermas which exhibit this strategy most clearly are: "Arbeit und Interaktion" (first published in H. Brown and M. Riedel, eds., *Natur und Geschichte: Karl Löwith zum 70. Geburtstag* (Stuttgart, 1967), pp. 132-55; "Zur Logik der Sozialwissenschaften" (first published in *Philosophische Rundschau,* Beiheft 5, February 1967); *Erkenntnis und Interesse* (Frankfurt, 1968), and the joint volume with N. Luhmann, *Theorie der Gesellschaft oder Sozialtechnologie* (Frankfurt, 1971).

4. J. Habermas, *Erkenntnis und Interesse,* ch. 1.

5. J. Habermas, *Legitimation Crisis,* p. 18.

6. See Hegel, *Encyclopädie* (1830), the remark to paragraph 276.

7. See K. Dove, "Alienation and the Concept of Modernity" in *Analectica Husserliana* V (Dordrecht-Holland, 1976), pp. 187-204.

8. For this theory of civil society see H. Arendt, *The Human Condition* (Chicago, 1958) and J. Habermas, *Strukturwandel der Öffentlichkeit* (Neuwied, 1962).

9. See J. Habermas, *Technik und Wissenschaft als Ideologie,* p. 163. J. Habermas, "Towards a Theory of Communicative Competence," *Inquiry* XIII (1970), pp. 360-75; J. Habermas "Der Universalitätsanspruch der Hermeneutik," in *Hermeneutik und Dialektik* I, ed. R. Bubner et al (Tübingen, 1970), pp. 73-103; J. Habermas, "Wahrheitstheorien," in *Wirklichkeit und Reflexion: Festschrift für Walter Schultz* (Pfullingen, 1973), pp. 211-65; K.-O. Apel, "Das Apriori der Kommunikationsgemeinschaft," in *Transformation der Philosophie* II (Frankfurt, 1973), pp. 358-435.

Response to the Commentary of Bernstein and Dove

by

JÜRGEN HABERMAS

When I first saw the announcement for tonight's panel I felt of course embarrassed; I soon realized, however, that this strange title invites comparison of the incomparable, in such an evident way, that I take this intentional overstatement as another example of that peculiar mixture of charm, generosity, and hospitality which visitors enjoy in this country.*

It is not easy for me to react to the two excellent comments. I do not want to deal with those flattering parallels which could easily trap me into a certain kind of narcissistic self-mirroring.

My attempt to write a small piece of history with a systematic intention, i.e., a piece of rational history, is only plausible within a Hegelian tradition. I became aware of this when I first saw some of the Anglo-American reviews of my book, *Knowledge and Human Interests*. These critics complained about the confusion of two distinct enterprises which should be kept apart: the empirical analysis of a historian, and the systematic analysis of a philosopher of science. These objections are, to an extent, well taken. Reading Hegel carefully, however, we will realize that he pursues not only two but actually four enterprises at once. We, today, no longer have the certainty that these four types of analysis will finally reveal only different aspects of one unified process. These four are, roughly speaking, the following:

(1) the rational reconstruction of universal presuppositions of paradigmatic types of cognition and communication; this is the Kantian enterprise of transcendental analysis, or what is left of it in, or integrated into, Hegel's philosophy;

(2) the rational reconstruction of developmental patterns for the genesis of transcendental universals; this is Hegel's genuine enterprise of discovering developmental logics;

(3) the phenomenological analysis of the experience of those involved in processes of self-reflection, that is, of a kind of self-reflection which step by step critically destroys the objective delusions arising from different modes and levels of false consciousness. This is an enterprise which starts with Kant's criticism of what he called *transzendentaler Schein,* and which, after Hegel, is continued by Feuerbach, Marx, and Freud with the assumption that self-reflection is instrumental for dissolving pathological deformations in the history of either collective or individual consciousness;

---

*The title listed on the program for this session was "Habermas and Hegel." Professor Habermas was at the time of the meeting on visiting appointment at Haverford College.—ED.

(4) the construction of a rational history, which can explain the observational and the narrative evidence of empirical regularities, not in terms of nomological theories, but in terms of the internal genesis of basic conceptual structures; this is the enterprise that Hegel attempted in his *Realphilosophien*, attempts which became, during the nineteenth century, famous, and almost totally discredited under the names of *Naturphilosophie* and *Geschichtsphilosophie*.

I think that both Bernstein and Dove have good reasons to focus on the problem: whether we still can pursue the enterprise of the rational reconstruction of universals, of their internal genesis, and of processes of self-reflection with the intention of explaining empirical, in particular, historical chains of events, and if so, how we can do it. Today, we no longer presuppose the unity of logic and history. If we separate, however, the enterprises of rational reconstruction, and of the phenomenology of self-reflection, then we have to face what Bernstein calls the "problem of agency." If we do not accept the dialectical movement of a spirit which determines itself, and gives itself a content, that is, if we do not presuppose an absolute mind which actively creates and engenders itself, what is, then, the concrete dynamics of a process which we want to explain with reference to internal, somehow logical rather than to external and casual relationship? Dove rightly points to some of the major difficulties in my preliminary attempts to answer this question from a Marxian point of view. I am not prepared directly to specify this answer tonight. Let me, instead, choose a detour, and draw your attention to certain features of the contemporary philosophical scene, which indicate the revival of a systematic interest in Hegel, and in Hegelian approaches. The rest of my comment must, of course, remain a rather superficial sketch. There are two areas of a special interest for me, and for Bernstein as well: (1) the post-empiricist philosophy of science; and (2) the non-objectivistic approaches in sociology.

1. In the debates started between Popper and Kuhn it became more and more apparent that categorial distinctions, well established by logical positivism, had to be revised or even abandoned. First, the clear-cut distinction between *observation and theory* was undermined, in a way which reminds us of Kant's distinction between sensations and judgements, intuition and understanding as they came under attack by Fichte, Schelling, and Hegel. Second, the dependence of theories on paradigms, and the discontinuity in paradigm-shifts, indicates the breakdown of another important categorial distinction, that between the *context of justification* and the *context of discovery*. With this, two further distinctions were challenged: the distinction between internal or logical, and external or empirical relationship, and, on the other hand, the distinction between facts and values. It is, of course, Quine who forcefully backs this liquidation of formally fixed categories, by blurring the line between analytic and synthetic and between descriptive and prescriptive propositions.

These challenges to the firm distinctions of understanding (*Verstand*) pose a severe problem for the project of a rational history of modern science, leaving us basically with three alternatives: (1) from an empiricist position, one could launch a counter-attack, with the aim of reestablishing the shaken ground of understanding. If this does not work, and one yet wants to maintain an empiricist position, the only way out of the dilemma seems to be: (2) to abandon the unity of the project of modern science, and to convert to a relativist position of a Diltheyian type of historicism (Elkana, in his recent presentations, relates every validity claim raised in the various communities of scientists in the last analysis to particular "images of science," while he does not allow for any systematic comparison between these images). If one is not willing to turn to a historically and sociologically informed descriptivism, and to pay the price of one or the other kind of cognitive relativism, one has to face a set of tasks which is essentially Hegelian, since there is no easy way back to an abstract universalism of a Popperian brand. The further alternative would be: (3) the project of a rational history of modern science, which takes into account not only the internal history of science but also the systematically related contexts of discovery, which are embedded in larger cultural traditions and connected with basic social changes. This project raises three questions which indicate the Hegelian dimension of thought.

If one wants to give a rational account of the history of science, including the contexts of discovery, one has, *first,* to look for a concept of rationality which is more comprehensive than the concept of understanding or *Verstand*, which is confined to the formation of nomological theories, the corroboration of, and the choice between them; one has, *second,* to inquire whether this concept of rationality can be extended under genetic aspects in such a way that it allows for an analysis of the logic of the development of modern science, which does bridge the gaps between different paradigms; and, *finally,* one has to face the problem of how conceptually to form those empirical hypotheses which could explain the contingencies within the history of science. Here I have in mind the problem of how we might conceive causal links between cognitive structures and the empirical conditions under which these structures emerge and get implemented within the institutional system of a process which is apparently mediated by the embodiment of cognitive structures within the research activities of scientific communities. It is this problem which is immediately related to the question of how it is possible to identify agents, collective and individual, of a rationally reconstructed history of science. There must be some communities which are capable of innovative learning processes, and which bring about what Kuhn calls "scientific revolutions." And, if I may make a big step, and look at history at large, it is suggestive to think that there have been social movements which were in quite a similar way the bearers of evolutionary innovations within the history of mankind.

2. I have mentioned the post-empiricist philosophy of science as an example for the emergence of a type of problem which also appear in recent sociology. If one looks at the revival of non-objectivistic approaches in this field one will observe a train of thought which is, under one aspect, the exact reverse of what happened in the philosophy of science. Here we can see a move from the objectivistic position of a nomological kind of social science towards a position which is almost exclusively preoccupied with internal structures of culture and society demanding rational reconstruction. This holds true for the post-Wittgensteinian and the structuralist approaches, which start

from the model of language-games or of the infra-structure of speech; for the phenomenological approaches which stress internal structures of the lived-in world; and for neo-Marxist approaches, particularly critical theory, which extend the analysis of internal structures to developmental patterns (it is here that I see a convergence between historical materialism and Piaget's genetic structuralism which was predicted many years ago by Lucien Goldmann).

If this sketch is not completely mistaken we are facing in this area the same problems, approached, however, from a different angle. This is *first* the problem of a concept of rationality which is sufficiently comprehensive to cover not only cognitive but communicative processes and their embodiment in social interactions. There is, *second,* the problem of discovering developmental patterns of rationality which can be identified in cognitive and moral belief system, in law, and in the basic institutions of social integration. And *finally,* and most difficult of all, there is the problem of how to link the rational reconstructions of all these internal structures with empirical assumptions about the conditions under which societies can and do learn by incorporating available cognitive structures into evolutionary new institutions and mechanisms. On a methodological level this problem takes the form of the connection between an analysis based on rational reconstruction, and a functional analysis of a systems theory type.

I am sure that we have to clarify these problems a lot more before we can provide a satisfactory answer to Bernstein's question: how we should conceptualize that very agency on which social evolution depends, an agency which reveals some sort of a developmental logic and is yet stripped from the necessity, the irreversibility, the unilinearity, and the foreclosure against an open future. These are the features incompatible with the fallability of the human mind, with the finiteness of basic human conditions, and the contingencies of history; and it is exactly these features which we would have to accept if we were still willing to endow the developmental patterns of internal structures with the power of self-realization. That we are not willing to start with this assumption is what separates us from Hegel, all the more if we face again problems of a Hegelian type.